D0849747

Andrew Johnson and the Negro

Andrew Johnson
and the Negro

David Warren Bowen

The University of Tennessee Press

KNOXVILLE

Copyright © 1989 by The University of Tennessee Press / Knoxville.
All Rights Reserved. Manufactured in the United States of America.
First Edition

The paper in this book meets the minimum requirements of the
American National Standard for Permanence of Paper for Printed
Library Materials. ∞ The binding materials have been chosen
for strength and durability.

Frontispiece: A cartoon showing President Andrew Johnson vetoing the bill
to protect civil rights of blacks. From *Harper's Weekly Magazine* (April 14,
1866).

Library of Congress Cataloging in Publication Data

Bowen, David Warren, 1944–
    Andrew Johnson and the Negro / David Warren Bowen.
        —1st. ed. p. cm.
    Bibliography: p.
    Includes index.
    ISBN 0-87049-584-4 (cloth: alk. paper)
    1. Johnson, Andrew, 1808–1875—Views on Afro-Americans.
2. Afro-Americans—History—To 1863. 3. Afro-Americans—
History—1863–1877. 4. Racism—United States—History—19th
century. 5. United States—Race relations. I. Title.
E667.B65   1988
973'.0496073—DC19   88-9668   CIP

To the editors and staff of
The Papers of Andrew Johnson

Contents

Preface

Like most southerners of my generation, I grew up in a segregated world — separate drinking fountains, separate restrooms, separate neighborhoods, and separate lives. The basic southern culture of my youth accepted black inferiority as a fact of life that could never be changed. Yet change came, in part, because the hallowed principle of white supremacy had for so long been an unpleasant and obvious island of hypocrisy within America's idealized conception of itself. The Civil Rights Movement of the modern era was, in a very real sense, a long-overdue effort to reconcile the difference between American myth and reality and, like it or not, was bound to have a profound effect on us all.

Black Americans could, of course, be confident that the American version of justice was on their side, but white southerners faced a difficult dilemma. They were forced either to repudiate their heritage, at least the part that rested on racism, or abandon the basic American principles so clearly illustrated by the civil rights crusade. As one of those latter-day "scalawags" who chose the former course, I do not pretend to approach the subject of race without some bias. The moral revulsion triggered by racism, whether it exists in the legend of the magnolia-scented plantation or the horror of a Nazi concentration camp, cannot be avoided. Denying or suppressing one's attitude toward something of that kind is far worse than being nonobjective; it is being dishonest. Nevertheless, a white southerner brought up in the environment of a segregated society is bound to bring a different perspective to the problem, a perspective that, in its own way, is uniquely southern.

Like the original, the modern scalawag is in a difficult position. In repudiating his region's traditional insistence on white supremacy, a southerner finds himself in intellectual and moral conflict with family and friends, people who are "good" people and who obviously cherish many of the same values as other Americans. While the conflict undoubtedly rests on a different attitude toward race, it is a conflict that always contains a uniquely personal dimension and brings up a question crucial to understanding such belief systems as racism, in the past or the present. Why me? To put the subject in less personal terms more suited for historical inquiry, why do people living in a similar environment develop different beliefs about the world? The answer to this question, however, is only the beginning and brings up a second "personal" dimension familiar to any southerner who has honestly thought about his culture. With racism, it is obvious that two people may hold exactly the same belief about the nature of a proscribed group yet act in a very different manner. How do the same general beliefs produce such varied reactions?

Unlike the social scientist who seeks to generalize from specifics, historians are intrigued by such personal differences, and I believe that this personal dimension holds a key to understanding a subject like racism. Whatever else racism may be, it is clearly an idea, a set of beliefs about the world. But ideas, standing alone, have little meaning. They must be put in the context of an individual personality in a unique time and place before they can influence human affairs. The problem then becomes how a particular mind-set operates in a specific individual to determine or, perhaps better, to influence action. Clearly the answer is neither simple nor one that has absolute validity outside a particular historical situation. How any belief influences history depends foremost on the man or woman under its influence.

In modern historical scholarship, the danger of ignoring this personal dimension is exaggerated by confusion over the meaning of the word "racism" itself. Many contemporary scholars refuse to use the term at all because of its pejorative connotations; others, following the lead of social scientists, have tried to avoid semantic confusion by defining the term rigidly. Some, for example, require that racism be used only to refer to a belief that divides races into a hierarchy based on immutable biological characteristics. Obviously such a definition has a certain utility. Modern racism often appeals to supposed biological differences, and a rigid definition certainly makes traditional "scientific" analysis seeking causes much easier. Others would go still further in the same direction and insist that racism be treated as a true ideology, which has the advantage of directly connecting the actions of a racist to an easily understood system of ideas.

In historical analysis rigid definitions can sometimes be counterproductive. In the first place, the term "racism" is used very broadly in modern society, and historians prefer to use standard language. More important, however, semantic rigidity can actually obscure understanding. For example, defining humans in terms of biological groups is clearly a post-Darwinian development. As a result, requiring that the phenomenon described by the term racism contain a biological element would mean that people living before the mid-nineteenth century could not be racists. This simply distorts what is normally meant by the word.

Labeling racism an ideology can be even more confusing. Implicit in this approach is the assumption that the logical *content* of the belief system in question leads directly to particular actions. With racism this distorts and oversimplifies causal relationships. A racist does not act toward people of a particular group solely or even primarily because of the *content* of his ideas. Such rationalizations are generally after the fact. In short, people do not discriminate against blacks or any other group "because" of some pseudo-scientific theory of group differences. The theory arose to explain the prejudice. Since the attitudes exist long before the explanation, the real origin and pattern of a racist's actions are far more complex and dependent ultimately on a myriad of factors within his personality and society.

This overemphasis on semantics in dealing with racism quite often leads to argument by definition or, to put it another way, mistaking the symptom for the disease. It is certainly plain that Americans were "race-conscious" in the eighteenth and nineteenth centuries and, in the South, built a society based on a kind of racism. In fact, southerners made racial purity one of the keys to their universe — justifying the belief, when justification appeared necessary, with simplistic or sophisticated arguments based on science, religion, or anything else that seemed to fit. Admittedly their rationalizations would be different from those of anyone in the twentieth century since the basic conception of the world was very different, but the similarity between the views would justify terming both "racism." Once this fact is accepted, it is possible to learn more about the real nature of the phenomenon by studying its variations.

To approach the problem from this perspective, racism must be understood as a phenomenon that has no narrowly definable nature — no real meaning beyond its relationship to other things at a particular point in time. It is best understood as a continuum of belief, bounded by normal ethnocentrism at one extreme and the madness of genocide at the other; but the extremes are less important than the relationships within the continuum. Our refusal to accept a narrow meaning for the word becomes an advantage since it helps illustrate one of the most fundamental aspects of racism. Though racism is definable in the general sense of being a kind of belief system requiring that society be divided according to inherent group differences, usually termed racial, its characteristics vary greatly. Appearing at different places, at different times, and in the minds of very different people, racism can produce many different attitudes and actions. For the historian, racism's meaning and its effect on society depend fundamentally on its context.

An examination of the human context of an idea is clearly within the province of traditional historical methodology. The approach I have chosen is very similar to the novelist's development of character yet concentrates on one aspect of a man's thought and its relationship to the total "character." Of course, unlike the novelist, the historian is not in control of events nor privy to the innermost thoughts of his subjects. As a result, the product will hardly be as tidy as a work of fiction. Moreover, though the process obviously contains many biographical elements, it should not be considered biography. Louis Namier once warned his fellow historians to avoid being distracted by the individual and to concentrate on studying the great forces that determine history. This is the study of one of those "great forces" and how it affected one man and, through him, his society. The focus is not Andrew Johnson, as in biography, but rather Johnson's racial attitudes.

Theoretically, of course, any individual living at the time in question would suffice. However, Andrew Johnson provides some unusual advantages in examining racism. As a practicing politician who had considerable success at his chosen vocation, the ideas of this self-proclaimed "plebeian" of the old South, especially as expressed in public speeches and political actions, had to mirror at least to some degree the thinking of his fellow southerners. This is particularly significant because of the type of politician he became. As a practitioner of an extreme variety of Jacksonian democracy and certainly no intellectual, the former tailor gloried in his very commonness. His political appeal was directed toward the South's mythical "average man"—the small farmer, the mechanic, and even the poor white—whose ideas are seldom part of the written record and are too often ignored. Though Johnson himself was hardly "average," as his obvious intelligence and driving ambition make evident, he shared many attitudes in common with his plebeian constituents and, no matter how far he advanced politically, always considered himself as their representative. Acutely conscious of his "class," he could never become the stereotypical planter-politician nor join the pseudo-aristocracy, which is usually the primary source for analyzing the southern mind.

Moreover, the events of Johnson's career in themselves are extremely important for understanding racism in nineteenth-century America. As he was President of the United States during the trying Reconstruction period, his actions and the attitudes that lay behind them, for good or ill, played an important role in the history of the Afro-American and helped mold attitudes about race for succeeding generations. As Frederick Douglass, speaking for black people, so poignantly warned the president: "In the order of Divine Providence you are placed in a position where you have the power to save or destroy us, bless or blast us — I mean our whole race."

Obviously Johnson's years in the White House provide the climax of most examinations of his career, and this study is no exception. However, I have chosen not to engage in a detailed chronological treatment of Reconstruction policy or politics for two reasons. In the first place, the presidency is the best-known part of Johnson's life. The work of modern revisionist scholars such as Eric L. McKitrick, John and LaWanda Cox, Michael Les Benedict, Hans Trefousse, and Michael Perman, as well as a host of others, has given us a reasonably clear picture of the period. To march over this well-trod ground once more would be redundant and detract from the primary focus, Johnson's racial attitudes. As a result, I have attempted to explain the president's actions with regard to the freedmen using examples and concentrating on the impact of his obvious racism. Second, I believe that too many Reconstruction scholars have concentrated exclusively on the events of Reconstruction, unconsciously de-emphasizing the influence of the war itself as well as prewar struggles over slavery. In the case of Johnson's racial attitudes, at any rate, I believe I have found a remarkable consistency throughout his life. This does not mean that Johnson never changed. He certainly did. The changes themselves, however, were oblique rather than direct and were based on earlier patterns of thought that often reveal the real nature of "new" ideas.

Whatever the ultimate value of this approach to racism in history, the results can hardly be considered a definitive explanation of the subject as a whole. The argument is not only limited to a particular place and time but is also limited to one individual — one small part of a broad continuum. The types of generalizations sought by a social scientist are simply beyond its scope. However, I suspect that the relation-

ship of ideas to action in most human events will defy concrete generalization, and we historians will be left to muddle through, depending in
the end on educated guesswork. Unlike novelists who create their own
world, historians will never know the real thoughts and feelings of
their characters. But to know anything aside from isolated facts, they
must try to recreate those thoughts and feelings.

Acknowledgments

This study would have been difficult if not impossible were it not for the Andrew Johnson Project at the University of Tennessee. My own association with the project, beginning while I was an undergraduate, gave me an unusual advantage. The numerous students and staff members who have worked on that collective venture have left a valuable legacy for the future. In particular, I would like to thank the original editors of *The Papers of Andrew Johnson*, Ralph W. Haskins and LeRoy P. Graf, who provided needed guidance to a sometimes troublesome student and acted as advisors on the dissertation that provided the raw material for this manuscript. I would also like to extend a special thanks to Pat Clark, who was key in the successful development of the Johnson Project and remains a good friend.

A number of historians have read this manuscript or parts of it during various stages of its evolution. While they may not accept all of the elements of my analysis, James C. Daniel, John Muldowny, W. T. M. Riches, Peyton McCrary, Allen W. Trelease, and Robert F. Engs have offered valuable suggestions that have undoubtedly improved the final product. I owe a special thanks to LaWanda Cox, whose book, *Politics, Principle, and Prejudice, 1865–1866,* coauthored with her late husband, John Cox, provided part of the inspiration for the approach I chose.

I would also like to thank my department chairman, Fred Sakon, whose introducing me into the mysteries of word processing was essential, and Joanna Overstreet, the typist who first placed this manuscript inside the confusing interior of a computer. Last, I owe a great deal to two ladies whose patient support makes any work I do possible: Mrs. Ruth W. Bowen, my mother, and Mary Bowen, my wife.

This book is dedicated to all the men and women who have worked on *The Papers of Andrew Johnson* over the past twenty-five years.

D.W.B.

NOTE ON SOURCES AND QUOTES

Although much of the research for this study was done from microfilm and original material in the Andrew Johnson Collection at The University of Tennessee, I have cited where possible the version published in *The Papers of Andrew Johnson*. Following the lead of the editors of that ongoing project, I have tried to avoid the use of *"sic"* when quoting directly except where necessary to avoid confusion; I have also inserted bracketed material to clarify meaning. The numerous misspellings that appear in quoted material are in the originals.

Andrew Johnson and the Negro

Prologue

On February 7, 1866, a group of black men called at the White House. That such men were received at all indicates the profound social revolution that had just taken place in the United States. A few years earlier some of these visitors had been slaves. Now all were free men — men who were as quick to rest their future on the "American dream" as any other American.

Representing an Afro-American convention meeting in Washington, the delegation came with an "official" mission: to inform the president of their deliberations. Black representatives from Wisconsin, Alabama, Florida, Pennsylvania, Maryland, New York, and the District of Columbia, as well as the six New England states, had spent several days in debate before passing resolutions calling for federal action to "guarantee and secure to all loyal citizens, irrespective of race and color, equal rights before the law, including the right to impartial suffrage."[1] It did not take extensive political experience to recognize that the individual with the most potential influence on the future of such "rights" was Abraham Lincoln's successor, Andrew Johnson.

Ironically, Johnson's presence in the White House was almost as remarkable as that of his black visitors. While the former tailor from Tennessee had been an extremely successful politician before the Civil War, the secession of his home state coupled with his unsuccessful opposition to the move had, only a few years earlier, put his political future in serious jeopardy. Even more important, given the bitter nature of the era's political struggles, the ultimate outcome of the secession crisis had left the Republican Party as the dominant force in American politics. Johnson had been a lifelong and extremely partisan Democrat. Before secession his attacks on "Black Republicanism" had been as vicious as those of southern "fire-eaters." Now through the strange operation of the "fortunes of war," this former political enemy found himself as the symbolic head of the party he had attacked so bitterly.

As fellow beneficiaries of the war, members of the black delegation were concerned primarily with the "fortunes" of peace. The delegation's chairman was George T. Downing, a well-known resident of Washington and leader of its Negro community, but the group was unquestionably dominated by the most famous black man in America, Frederick Douglass. What Douglass and his colleagues really hoped to accomplish by visiting the president is less clear than their official goal. Certainly they had reason to expect a less-than-enthusiastic response. Douglass himself was rumored to have long been suspicious of the new occupant of the White House. A year earlier during the inaugural ceremonies, President Lincoln had pointed out the famous black abolitionist to Johnson. Glancing toward Douglass, the new vice-president visibly scowled. Somewhat taken aback, Douglass is reported to have whispered to a companion, "Whatever Andrew Johnson may be, he certainly is no friend of our race." Apocryphal or not, the supposed incident was prophetic and represents a perception of Johnson that would become more and more common in the ensuing months. Disillusioned with the results of the president's policies in the South, Douglass had already made several public assaults on the administration's approach to Reconstruction.[2] Such attacks seldom go unnoticed. It is quite possible that some in the delegation actually hoped to provoke a hostile reaction that could provide ammunition in the escalating but still muddled propaganda war between the executive branch and a small group of radicals in Congress. If this were the case, they would not be disappointed.

When the delegation was presented, the president was slouched in his chair, "hands in his pockets . . . looking a trifle sour." After a round of perfunctory handshaking, Downing introduced his friends and gave a brief prepared address in the typically obsequious rhetoric reserved for formal state occasions. He observed, perhaps with tongue in cheek, "that we come feeling that we are friends meeting a friend" and praised Johnson's record before concluding with an appeal for equal rights before the law, including suffrage.[3]

Frederick Douglass followed and, though maintaining the obligatory formality, was more direct and to the point:

> Mr. President, we are not here to enlighten you, sir, as to your duties as the Chief Magistrate of this Republic, but to show our respect, and to

present in brief the claims of our race to your favorable consideration. In the order of Divine Providence you are placed in a position where you have the power to save or destroy us, to bless or blast us – I mean our whole race. Your noble and humane predecessor placed in our hands the sword to assist in saving the nation, and we do hope that you, his able successor, will favorably regard the placing in our hands the ballot with which to save ourselves.

Even if a hostile response was anticipated, there must have been a lingering hope that Johnson would at least acquiesce in the basic principles behind such remarks. Certainly for a man elected by Republican votes, political expediency would dictate a token acceptance of the position held by his party's moderate wing. But tokenism had never been a visible part of Andrew Johnson's arsenal of political skills, and he responded with a harangue that lasted for forty-five minutes in a tone later described as "repressed anger."[4]

Starting with a promise not to make a speech – a phrase that would become familiar before his term was finished – the president emphasized his record. If he had not given evidence that he was a "friend of humanity, and especially the friend of the colored man," he claimed, there was nothing he could do now. He reminded his guests of his many sacrifices, assuring them that the feelings of his own heart had always "been for the colored man." He then became even more personal:

> I have owned slaves and bought slaves, but I never sold one. I might say, however, that practically, so far as my connection with slaves has gone, I have been their slave instead of their being mine. Some have even followed me here, while others are occupying and enjoying my property with my consent. For the colored race my means, my time, my all has been perilled; and now at this late date, after giving evidence that is tangible, that is practical, I am free to say to you that I do not like to be arraigned by some who can get up handsomely-rounded periods and deal in rhetoric, and talk about the abstract ideas of liberty, who never perilled life, liberty, or property. This kind of theoretical, hollow, unpractical friendship amounts to but very little. While I say that I am a friend of the colored man, I do not want to adopt a policy that I believe will end in a contest between the races, which if persisted in will result in the extermination of one or the other. God forbid that I should be engaged in such work!

Apparently emotions had gotten the best of the president. The formal remarks of Downing and Douglass were hardly an "arraignment," yet the lecture continued in the same belligerent tone. He would be happy, Johnson asserted, to lead the black man "from bondage to freedom," but that freedom would not include the right to vote. Approaching closely and appearing to direct his remarks toward Douglass, he provided his own interpretation of slavery to the former slave:

> Now, let us get closer up to this subject, and talk about it. . . . What relation has the colored man and the white man heretofore occupied in the South? I opposed slavery upon two grounds. First, it was a great monopoly, enabling those who controlled and owned it to constitute an aristocracy, enabling the few to derive great profits and rule the many with an iron rod, as it were. And this is one great objection to it in a government, being a monopoly. I was opposed to it secondly upon the abstract principle of slavery. Hence, in getting clear of a monopoly, we are getting clear of slavery at the same time. So you see there were two right ends accomplished in the accomplishment of the one.

At this point Douglass made an effort to interrupt but was cut off by the president, who continued his tirade, pointing out that most white southerners had not owned slaves, yet their status had been judged, even by blacks themselves, according to the number of servants owned. When Douglass failed to agree and attempted to explain the slaves' understandable antipathy and fear of the non-slaveholding white southerner, Johnson refused to listen and retorted that the poor white man "was opposed to the slave and his master." These two had combined to keep the poor whites "in slavery" and deny them an equal chance. Most important in the present situation, however, was the fact that the poor white had always been a part of the government. The government, Johnson declared, "derived from him." Freeing slaves had not been one of the objects of the war but came "as an incident to the suppression of a great rebellion — as an incident, and as an incident we would give it proper direction." When the rebellion began the black had been in bondage; he had gained everything. The poor white, "forced into the rebellion," had lost a great deal. Was it just to change their positions further, especially to the extent of forcing black suffrage on a people without their consent?

> Now, where do you begin? Government must have controlling power — must have a lodgement. For instance, suppose Congress should pass a law authorizing an election to be held at which all over twenty-one years of age, without regard to color, should be allowed to vote, and a majority should decide at such an election that the elective franchise should not be universal; what would you do about it? Who would settle it? Do you deny that first great principle of the right of the people to govern themselves? Will you re-

sort to arbitrary power, and say a majority of the people shall receive a state of things they are opposed to?

When Douglass, with considerable accuracy, pointed out that such an interpretation of democracy had been prominent in the South before the war, the president merely replied that the war had not changed the "principle." Even George Downing's request that the president apply this interpretation of democracy to South Carolina, where a majority of the inhabitants were colored, had little effect. Each community, the president insisted, was better situated "to determine the depository of its political power than anybody else." State legislatures should decide who should vote, not Congress. It was a fundamental tenet of his creed "that the will of the people must be obeyed." Could there be anything wrong or unfair in that?

Mr. Douglass, who had firsthand experience with the "will" of the southern people, smiled, and replied "A great deal that is wrong Mr. President, with all respect."

Johnson would not, or perhaps could not, understand Douglass's objections. He claimed to have confidence in the fairness of the people of each community. Problems would work out "harmoniously" only if unacceptable things were not forced upon the people:

> God knows I have no desire but the good of the whole human race. I would it were so that all you advocate could be done in the twinkling of an eye; but it is not in the nature of things, and I do not assume or pretend to be wiser than Providence, or stronger than the laws of nature.

After a few more words, the president thanked his visitors for the "compliment" they had paid him and attempted to bring the interview to a close, but the black leaders were far from satisfied. Both Douglass and Downing wished to make it clear that they did not concur with the arguments they had heard and asked for permission to answer for their people. Still attempting to end the session and apparently not wishing to hear their views, Johnson observed that it was his impression that they had only requested his honest opinion. Douglass then pointedly complained to the president, "You enfranchise your enemies and disfranchise your friends."

The tense exchange continued for a few moments until Johnson made a final suggestion. The freedmen, he advised, would be better served if their leaders would encourage them to leave the South. They could "live and advance in civilization" more easily if they were not crowded into one section of the country. Douglass tried to point out that as things stood poor whites and blacks were natural political allies, but the president refused to listen. Definitely concluding the interview, he ignored the obvious gulf between his guests and him, claiming that they were "both desirous of accomplishing the same ends, but proposed to do so by following different roads." Turning to leave, Douglass remarked to his fellow delegates, "The President sends us to the people, and we go to the people." Overhearing the statement, Johnson made a characteristic retort: "Yes, sir; I have great faith in the people. I believe they will do what is right."

Immediately after leaving the White House, the delegation discussed the situation with several Republican congressmen. The news was not good, and the black leaders were worried. The president would most certainly oppose their program for black suffrage. Both the blacks and their allies would have been even more alarmed had they heard Johnson's candid remarks following the group's departure. One of the president's private secretaries, present during the interview, remembered his description of the "darky delegation." "Those d——d sons of b——s thought they had me in a trap! I know that d——d Douglass; he's just like any nigger, and he would sooner cut a white man's throat as not."[5]

Though their disagreement over policy was real and important, neither Johnson nor Douglass was in a position to actually come to grips with the basis of their mutual hostility. The nineteenth-century mind was obviously well aware of racial prejudice but was not prepared to understand its deep social and psychological roots, much less the subtle and often hidden operation of racism in human affairs. Booker T. Washington, in his biography of Douglass, would later claim that what the country really needed at the time was a modern sociologist.[6] Yet even in the "enlightened" twentieth century, with its plethora of social scientists and psychologists, complete understanding often seems beyond our grasp. When Johnson faced Douglass he simply *felt* that blacks were inferior and would always remain so. Moreover, they somehow represented a danger to him and to what he defined as "the people." He could have explained his feelings in what he would have called "rational" terms if requested, but explanations were seldom needed. In fact, most white Americans shared his general conception of blacks as inferior even if they might disagree on particulars. Their attitude did not come from rational analysis but from an emotional reaction to what they considered a different species. It came from a perception created in their own minds — minds distorted by their society and its history.

In a sense, then, Johnson, Douglass, and most of their fellow Americans were victims of racism. Yet the results of this victimization depended not so much on the belief system itself as on how that system evolved and influenced the actions of each individual. Of course, in Andrew Johnson's case racial attitudes would exert influence far beyond a clash of personality between two men. Andrew Johnson's basic racism would help distort the immediate future and leave a bitter legacy for generations to come.

Chapter 1

Andrew Johnson's World

Can the Ethiopian change his skin, or the leopard his spots?
then may ye also do good, that are accustomed to do evil.

Jeremiah 14:23

No man, at least no man considered sane, can escape the world he lives in any more than he can change the color of his skin. Andrew Johnson was a nineteenth-century American. He could be nothing else. His reaction to blacks had to be rooted, generally at least, in the conceptions of race held in his own time. Existing ideology and social attitudes provide the fixed boundary, the "setting," within which individual ideas of a historical "character" develop. Although a complete description of nineteenth-century thinking about race is obviously beyond the scope of this book, it might be useful to at least establish an outline of the world of ideas in which Johnson and his contemporaries operated.

Sketching what might be called the perimeter of alternatives, however, is only a first step since questions concerning the relation of environment to personality must ultimately play a part. Such questions are always particularly difficult in a historical context. Because of the nature of the craft, a historian appears in the guise of a simple empiricist. The past is explained by a description of events, a complex pattern of empirical facts that seem to produce an understandable narrative. As a result, the personality, no matter how complex, seems purely a creature of environment. That such a view often oversimplifies reality is obvious. The personality is, of course, influenced by environment, but that influence must be understood as a complicated system of exchange between a person and the world as experienced. Moreover, the individual is always changing, just as ideas about the world available to him or her constantly undergo change.[1]

Perhaps the least difficult way to deal with the problem, avoiding some of the more esoteric theories entertained by philosophers and psychologists, is to imagine the individual as a shopper in a modern supermarket. The shelves are filled with a myriad of ideas, attitudes, and observations. In the case of most complex, value-laden subjects, race for instance, the selection process is clearly not rational. The shopper does not carefully choose from the wares displayed. Rather, he grabs at random, depending on what is near at hand, what is already in his basket, and the whims of his own personality. Nor are most people, certainly not Andrew Johnson, cosmopolitan intellectuals with broad choices. They are limited to immediate environment. In the past century, given the relatively low level of general education and the lack of a true mass media, most people would be shopping from the equivalent of a small country store.

This narrowness of choice on matters concerning race for almost everyone living in the nineteenth century has often been given insufficient emphasis by historians concerned with the subject. Some writers seem to forget the simple fact that the last hundred years have witnessed extensive development in the ability of humans to understand themselves. While our knowledge is still obviously limited, we know far more about our species and our social order than our ancestors could have, and, as a result, our system of values has also changed. The modern concept of race has been an important part of this growing self-awareness. Today we have the means, however imperfect, of objectively measuring group differences. Hence, any conceivable defense of the idea of racial supremacy has long since vanished. To the nineteenth-century mind, however, our concept of race and what is meant when we use the word "racism" would be difficult to understand. Certainly most people in the era did not consider racial prejudice morally unacceptable.

For historians, the distortion produced by our modern perspective is aggravated by a temptation to deal exclusively with the involvement of race in politics or with what individuals, especially intellectuals, wrote about the subject. Voluminous and easily accessible, these sources provide only the tip of the iceberg. Laws and debates are more often rationalizations after the fact. Response to another group is not formulated by reason following the careful consideration of empirical evidence. Nor are people apt to talk about the real origin of such opinions, since they are not consciously aware of them.[2]

Though the foundations of racial prejudice are the subject of considerable controversy, psychologists would generally agree that they are deeply buried in the human psyche. In most cases it would be impossible for an historian to explain and document their effect, but their existence should never be ignored. Sigmund Freud, for example, argues that the tendency of humans to accept and identify with the familiar, with their own value system or group in opposition to difference, is related to basic ego-centered drives. "In the undisguised antipathies and aversion which people feel toward strangers with whom they have to do, we recognize the expression of self-love, of narcissism." One need not accept Freud's hypothesis to be aware of ingroup identification in almost all humans. It is one source of what sociologists call "ethnocentrism" and is probably a normal, or perhaps necessary, response. Gordon Allport, the noted psychologist of prejudice, generalizes from considerable evidence that groups do, in fact, "tend to stay apart" by choice. This is not necessarily prejudice or racism; it may well be the product of other factors. Yet once separation exists, "the ground is laid for all sorts of psychological elaboration."[3]

Most important in black-white relations is the impact of glaring physical difference. Harmannus Hoetink, the noted Dutch sociologist, stresses this factor in understanding the varied patterns of race relations and develops terms like "somatic norm image" and "somatic distance" to describe the culturally determined esthetic ideals that define acceptable criteria for physical appearance.[4] In nineteenth-century America the dominant whites inherited, at a cultural level so basic as to seem *almost* biological, an image of what people were supposed to look like, and this image excluded Negroes.

In Western society the handicap for dark-skinned people does not end with appearance. The very meaning of blackness has strong negative connotations within all European cultures. Frantz Fanon explains the symbolic implications:

> *In Europe, the black man is the symbol of evil.* . . . The torturer is the black man, Satan is black, one talks of shadows, when one is dirty one is black—whether one is thinking of physical dirtiness or moral dirtiness. It would be astonishing, if the trouble were taken to bring them all together, to see the vast number of expressions that make the black man the equivalent of sin. In Europe, whether concretely or symbolically, the black man stands for the bad side of character. As long as one cannot understand this fact, one is doomed to talk in circles about the "black problem."[5]

Basic attitudes firmly embedded in the human personality and, in the Western world, the general culture, would mean that our shopper in the nineteenth-century supermarket of ideas, like Andrew Johnson, would be predisposed to certain general beliefs. Because much of the selection process is unconscious and almost completely unperceived by the contemporary equivalent of social science, the impact is exaggerated. In such a world it is hard to imagine how a person, without some kind of strong contradictory force, could be other than a racist. Looking at racism in this manner means that one key to understanding its existence in the nineteenth century lies in identifying the social forces in a particular culture that might work against it and how such forces operate within the individual personality.

Certainly in a country that claimed to be built on the precept that "all men are created equal," there must have been some sort of ideological resistance to the conversion of ethnocentrism into racism. On the level of political theory, the ideas of the Enlightenment, which form the basis of American political thought, had emphasized the importance of the individual human being and declared perpetual war on the value system that lay beneath the established social order in Europe, a social order that for thousands of years had simply accepted, as a matter of course, exploitation, inhumanity, slavery, and oppression. Clearly this "American ideology" was a key part of the first assault on slavery, which took place during the Revolutionary era and led to emancipation in the northern states. But that assault had not been based on a theory of "racial" equality. Moreover, rhetoric aside, these revolutionary ideas remained largely that—ideas. Americans may have rejected the basis and the rigidity of the European class system, but a system of classes was still the social norm even if the criteria for position had changed.

One of the best illustrations of the resulting war between ideals and reality was the struggle carried on in the mind of the author of the Declaration of Independence himself. Thomas Jefferson, one of the preeminent American intellectuals of his time, had a mind steeped in the spirit of the Enlightenment and a belief in the "natural rights" of man that bordered on a religion. Yet Jefferson was also a slaveholder and, in spite of theoretical opposition, could never bring himself to free his own slaves. Part of the rationale for participating in a system he professed to abhor was pure self-interest. Freeing his slaves would have condemned him and his descendants to poverty.[6] Nevertheless, his reluctant support of slavery was buttressed by an attitude, no matter how much Jefferson qualified it, that could only be characterized as a kind of racism.

He made his views clear in *Notes on the State of Virginia.* Negroes were "in reason much inferior" to whites. In spite of all the advantages available to some in America, he had never found a black capable of uttering "a thought above the level of plain narration." When faced with contrary evidence Jefferson chose to ignore it, warping logic to fit his argument. For example, in his opinion Negroes had never produced a poet even though their melancholy condition should have been excellent raw material for verse. Phyllis Wheatly, the contemporary black writer, was "not a poet. The compositions published under her name are below the dignity of criticism." Of course, this man of the Enlightenment was willing to suspend judgment and await the verdict of natural history, even if forced to advance the idea as a "suspicion only" that Africans, whatever the reason, were innately inferior.[7] Though it may seem less than charitable, one cannot avoid concluding, as a "suspicion only," that no matter how strong the scientific evidence to the contrary, Jefferson would still *feel* Negroes to be inferior.

If a mind like Jefferson's, with its ideological foundation, could not overcome the patterns of racial inequality built into society, how many others could? Clearly some American writers and thinkers, especially those without the obvious handicap of living intimately with slavery, advanced ideas approaching a conception of human equality, but one can still detect in these speculations the imprint of feelings of racial superiority. Almost nowhere in the United States was the social structure anything other than avowedly racist. And it is also significant that many of the antislavery–pro-Negro writers began not from a basis of Enlightenment philosophy but from Christianity's much older belief in the unity of the human race. In the mid-nineteenth century this belief was strongly challenged by science — the science that Jefferson claimed would solve the problem of the Negro's place in society. With the rise of the "American school" of anthropology, natural history gave its answer: Blacks belonged to a different, inferior species.

Samuel George Morton, originator of the "American school," was a physician who became president of the Academy of Natural Science in Philadelphia. His considerable reputation was based on the study of natural history, and his primary interest seems to have been skulls. In his early twenties he became fascinated with these human remnants and amassed the largest known collection, called poetically the "American Golgotha." Precise measurement of crania, coupled with the common belief that mulattoes were less fertile than either parent, convinced him that whites and blacks belonged to different species. In his most noted work, *Crania America* (1839), Morton drew back from an out-right declaration of innate Negro inferiority, but his research paved the way for disciples without his rigid scientific scruples.

The most widely read apostles of the "American school" were two characters closer to medicine-show vendors than modern scientists. George Robin Glidden was an Englishman who served as American vice-counsul at Cairo and later parlayed his acquaintance with Egypt into a lucrative career on the lecture tour. His collaborator, Josiah Clark Nott, practiced medicine in Mobile and made an avocation of defending slavery. Popularizers of Morton's ideas, buttressed with some of their own dubious interpretations, these two produced what might be considered the master work of nineteenth-century American racism, *Types of Mankind* (1854). With considerable elaboration the book argued that the races of mankind belonged to different species — the white the superior and the black the obvious inferior.[8]

In spite of its pejorative tone, *Types of Mankind* cannot be dismissed as mere propaganda, though it certainly contained that element. The view received considerable support from the scientific community — not the least of which was Louis Agassiz, the noted Swiss naturalist. Recognized as one of the leading scientists of his time, Agassiz settled in the United States in 1846. Shortly after his arrival, he made a pilgrimage to Morton's "Golgotha" and became convinced of the separate origin of the races, a belief he held the rest of his life in defiance of Charles Darwin's theories.

The background of Agassiz's conversion is extremely revealing. Not long after arriving he had his first physical contact with blacks, who were waiting tables at a Philadelphia hotel. He wrote his mother describing shock at their appearance. The color, the big lips, the odd limbs, and the heads covered with wool rather than hair almost caused him to bolt the room in disgust. These creatures, though human, were not of the same species as Europeans. It was easy to see they were not the equals of white men, and he claimed that almost all Americans, even abolitionists, considered them inferior.[9] If appearance could have had such an effect on an "objective" scientist, what must have been the impact on the less educated and less objective, especially when the social structure required the black to appear always in the role of an inferior?

It would be a mistake to consider the scientific arguments of Agassiz or the "American school" typical; such an approach required a sophistication of mind and a level of concern beyond the average man. Moreover, in Christian America one did not need recourse to the infidel theories of scientists to defend the existing social structure when the Bible itself provided a convenient tool for all sorts of rationalization. The legend of Ham was the most commonly cited piece of scriptural evidence, but numerous other examples were used.[10] Most, of course, would never need even this rationale; the reality of separation reinforced belief daily. In short, at all levels of society white Americans, like Andrew Johnson, began life in the nineteenth century with the odds heavily in favor of the acceptance of some form of racism.

Still, in the United States, especially in the exalted image Americans had of their revolutionary system, there remained fundamental opposition to the principles underlying slavery, if not racism. Nowhere is this more evident than in the humanitarian reform movement of the early nineteenth century and the eventual success of its offspring, abolitionism. Yet the reformers, no matter how popular their ideas in the abstract, remained outside the mainstream of society. Moreover, abhorrence of the peculiar institution did not require the acceptance of an equal status for its victims. Nor did it hinder men of basic good will, intelligence, and what passed for objectivity from concluding, whatever the rationale, that Negroes were somehow less than human. The legal status of free blacks in the North, the writings of most intellectuals, and the social ostracism that existed, even in such hotbeds of freedom as Massachusetts, tell the same basic story albeit with variable plots.[11] In short, even nineteenth-century humanitarianism, itself something of an anomaly, did not lead to the general acceptance of racial equality.

This is perhaps the most significant element of uniqueness in nineteenth-century American racial thought. In direct contradiction to an equalitarian ideology, most Americans held a conception of race involving some kind of hierarchy with the white at the top and the black at the bottom. Whatever the justification, and there were many, only a racist division of humanity could create psychological agreement between American myth and reality.

Although racism was a national condition, the actual pattern differed from section to section. One might expect it to be harsher — or at least possess a different "quality" — in the slave South, Andrew Johnson's section. Generalization, however, is more difficult than it appears; the South was never monolithic. The distribution of slaves in relation to whites is a prime illustration. In Tennessee the number at no time exceeded a quarter of the population — a ratio that needs only to be compared to statistics from a state of the deep South to illustrate the point.[12] Certainly a difference in relative numbers must have had considerable impact on the development of the socioracial structure.

This lack of uniformity was very important in the narrow world of Andrew Johnson. No state was more influenced by intrastate sectionalism than Tennessee, and slavery was clearly part of the problem. East Tennessee, Johnson's section, had in 1839 only 7,878 taxable slaves valued at $3,712,033. At the same time, Middle and West Tennessee had 46,067 and 24,073 taxable slaves, respectively, valued considerably higher. Plainly having nothing to do with social origins, the difference was rooted in geography. Suitable for large-scale cultivation and easily accessible to water transportation, the land of Middle and West Tennessee made the production of large-scale money crops by slave labor profitable. East Tennessee's mountain terrain, poor by comparison, forced its farmers into subsistence production and livestock raising. Here, and in other similar regions in the South, economic well-being did not revolve around the slave system. The non-slaveholder or small-scale slaveholder was dominant, economically and politically.[13]

The lack of a strong economic commitment to slavery explains, in part, the presence of hostility toward the institution in that area throughout the antebellum period. With regularity, East Tennessee representatives to the General Assembly advocated measures essentially in opposition to slavery or, at least, to the interest of slaveowners. As late as 1834, at the state constitutional convention, a small group even made a futile effort to insert into the constitution a scheme for gradual emancipation. The region was also, for a short time, the center of an embryo abolition movement. The first organization clearly dedicated to emancipation was founded in Jefferson County in 1814, and the movement grew until it encompassed at least twenty-five active societies by the late 1820s. In March 1819, Elihu Embree, a Quaker slaveholder, started the weekly *Manumission Intelligencer* at Jonesboro, sponsored by the Tennessee Manumission Society; his paper was, for a brief period, the only periodical in the country dedicated solely to the antislavery cause. After Embree's death a few inhabitants encouraged Benjamin Lundy to bring his *Genius of Universal Emancipation* to Greeneville, where he began publication in 1822, remaining for more than two years before moving to Baltimore.[14]

The burst of abolition activity in these early decades was short-lived and not always popular. Lundy reported that he had been threatened in "many ways" in Tennessee, and the membership in antislavery societies, led essentially by Quakers and a few Presbyterians, never seems to have been over one thousand. Moreover, organized opposition to slavery disappeared altogether in the late 1830s, the last society apparently ceasing to function in 1837. Chase Mooney, the historian of Tennessee's peculiar institution, explains this collapse as the result of a number of related factors. Never radical, Tennessee abolitionists had little real influence, and after the beginning of a more uncompromising abolition crusade in the North coupled with the specter of slave revolt following the Nat Turner uprising, their position became increasingly uncomfortable. Many of the most energetic advocates of freedom in Tennessee moved to the Old Northwest. Also, and perhaps equally important, the center of population as well as political power had shifted westward into regions more hospitable to unfree labor.[15]

As pointed out earlier, opposition to slavery did not mean absence of racism or a lack of hostility to black people. In fact, there is reason to believe that general attitudes toward the Negro were more antagonistic in the mountain regions of the South than in regions where slavery dominated. In one of his descriptions of the area, Frederick Law Olmsted gave an account of a conversation with an old East Tennessee squire and his wife:

> He asked if New York were not a free State, and how I liked that. I answered and he said He'd always wished there hadn't been any niggers here (the old woman called out from the other room that she wished so, too), but he wouldn't like to have them free. As they had got them here he didn't think there was any better way of getting along with them than they had.[16]

This same perception was visible to John Eaton, at one time General Superintendent of Freedmen, Department of Tennessee. He reported in his memoirs that although the colored refugee problem was not as severe in East Tennessee as far as numbers were concerned, " the prejudice of the whites against the Negro was even more acute." Perhaps the most extreme example of this kind of hostility was Hinton Rowan Helper, North Carolina mountain white and famous, or perhaps infamous, author of *The Impending Crisis*. It is hard to imagine a stronger opponent of slavery than this one-time darling of the antislavery Republicans, yet Helper maintained a venomous hatred for Negroes and other "inferior races."[17]

Since the planter class hardly existed in the mountains, it is possible to view this intense race hostility as, in part, a product of social position. It simply appeared stronger because the self-serving paternalism of the planter was not present to soften public expressions of hatred. Olmsted implies that lower-class whites everywhere in the South harbored intense feelings against the black, and he assumed that the attitude stemmed largely from the direct economic threat posed by the Negro, slave or free.[18] While there is much truth in such an assessment, it needs qualification in the light of modern understanding about personality.

In his classic study of modern racism, *Caste and Class in a Southern Town*, John Dollard maintains that the severest hostility came not from the lowest-class whites but from the middle class. Negroes in *Southern Town* had a name for these people that was quite appropriate; they were "strainers"—those straining to maintain their shaky position in society. Upwardly mobile, middle-class whites were much more concerned with status and therefore determined to preserve the rigid color line.[19] Applying similar logic to nineteenth-century conditions might well explain the intense race hostility of the nonslaveholding yeoman and the mountaineer, far more numerous and influential politically and socially than the stereotypical "poor whites." The yeoman and the mountaineer, the nineteenth-century version of a southern middle class, felt most strongly the threat to status represented by blacks. To the classic "poor white," status was not that important. He had none and was unlikely to acquire any. He may have been capable of great violence toward Negroes, or anyone else for that matter, but would be less able to maintain rigid racial barriers.

This view is reinforced by the well-documented existence of intense race hostility in the Old Northwest, also a frontier area with a small farm economy. As astute an observer as Alexis de Tocqueville commented on the attitude and, in fact, maintained that during his trip to the United States in the 1830s he found the prejudice against blacks more severe in "those states where slavery has never been known." Eugene H. Berwanger's *Frontier Against Slavery*, an excellent study of race prejudice in the area, gives considerable credence to the observation.[20]

Looking at race thinking in this manner—admittedly a hypothesis only—and reducing it to a personal level suggests that racial attitudes were more strongly influenced by one's definition of his own social position: his status. The yeoman, the mountaineer, the mechanic, and the frontiersman of the Old Northwest, all taught in the democratic age of the nineteenth century to consider themselves "as good as any man" yet facing an increasingly unequal social structure, were pushed toward ever greater expressions of race hatred. Such an approach also suggests that attitudes varied greatly, depending on how each individual defined his status rather than his actual economic position, and could change should the individual's definition of his social position change.

An individual's perception of status and his exposure to ideas depends in large part on the alternatives available in his own small corner of the world—his local supermarket of opinion. In 1826, when seventeen-year-old Andrew Johnson arrived in Greeneville, no one would call the backwoods village a center of culture. J. S. Buckingham, an English traveler who visited the area in the late 1830s, was so unimpressed that his description consisted largely of complaints about the "most disagreeable road" encountered and the crude accommodations at the inn of one "Major Malony."[21] One might ignore Buckingham's priggish comments as an example of British snobbery, but O. P. Temple, East Tennessee's self-appointed historian, was a native of Greene County, if no lover of Greeneville. He described the village as having a "reasonable percentage of culture" and in general "on a par with its neighbors." But nowhere in town was there "a single man of wide intelligence who could act as an example for the young. . . . Good books were rare and perhaps there were not one hundred standard works of literature in town." In those days there were "no popular lectures, no magazines, certainly none for remote Greeneville."[22]

That Temple was probably exaggerating for effect should not obscure the essential accuracy of his description. No matter how much one may glorify the coonskin cap and the independent spirit, one of the basic elements of frontier life was the absence of intellectual stimulation. The pioneer, with few exceptions, remained fundamentally ignorant of the world outside, and East Tennessee, though settled for many years, remained a kind of frontier. Greeneville, like hundreds of other remote nineteenth-century villages, was separated from the mainstream of life by bad roads, poor communications, and, perhaps, a willful ignorance on the part of her population. Life was rugged, and most people, occupied with the hard work of living, could not spare the time to cultivate their minds or wrestle with complex new ideas. What worked for their fathers would work as well for them. Ideas that might contradict the established patterns of society were rare or much diluted by the time they reached Greeneville.

The one modern conception that did trickle down seems to have been Jacksonian democracy—or at least its rhetoric. Even in this remote mountain village, however, such an idea ran afoul of established structure. Though the lines were seldom rigidly drawn and the gulf between groups never large, class had considerable influence on the frontier. Greeneville's own version of an aristocracy was made up of a group of merchants and early arrivals who had secured the best land. Men like William and John Dickson, Valentine Sevier, and Dr. Alexander Williams, the "Grand Duke of Lick Creek," dominated the social and political life of the county. They built pretentious homes, amassed moderate amounts of wealth, and usually owned a few slaves. Holding themselves above the "common sort," these men helped create a definite class hierarchy. To an outside observer the difference might not have appeared great, but it certainly had an effect on those who lived within such a system.[23]

However, in the case of Greeneville, it is at least possible to speculate that those excluded from the "social register," the vast majority, may have been somewhat unique. They seem to have been willing receptacles of democratic mythology. If popular legend is to be believed, there was considerable class and political consciousness and, after 1830, the plebeians challenged the political control of the "aristocratic clique." Even Temple, a hostile Whig, saw a kind of vibrancy in Greene County democracy, calling it the "genuine article." There is little doubt that he meant his assessment in a pejorative sense, but in his description of the rough-and-tumble world of the county's politics, one does sense an exaggeration in the Jacksonian appeal to the common man. This does not mean that the actual result of politics was much different from that in other areas. As Thomas P. Abernethy has pointed out, there was a great deal more rhetoric than reality in nineteenth-century democracy, and certainly the people of Greene County usually followed the dictates of their leaders, as the career of Andrew Johnson would illustrate. Still, the leaders, either by desire or political necessity, felt the need to dwell on their identification with the common man.[24] Even if this vaunted democracy is simply fable, the existence of such a legend would indicate the importance that class position assumed in the minds of the citizens of Greene. Here, as probably elsewhere in Jacksonian America, egalitarian philosophy ran headlong into a much older means of organizing society, producing a peculiar American version of class conflict.

If anything, the social structure as it related to race may have reinforced the democratic atmosphere. As in the rest of East Tennessee, slavery was not a key element in the economic life of Greene County. In 1800 there were only 471 slaves out of 7610 inhabitants, a little over

6 percent of the population. Though the absolute number of bondsmen would grow with the population, the percentage would never approximate the state average. Equally important, most of the slaveowners held relatively few Negroes. In 1850, at the apex of the institution nationally, only eleven men in the county had fifteen or more slaves and only two of these owned more than twenty. Also, during the early decades of the century, Greeneville was the veritable center of East Tennessee abolitionism. The first convention of the Tennessee Manumission Society, which created the statewide organization, met at the Lick Creek Meeting House of Friends on November 21, 1815, and, probably more important, Benjamin Lundy's abolition paper was actually published in Greeneville.[25]

It is difficult to gauge the impact of the antislavery movement on the community at large. Lundy clearly tried to direct his publication to a national audience, and it is safe to assume that a large number of subscribers came from outside the immediate area. Moreover, the gradualist approach of all Tennessee antislavery advocates was quite evident, and never did they call for anything approaching social equality. In 1823 the Manumission Society even endorsed the idea of colonization, an alternative repudiated later by more radical northern abolitionists because it was considered essentially antiblack. On the other hand, it should also be remembered that Greeneville at least tolerated Lundy's antislavery views, something that would have been impossible in many southern communities, particularly after 1830. No organized opposition ever seems to have developed, and his other newspaper, a weekly devoted to agriculture and general news, had no great difficulty in acquiring sufficient advertising.[26]

No matter how widespread the support of the moderate antislavery position, it is still doubtful that Lundy and his cohorts had much impact on the commonly held opinions about people of color — opinions that amounted to a general dehumanization. This attitude could even find expression in the abolitionist editor's own publications. In 1824, the *American Economist and East Tennessee Statesman* printed a Fourth of July address delivered by J. F. Deadrick at Greeneville College, the local citadel of learning. The view of race might be considered typical and apparently did not alarm Lundy. After suitable patriotic rumblings, the speaker launched into an analysis of American republicanism that leasted for what must have seemed to his listeners an interminable time. America's revolution had been of a far nobler character than other similar movements because its triumphs were "victories of reason – of justice – of humanity" and, of course, had the specific approval of the Almighty. The key to success was "civil liberty," the most important "blessing civilized man" possessed and "heaven's noblest – dearest and most precious gift. . . . " The lack of civil liberty was slavery:

> When Slavery rears her sickly head among the habitations of men, how debasing the effects she spreads around! imagination droops – the loftiest energies that enoble man are doomed to languish in supine sluggishness – the expanding buds of genius are crushed in embryo – and human nature is reduced to its lowest state of mental degradation. . . .[27]

If the listener were not careful, these passionate words might be mistaken for the ravings of a wild-eyed abolitionist, but nothing could have been further from the speaker's mind. When the statement is placed in context it becomes clear that, with no apparent self-consciousness about word selection, the reference was not to Negro slavery at all. Slavery simply meant the absence of republicanism – the lack of civil liberty for whites. The speaker plainly could never imagine blacks as capable of such an exalted system and seemed naively unaware of the contradiction. In short, in his mind the enslavement of *men* was obviously different from the enslavement of *blacks.* The rationale is made clear in a description of the remainder of the benighted world – in other words, that portion of the globe beyond America:

> From the cold and barren region of Kamschatha to the southern country of the sluggish Hottentot – from the western extremity of Erin, to the remote isles of Sunda, the deadly sway of despotism and ignorance chains the intellect – cramps the virtue and curbs the noblest aspirations of man. In Asia the clouds of superstition and ignorance veil the eyes of the inhabitants to the proper dignity of the species; and make them cringe with slavish alacrity to the capricious tyranny of their idolized despots. The effeminate Persian – the superstitious Hindoo – the slavish Russian – the heartless suspicious Chinese, all furnish striking example of the depth of degradation to which human nature is capable of descending – Benighted Africa's barren sands are but a faint symbol of the moral sterility which reigns throughout the land. The wandering Arab's savage yell – the stupid ignorance of the sottish Hottentot – and the contemptible idolatry of the meanhearted Egyptian peasant, in general, the degraded features of a people, long since resigned to the arms of barbarism. In Europe we behold here and there a spark of the sacred fire, but crimes and corruption darken its brightness, and smother it, ere it breaks into a flame. The grandeur of Italy is gone. Russia's vast

population crouches to a despot. France and Spain bear upon their necks the heavy yoke of tyranny. Degenerate England joins the general throng — and Scandinavia's icy realms still languish in their wonted insignificancy.[28]

Popular as this attitude might have been in East Tennessee, one would shudder to think what might have happened to American diplomacy in Deadrick's hands. But far more important, his chauvinistic babblings reveal a conception of man in the universe, whatever the rationale, that groups people into a hierarchical arrangement, everyone inferior to Deadrick's own group. Western Europeans represented the best of a bad lot. They were not innately inferior and might have been as good as Americans had it not been for "crime and corruption." Never referred to as a kind of people, with one exception, these decadent Europeans were denounced by place names. The rest of the world — the non-white world — is damned in very personal terms. Asians were "effeminate," "superstitious," "heartless," or "suspicious" and illustrated how low human beings could sink. It was the people themselves, not nations, that were at fault. Still, with the Asians human status was recognized and an act of will implied. One is superstitious or effeminate because one wants to be. The poor, benighted African, especially the black, seems to have been much worse off; he had no choice in the matter at all. The Hottentot, for example, was "sluggish" or "sottish." Such adjectives refer directly to innate physical characteristics, and it is not likely that anyone possessing such attributes would ever be admitted into the glorious fraternity of republican liberty. Given such logic, American ideals could actually become a contributing factor in the evolution of ethnocentrism into racism and with very little dissonance provide sanction for an unequal social system based on color.

Such was the normal place of the Negro in Andrew Johnson's world. Whether scientist, theologian, or backwoodsman, the white American, with few exceptions, usually viewed mankind as a hierarchy — with himself at the top or at least intrinsically capable of being there. The black could fit in only at the bottom. Even those who professed to believe otherwise and who opposed the obvious evil of slavery drew back from affirming complete equality and thereby lost their best argument. Inclusion of creatures not actually equal would be a disaster in a democratic system, destroying the newly won self-respect of the common man and, more important, destroying the logic underpinning a democratic form of government.

In a place like Greeneville — Johnson's country store of opinion — the situation would be exaggerated. Nineteenth-century ideas, weak tools in any case, which might have been used to counter the natural development of ethnocentrism or the patterns of society that directed such an attitude toward racism, seldom reached the isolated backwoods. When the most powerful idea of the first half of the nineteenth century, Jacksonian democracy, did trickle down it probably reinforced "group" identification. Democracy was easily narrowed to include only those true members of the family of man — whites. It is asking a great deal to expect men struggling against an oppressive class structure to accept equality with those already considered by almost everyone to be below them. It was so much easier to be brother to the master than to the slave. By standing on the shoulders of the black man, the nineteenth-century believer in democracy — the "strainer" — could join, at least symbolically, his betters. Andrew Johnson was one man who clearly wished to join his "betters."

Chapter 2

The Self-made Man

If Andy Johnson was a snake, he would hide in the grass
and bite the heels of rich men's children.

Isham G. Harris
Governor of Tennessee[1]

A courageous man of the people, a bitter demagogue, a snake in
the grass — in his own time opinions about Andrew Johnson were seldom expressed with moderation. Adversaries like Isham Harris reserved
their most caustic phrases for his benefit, while admirers spoke of their
champion in glowing superlatives. Intemperate rhetoric was, of course,
part of mid–nineteenth-century politics; yet modern historians, far
removed from the political struggles of the post-Jacksonian world and
the violence of civil war, continue the debate, albeit in more subdued
tones. These differing perceptions are, in part, reflections of a complex,
dynamic personality in difficult times, but they also illustrate that many
of the "old" issues have never been resolved, most important the seemingly endless conflict over race relations.

The demise of slavery left the future status of the freedmen as a burning residue, and nearly all other problems in the Reconstruction era
seemed to touch this issue and be affected by it. As president, Johnson
took an approach that was interpreted by contemporaries as essentially
hostile to the integration of blacks into American society and politics.
Few modern historians would challenge this viewpoint and, since the
majority of works about Johnson have concentrated on the presidency,
his response to the Negro assumes an exaggerated role in historical assessments of his character. In fact, his obvious racism and a writer's
reaction to it are often the keys to understanding interpretations of the
man.

In the first half of this century, avowedly pro-Johnson writers usually reflected the prevailing notions about Negro inferiority and saw Reconstruction as the president's finest hour. Biographers, in particular, threw objectivity to the winds, often finding Johnson the beau ideal of American statesmanship and the Negro — after suitable homage to paternalism — something less than a white man. The best of a bad lot, Robert Winston, ironically using Louis Agassiz as scientific authority, stated his position without equivocation. "Social equality is impracticable, and the negroes are 'a people within a people'."[2] With such an attitude, it is easy to understand why the bitter struggle with the so-called radicals is seen as positively heroic.

Once the latter-day Confederate is excepted, modern Reconstruction scholarship, especially of the revisionist variety, has totally reversed the image. Living in an age in which "racist" has become a pejorative and belief in racial inferiority a refuge for the ignorant, contemporary historians are almost required to look with some degree of disfavor at Johnson's policies and often at the man himself, whatever the motive for his actions. The minority who continue to insist on a more benevolent view of the president invariably de-emphasize the influence of racial attitudes during Reconstruction. This relationship between race thinking and judgments about Johnson's character is obviously no accident. It is a function of the actual role that such ideas play in human affairs.

The development of a set of beliefs, like racism, and the actions taken at least partially in response to such beliefs are the result of a complicated interaction among ideas, events, and that mysterious collection of unknowns called the human personality. Which element makes the greatest contribution in a given case is often more a question of perspective than anything else. Certainly ideas, which seem so clear in the abstract, become part of a tangled web when we try to decipher their influence on action. Further, the more deeply held a particular belief, the more difficult it is to separate from personality.

For historians, our own attitudes and the prevailing views of our time naturally enter the picture and become part of the equation. This has clearly been the case in the historical debate over Reconstruction. Moreover, restricted by the chronological limits of a single inquiry, historians often concentrate on one period of an individual's career, distorting his actual beliefs through the haze of specific events. Just as historians have changed with time, the personality of an historical character evolves throughout his life. Deeply held beliefs, such as racism, may be resistant to change, but they are hardly static and must be understood as part of this evolutionary process.

One of the few times the controversy that always seemed to swirl about Johnson's personality became restrained was during the natural rush of sympathy following his death, yet, even here, the picture that emerged from dozens of eulogies was of a man whose life could be described only in extreme terms. In the United States Senate, for example, none of his former colleagues, even old foes, who rose to pronounce the obligatory eulogy for a fallen statesman, could resist hyperbole. In particular, almost no senator seemed able to avoid making some reference to the former tailor as the prototypical self-made man. Oliver P. Morton, the tough-minded Republican governor of Indiana during the Civil War, began his oration by refusing to apologize for having been in favor of Johnson's impeachment but followed with what became a familiar litany before the day was finished. Andrew Johnson "was born in the humble walks of life; he lived in poverty and had no advantages of an early education." Seeming to intimate that success in the face of such adversity was, in itself, a great virtue, Morton went on to catalog the triumphs of the man he had once tried to remove from office — a man who had climbed "step by step" up the ladder of political success.[3]

This idea of climbing things, moving upward and onward, seems to have had important symbolic meaning for Andrew Johnson himself. In his first inaugural address as governor of Tennessee, he conjured up a vision of democracy with implications far beyond the glorification of party:

> It will be readily perceived by all discerning young men, that Democracy is a ladder, corresponding in politics, to the one spiritual which Jacob saw in his vision: one up which all, in proportion to their merit, may ascend. While it extends to the humblest of all created beings here on earth below, it reaches to God on high; . . .[4]

The metaphor was not simply a rhetorical device; to Johnson, it was an obsession. His whole life, as he reminded contemporaries in speech after speech, was a persistent assault on his own version of Jacob's ladder. Each success in his remarkable career became, in his own mind, an example of the opportunity available within the democratic system, as well as a private vindication. Nearly every address he made contained at least one passage praising democracy and offering Andy Johnson as its embodiment. It was his true religion, and he made proselytizing an integral part of politics.

His constituents obviously heard and believed; the "masses," as Johnson loved to call them, responded with votes. Prior to his ill-fated debacle as president, he was defeated in a popular election only once and held almost every elective office possible from city alderman to president. Even detractors, as much as they might have snickered in private at his social origins or laughed at the numerous "andy johnsonisms," accepted his self-proclaimed status as an American success story and, at times, admitted a grudging admiration for his dogged climb.[5]

In American mythology, no image is more potent than that of the self-made man. Listening to any of the Fourth of July speeches that annually canonize American political leadership, one might acquire the distinct impression that a humble birth is an important prerequisite for political success. Daniel Webster is reported to have once lamented the fact that he was not born in a log cabin, and certainly most Americans remember that Abraham Lincoln was born in just such a cabin. Yet, once common sense replaces inflated rhetoric, it is obvious that an early life of hardship and a long struggle to raise oneself does not guarantee virtue or, in the case of leadership, political acumen. Poverty can hardly be a real advantage when, in Johnson's case as in Lincoln's, it is not political cant. It was the simple, grinding truth.

There is another side to the hallowed image of the self-made man, one seldom mentioned by those wishing to praise. Early adversity, particularly in an individual who feels himself gifted beyond his station, seems as apt to breed bitterness and hatred as admirable characteristics. Johnson's enemies — and he was never without them in reality or in his own mind — left ample evidence that his character contained elements that were less than attractive. Isham Harris's picture of the self-appointed plebeian as a snake hiding in the grass to bite those more fortunate than he would have found many who agreed, and did not stem from simple political difference. Johnson made no effort to hide resentment and bitterness toward anyone who disagreed with him and always answered vicious attacks in kind. Living in an age and section where stump debate was only a level above common brawling, most of Johnson's contemporaries would agree that the tailor-politician usually bettered his opponents and excelled, especially with invective. His rare sparks of humor, when they came in speeches or letters to intimates, were most often jibes directed toward opponents or imagined enemies. Even the sympathetic William H. Crook, who served as personal guard in the White House, summed up his employer as "the best hater I ever knew."[6]

Harold D. Lasswell's controversial and provocative study *Power and Personality* advances an hypothesis that explains in part Johnson's aggressive ambition. The power seeker "pursues power as a means of compensation against deprivation. *Power is expected to overcome low estimates of the self,* by changing either the traits of the self or the environment in which it functions."[7] Such a broad generalization can hardly be accepted as a universal theory of political leadership because of the vast number of personality types involved. Yet when the major focus is on one individual whose life follows the revered pattern of the self-made man, the idea provides a starting point.

In Johnson's case, there can be little doubt that life began in circumstances likely to produce "low estimates of the self." His father, endowed by the rose-tinted spectacles of sympathetic biographers with all sorts of hidden virtues, actually occupied one of the lowest rungs on the southern social ladder. Jacob Johnson was a janitor at Casso's Inn in Raleigh, North Carolina, while his wife was apparently a servant there. In a slave society where landowning was widespread and, in part, the index of social status, whites who stooped to the position of servant inherited some of the contempt normally reserved for slaves. Even as a child, Andrew must have had to face the social stigma of being the son of a white version of Uncle Tom. The situation was not helped by his father's early death and his mother's remarriage to a man in whom even sympathetic biographers find little virtue.[8]

The cycle of social deprivation and grinding poverty was not breached until the "wild, harum-scarum boy" of fourteen, still illiterate, was apprenticed to a local tailor. James J. Selby's shop proved a turning-point. Not only did the young Johnson learn a trade, which eventually led to moderate financial success, but he also picked up a rudimentary knowledge of reading. In addition, the brief stint as an apprentice indicated that the erstwhile tailor had considerable native ability. When he and his older brother ran away in June 1824, Andrew had been an apprentice for only a little over two years, yet he seems to have acquired enough knowledge to become a financially successful tailor working on his own. Equally revealing was Selby's appreciation of the younger Johnson's abilities. In advertising a reward of ten dollars for the return of the wayward boys, he was careful to point out that he would pay the whole sum for Andrew alone.[9]

The next few years of Johnson's life are known only through legend. He seems to have lived in several small towns in the backcountry of the Carolinas, practicing his trade. According to local lore one of these villages, Laurens, South Carolina, became the scene of an almost necessary ingredient in romantic myth — the unsuccessful love affair. The young tailor is supposed to have become infatuated with Sarah Word, the daughter of a local aristocrat, but his suit was rejected because of his family background and penniless condition. The story is almost too ironical and, unfortunately, supported by little hard factual evidence. However, true or not, the rejected-suitor image does provide a kind of metaphor for Johnson's youth, and it is not too much to speculate that at least the metaphor is accurate. The future president faced a society that erected numerous barriers in the path of an ambitious and impatient young man without social status. Each rejection, major or minor, would result in considerable personal anguish and leave its residue. Like many other Americans of his time, Johnson tried to avoid some of these hurdles by moving west — but not too far west.[10]

Upon arriving in his adopted home, Greeneville, Tennessee, Johnson immediately set to work carving a niche for himself and making the requisite moves supposedly guaranteed, in his Jacob's-ladder world, to result in recognition and social advancement. While still young he married a local girl of respectable though certainly not high birth, and established a family; he applied himself diligently to his trade and acquired considerable property; and perhaps most important, he struggled with a vengeance to make up for the absence of an early education. His course in self-improvement consisted of considerable if shallow reading (he actually hired a boy to read to him while he worked) and oratory, usually in the form of debate with a local club or visitors to his shop.[11] The latter pursuit was clearly visible to most of his neighbors and probably indicates that the young man had an image of himself that included something beyond the tailor shop. It was a vision he never tried to hide.

Exactly when politics became Johnson's personal path upward is unclear. It is conceivable that the idea was planted early in his apprentice years. He is supposed to have learned to read from a book of political speeches, later kept as a cherished memento, and he perhaps unconsciously connected politics with success.[12] Whatever the deep personal reason, it was an obvious choice. Politics in the American system is always, in part, a personal popularity contest. Election to local office is not only an indication of the esteem in which the victor is held by his neighbors, but it also provides a shortcut to status. Political office was democratic America's most available equivalent to European nobility.

In 1829, after only three years of residence, Johnson started his climb in Greeneville politics with election as city alderman. He was soon mayor and, in 1835, was sent to the lower house of the Tennessee General Assembly.[13] Quick success must have been gratifying to the would-be statesman. For a man still illiterate at fourteen, election to the state legislature at twenty-seven was no mean accomplishment. He had made himself respected in the community, and further heights must have seemed just beyond his grasp. Unfortunately, the just world envisioned in his own rhetoric was an ideal only, and Andrew Johnson was much more than just an ambitious young man. The obstacles he faced were still very real and would never completely disappear.

One stumbling block was internal. Most pictures of the president show a dark countenance and a grim expression. His scowl may have been the product of artistic fashion or the imprint of a hard life, but there are few indications that Johnson was ever a happy man. Numerous observers have commented on his generally morose and gloomy character. Even as a youth he probably carried the proverbial chip on his shoulder. In describing his missing apprentice, James Selby noted that he was "of dark complexion, black hair, eyes, and habits," perhaps indicating that he and the young man did not get along very well. In fact, one version attributes the flight to a supposed altercation in which Johnson gave his employer a good whipping. It is possible that Selby's seeming eagerness to get the apprentice back stemmed as much from a desire for revenge as regret over lost services. At any rate, on moving to Tennessee the young tailor was apparently determined to work for no man but himself.[14]

Throughout his life, Johnson remained sensitive to any act that could be even remotely imagined a slur on his origin or class position. Stories about his vindictiveness toward his social "betters" are legion. One of the best, preserved by the son of his old archenemy, William G. Brownlow, illustrates how petty the self-proclaimed tribune of the people could be and how long he could bear a grudge. As soon as finances made it possible, Johnson moved his family from the back of the tailor shop to a more pretentious dwelling. However, a tailor's family was not completely welcome, at least to one set of neighbors who assumed to belong to a better social class, and the neighborhood was soon embroiled in a "wordy war." The opening salvo apparently involved the

Johnson family's calf, whose daily separation from its mother as the cow was led to pasture resulted in "a most infernal bellowing." The racket caused a complaint from the more aristocratic neighbors, who were told in no uncertain terms that the tailor would have a dozen calves on his property if he wished. One word led to another in a typical neighborhood squabble, but the words were never forgotten. Years later, after Johnson's political and financial success, the neighbor fell on hard times and his property was sold at auction. The now-recognized leader of Greene County democracy was in the crowd and outbid all comers. When asked by a fellow Democrat why he bid on the property, since he obviously did not need it, he replied in a loud voice so that bystanders, including the bankrupted family, could hear: "I want it, by God, for a calf pasture."[15]

Attitudes of this kind would not make anyone popular with the upper orders of society and are certainly not flattering attributes of character. Still, it is well to remember that such bitterness, though exaggerated, was not totally unjustified. The plutocrats of Greeneville, of the South, or of America were not prepared to accept a tailor, no matter how talented, as a social equal. Simple snobbishness was no stranger to the Jacksonian world and, in the South, was possibly exaggerated by the system of slavery. For a member of the "mechanic" class, the situation was particularly difficult. Thomas P. Abernethy, whose iconoclastic view of the era in Tennessee has done much to deflate Jacksonian bombast, gives one of the best descriptions of the social position Johnson was forced by circumstances to occupy. Mechanics "were considered as of no social consequence and, as 'laborers', ranked below even the poorest farmer in point of respectability. . . ." Had it been possible for Johnson to choose a different occupation—one more respectable than a tailor—his outlook might have been altered. Abraham Lincoln, by choosing the law and making a "good" marriage, overcame a bad start in frontier Illinois; in Tennessee, Andrew Jackson himself, whose birth was hardly aristocratic, parlayed land speculation, the bar, and planting into a relatively acceptable social position. But Andrew Johnson was a tailor. He would never forget and, in later years, never let others forget.[16]

It is likely that his own reasonable perception of class prejudice had a primary influence in molding the later advocate of radical Jacksonianism. There is, however, little evidence suggesting that the future evangelist of democracy arrived at the extreme ideological position through a process of reason. Like so many other aspects of his career, conversion seems to have been on purely personal grounds. It is, of course, difficult to speculate exactly when the spirit moved him, but a good estimate might be sometime during, or following, the campaign for the state legislature in 1837, when Johnson suffered his first political defeat.

Some observers, supported by tradition, argue that the "tailor shop crowd" had scored a minor political revolution over the Greeneville aristocrats with Johnson's election as alderman in 1829. Yet the editors of *The Papers of Andrew Johnson*, far more careful with source material, have found "no conclusive evidence" that Johnson and the Greeneville plutocracy were on opposite sides of the political fence in the early thirties. In fact, there is reason to believe he worked closely with his later political foes. His earliest extant letter, written in 1832, was addressed to Valentine Sevier, scion of the famous Sevier family, member of Greeneville's establishment, and influential Whig. In the letter Johnson suggests a meeting to discuss matters that concern him, promising to "unbosom" himself; he also sends compliments to "the Doctor and all your families." The "Doctor" was probably Alexander Williams, the "Grand Duke of Lick Creek" himself and the self-acknowledged capstone of Greeneville's social register.[17]

Such a letter supports O. P. Temple's assertion that in the 1830s Johnson had been known as a Whig. It is possible to carry this party label too far since the political situation in Tennessee was still in flux and party lines were by no means firm, but Johnson was very likely working with the men who would later become the nucleus of the Whig Party in the region. This seeming paradox with Johnson's later career can be partially explained by Abernethy's analysis of the Jacksonian mind. The supposedly democratic frontiersmen of the West actually followed with "unthinking devotion" their "self-appointed leaders," no matter what the issue. When leadership was demanded, "political office fell as a natural heritage to those who commanded in other fields." In the narrow world of Greeneville, tailors commanded nothing. For an ambitious young man there was no other choice. Johnson almost had to cooperate with the ruling clique of his region, at least until his own name and qualifications were established.[18]

The tailor might have been willing to continuing the alliance if the local politicos had been willing to do so. But they were not—at least not without being the dominant partners. The truth was made clear to Johnson in the election of 1837. The first term in the legislature had whetted his appetite for more, but he had made a fatal mistake by taking positions contrary to the wishes of Dr. Alexander Williams and other Greeneville leaders — in particular his opposition to a projected railroad for the area. Greeneville's establishment was determined to bring the upstart into line. When the legislators returned home, the "friends of internal improvements" held a banquet in honor of Brookins Campbell, Johnson's political rival who had voted more to their liking. The gathering, to which Johnson was not invited, was intended as a public rebuke for his course, and the now politically isolated tailor interpreted it correctly. On his way home from the affair, O. P. Temple met a bitter Johnson. According to Temple, the rejected politician, slightly inebriated, was in a "towering rage," swearing vengeance on Williams, Campbell, and others. Revenge had to wait. Without the support of the local leadership, Johnson was defeated by Campbell in the subsequent election.[19]

The traditional explanation for this loss rests on the ideological opposition to internal improvements. To this should be added Johnson's support of Hugh Lawson White instead of Martin Van Buren in 1836, which would have alienated hardshell Jacksonians. But these issue-oriented factors, as important as they were, may not have been primary. Temple describes Brookins Campbell as "Educated, amiable in disposition, honorable in deportment," and highly regarded by his friends.[20] In short, Campbell was everything Andy Johnson was not. He was of the same class as the traditional leaders — a gentleman, not a mechanic — and, especially when he supported the same political positions, was preferable to a pushy tailor.

If the Greeneville aristocrats actually hoped to finish Johnson politically, they had made a serious miscalculation. In the first place repudiation came too late. Already an established political figure, the tailor was now acceptable to his fellow townsmen in the role of leader, especially to those who felt the pangs of class prejudice as he did. In short, he became a lightning rod attracting those antagonistic to the traditional leadership. Moreover, the establishment's opposition — Johnson considered it a betrayal — in the election of 1837 and in hundreds of other major and minor political squabbles only channeled his boundless energy and determination in one direction: politics, translated in his own mind to mean personal vindication. He always seemed strongest fighting against the odds, particularly when enemies could be faced on personal grounds.

In addition, an important political weapon had been unwittingly placed in his hands by the Greeneviille leaders. Excluding Johnson partly because of his class made it natural to counterattack on the same basis.

The tailor-politician became an advocate of the "people," the "masses," against entrenched privilege. Twenty years earlier his leveling might have fallen on deaf ears, but times had changed. These were the years of Jacksonian Democracy. Homage to the "common man" was becoming a necessary ingredient in political success. In Johnson the rhetoric contained less hypocrisy than with the most political leaders as he remained, in many ways, a common man.

It would be incorrect to see his as an intellectual conversion easily accomplished. Johnson simply did not think in those terms. He found his political home almost by instinct. Jackson had certainly not been his patron saint when the East Tennessean supported Hugh Lawson White for the presidency. It is also possible that he flirted for a time with the doctrines of the arch-heretic John C. Calhoun. But in Tennessee his personal enemies were the opponents of the party of Jackson. Therefore, Johnson became that party's ardent supporter.[21]

In spite of the opportunism involved in the decision, there was also another element, perhaps in the long run more important. Johnson came to believe deeply in what he preached. It was a belief made natural by the style of politics he practiced. In the East Tennessean, political hucksterism was almost an art. He became a master demagogue in an age of demagoguery, able to make a grandiose gesture or to carefully orchestrate events and appearance for the pleasure of the crowd. He was never better than during the campaign for governor, in 1855, facing the champion of the Whigs and Know-nothings, Meredith P. Gentry. The political situation was tense and the canvass produced vicious personal attacks launched from both camps. At one point, tempers became so hot that threats on Johnson's life were rumored. The wily politician took advantage of the situation. In one Whig community, he is actually supposed to have mounted the rostrum with a pistol and informed the crowd that certain individuals were apparently bent on his assassination. With his hand on the weapon, he asked the gentlemen in question to get their business out of the way before he started speaking so as not to interrupt him.[22] The whole thing was obvious nonsense. It is unlikely that anyone actually intended to shoot Johnson, especially after he made his announcement to the crowd, but it was just the sort of bravado calculated to appeal to the "one-gallused" voter of East Tennessee.

Theatrics were supported by more subtle appeals. In the same campaign Gentry, definitely a "gentleman," carried a large, expensive gold watch attached by a fob chain. Johnson, on the other hand, displayed a cheaper version attached by a leather shoestring. Obviously able to afford a better timepiece, Johnson exploited the contrast, continually brandishing his "bulls-eye" before the audience at joint speaking engagements. Enemies would never tire of denouncing such tactics, but since it is clear that ballyhoo was the order of the day, detractors were probably more envious than actually offended.[23]

Certainly when it came to stump speaking, even the opposition was forced to admit that the tailor-politician had few peers. O. P. Temple lets admiration slip in between the apparent sarcasm in his colorful description of one of Johnson's harangues:

> As Mr. Johnson grew warm and hurled the terrible thunder of his wrath against the old Federalists, the shouts sent up by the Democracy could be heard far and wide among the surrounding hills. As he pictured the old Federal party in fearful colors, and pathetically entreated the people to stand firm upon the Constitution, his hearers would plant their feet more firmly upon the ground. When he informed them, as he never perhaps once in his life failed to do, that "eternal vigilance was the price of liberty," and that "power was always stealing from the many to give to the few," they would furtively glance around to see if anyone was trying to steal from them! After traversing the whole wide field of politics, Mr. Johnson wound up by the use of a figure drawn from the road, exhorting the party in an impassioned appeal to stand together "hand in hand, shoulder to shoulder, foot to foot, and to make a long pull, a strong pull and a pull altogether. . . ." The crowd became tumultuous. Its hurrahs were like the sound of many waters. The din and uproar became almost infernal.[24]

The magnetism of these philippics was not based on rhetoric, as any casual reading of the Tennessean's speeches would indicate. His florid allusions were often overdrawn, sophomoric, repetitive, and at times frankly silly. The real source of his appeal lay in the power and energy of his delivery buttressed by the aura of genuine sincerity. Political enemies became evil specters conjured up for his audience. Evil must be vanquished, and words were Johnson's weapons. As a correspondent from the *New York Times* described it in 1849, "He thrusts his opponents through and through, as with a rusty and jagged weapon, tearing a big hole and leaving something behind to fester and be remembered."[25]

In addition to avoiding such verbal swordplay, Johnson's adversaries were also forced to dodge bits of information hurled like bricks at their heads. His usual barrage of statistics was possible because the East Tennessean, always sensitive about his lack of formal education, studied each issue carefully, gathering a veritable encyclopedia of material to support his positions. This does not mean that specifics were used to arrive at general conclusions. Quite the contrary: Johnson preferred simple arguments and simple reasoning. Contradictions made apparent in the careful study of complex questions might embarrass some men—but Johnson never. Factual information was not necessary for understanding a complex issue; it was necessary only as a basis for a preconceived position. In Johnson's mind this was politics based on principle. Early life, he claimed, had taught him a significant truth: "In pursuit of a great principle, you can never reach a wrong conclusion." No matter how complex the question, a man needed only one guide, "and that was to pursue principle and . . . let the consquines be what they may—."[26]

Eric L. McKitrick, author of one of the classic studies of presidential Reconstruction, captures this element of thought in his conception of the tailor-politician as the perennial "outsider." He feels that "The texture of Johnson's mind was essentially abstract. Concrete problems never had the power to engage his interest. . . ." This kind of mental disposition does much to explain his almost Neanderthal attitude toward public spending, the reverence for hard-money economics, and the fetish-like worship of the Constitution, strictly interpreted of course. Johnson, in McKitrick's view, was "temperamentally and sociologically 'radical'" and, as a result, unable to find a home within the pragmatically defined limits of any political party. He, therefore, remained a political and social outsider unfortunately able to gain power in the complex world of Reconstruction—a world ill-suited for his style, or perhaps lack, of leadership.[27]

Difficulties in executive positions, both as governor of Tennessee and as president, were at least partially attributable to Johnson's tendency toward abstraction; and he might have agreed at times with a portion of the assessment himself, especially the term "radical." Johnson enjoyed thinking of himself and his positions as radical. Conservatism was the opponent of democracy. "What was Conservatism? 'A little more sleep, a little more slumber, a little more folding of the hands to sleep.'"[28] If his speeches are to be believed, he never compromised on any issue. Compromise was evil in principle:

The Devil, who rules the regions of despair, or his Satanic Majesty, who presides over the grand councils held in Pandemonium, would at all times be willing to be involved in a controversy with the Deity who rules on high, if he could have a settlement of the differences between them in a compromise which would be an inducement to another, and another, until Heaven itself would be comprised away, and the infernal regions would gain the ascendancy.[29]

Some of Johnson's finest hours in politics came when battling against compromise, against a violation of his "principles." In the election of 1855, disregarding personal and political danger, he defended freedom of religion and attacked Know-nothingism as unAmerican; he was acting in part from principle. His long and, at times, unpopular advocacy of the homestead idea was based on a sincere, if overenthusiastic, belief in the measure as salvation for the working man. And certainly, loyalty to the Union in the face of his own state's secession was at least partially influenced by principle.[30] Yet if politics is the art of compromise, it is hard to see how Johnson could have been so successful if he was as much an "outsider" as McKitrick believes or as much a man of principle as he saw himself.

Enemies in East Tennessee, who dealt with Johnson on a day-to-day basis for years, saw a very different man. Writing to O. P. Temple near the turn of the century, John Bell Brownlow compared his flamboyant father, "Parson" Brownlow, with his old archenemy:

> Their temperaments were almost the antipodes of each other. Johnson was an impassive and usually self-controlled man; Brownlow was demonstrative and impetuous. Johnson was a politician who knew how to withold opinions which he doubted the popularity of; Brownlow was under a dominant impulse to speak out what he felt without reference to policy and hardly to prudence. The one [Johnson] led men by the cool study of the influences likely to be potent with them, and knew how to bend to a drift of current opinion in order to preserve his lead; the other [Brownlow] controlled men by the sympathies which were aroused by his unrestrained disclosure of his strong personality and the openness with which he avowed and fought [for] the ends which seemed to him right.[31]

The obvious tendency to overdraw the contrast is attributable to filial piety. Johnson was not quite the Machiavellian of his enemies' imagination, nor was the fighting "parson" quite the fearless crusader of his son's rose-colored memory. But the fact that John Bell Brownlow envisioned his father as exactly the kind of impetuous man of principle Johnson claimed to be provides an important insight into the personalities of both men. Many American political figures think of themselves as men of principle, never willing to compromise, and like to project— in fact cultivate—just such an image, as Johnson certainly did. This does not mean that McKitrick's analysis is completely inaccurate; the abstract nature of Johnson's mind is very evident. It means that McKitrick captures only one dimension of a multidimensional character.

Johnson could also be a crafty, shrewd, and at times ruthless politician, especially when dealing with personalities. In a letter to his daughter Mary, attending Rogersville Female Academy, this impetuous man of principle gave an odd piece of advice:

> There is one other thing I will suggest and that is — in making up your acquaintance among strangers, be careful who you make intermit friends — have but few if any secret keepers or in other words have no secrets to keep. To day persons are friendly tomorrow they burst into as many pieces as a touchmenot — The true policy is to be friendly with all and too friendly with none — Infine so demean yourself as to command the love and respect of all teachers and pupils and the censure and ill will of none — [32]

The politician advising his daughter to keep up appearances was also a father warning his child of the world's cruelty, which he knew only too well. The embittered tailor was remembering the painful slights received at the hands of others.

Politics to Johnson remained a very personal thing. It should be no surprise that his speeches are filled with the first-person pronoun. Each issue was seen through his own unique perspective. Opponents were always "my enemies," supporters always "my friends," and a political position always "my policy." Loyalty was demanded from all who would follow and disagreement considered a personal attack. An old friend could be dropped overnight and become "by nature treacherous and by practice a liar," merely for standing in the way of his ambition.[33] Though others might see this approach as opportunistic, to Johnson it was justified. Individuals, with few exceptions, were not to be trusted. He could never forget what he considered betrayals in his early career, and the harsh world of practical politics continually reinforced the attitude. Moreover, Johnson himself would never have seen his own actions as purely opportunistic. Enemies were the ones who were unprincipled, while he always stood for principle. The radical democrat actually came to believe his own rhetoric.

This apparent dichotomy is the key to understanding Johnson's process of decision making as well as his political effectiveness. Most people, from time to time, hide from themselves the real motives behind their actions. Indeed, in view of the findings of modern psychology, whatever the school of thought, few of us can be sure of the ultimate source of our ideas, beliefs, or feelings, yet we act on them just as Johnson acted on his. In the former tailor's case, however, the tendency, or perhaps better ability, to rationalize real concrete needs in abstract terms — what he would have called principle — was clearly exaggerated. It is as if the abstract and practical levels of Johnson's mind maintained an unconscious symbiotic relationship. Whether this pattern of thought was inherent or the product of early experience remains unclear but, regardless of the origin, the pattern repeated itself again and again throughout his political life. Decisions, no matter what the basis, once made were quickly clothed in the abstract raiment of his version of democratic principle. The garments quickly became a suit of armor strengthening his commitment and making compromise difficult if not impossible.

Such an approach could be very effective politically. It allowed Johnson to transform the more prosaic needs, as well as the prejudices, of his backwoods constituents into the poetic language of ideology. As Johnson claimed, he did speak for many among the uneducated "masses" of Tennessee and, in doing so, raised their words to another, apparently higher, plane. That the process worked is amply illustrated by his repeated election successes, often against the odds. Moreover, his "commitment" to ideology never really interfered with the obligatory political maneuvering so necessary in the successful politician. In fact, the former tailor was able to mold "his friends" in Greeneville into a small but efficient political organization. Though hardly a machine in the modern sense of the word, his network of contacts and loyalties spread as the focus of his interest moved from local to state, then national politics. By the late 1850s, the East Tennessean was the dominant figure in Tennessee's Democratic Party, in spite of the opposition of many of its leaders and his own hard-headed, abstract ideas. He had actually risen far enough, by 1860, to entertain serious hopes for the Democratic nomination as a dark horse candidate, until the unpleasantness over slavery fragmented the party.[34] This was not the career of a complete outsider.

Credit for the climb belonged to him and "his friends," certainly not to the Democratic leadership, and Johnson always rewarded loyalty. Old Greeneville cronies, those who remained true like Sam Milligan or Blackston McDannel, were never forgotten. His constituents, who put him in office, were taken care of whether their problems were personal or political. Even his obvious demagoguery with the "masses" was probably, in part, honest enjoyment of the company of those who looked up to him and thought him worthwhile. In his exaggerated, first-person rhetoric and in the image of a politician treating voters at the local public house, slapping backs in friendship, sharing a jar of cheap mountain whiskey, and being one of the boys, there is an almost pathetic appeal for acceptance.[35]

His image, how he appeared in the eyes of others, was one of the most important elements in Johnson's thinking. He saw himself in these terms, and the concern was evident at all levels. For example, though he professed to be a working man, he was always fastidious in matters of dress and careful, when in public, to be neatly attired.[36] Also, working much of his adult life in a profession not noted for its honesty, there was almost no breath of scandal about his handling of public funds. In their most scurrilous attacks, enemies hesitated to impugn his fidelity in money matters. Wealth was never as important as reputation. When this same attitude intruded into practical politics, it could be very effective. To use the modern phraseology, Johnson always made sure his positions would "play in Peoria," in his case Greeneville. Given his way of thinking, even rigid principles could be twisted to pass muster.

In 1859 he wrote a letter giving advice to his son Robert, then serving in the Tennessee General Assembly. The specific question involved a proposed rise in the interest rates. In view of Johnson's hard-money, laissez faire economics, it is not surprising that he was forced to admit that "there can be much said of such a measure: but it has to be said and the public mind prepared before the public mind would be reconciled to it, . . ." For the present the experienced politician, possibly thinking as much about his own future as his son's, counseled the purdent course:

> It is always safest to be first certain that the thing or principle we assume to Justify another by is right in itself and that it can [be] defended as such before an honest community— Infine I would let those who thought it proper at the present increase the rate of interest— It is safe to go against it and might require a great deal [of] expla[na]tion of those who voted for it—[37]

To see Johnson's politics as purely the result of conscious self-interest would be unfair and touch only the surface. Concern over image was rooted much deeper in his mind, and its operation was unconscious.

After all, the desire for self-esteem was perhaps the real reason for being in politics in the first place, and success meant much more than just another political or ideological victory. It meant that Andrew Johnson was somebody — somebody worthy of other men's admiration.

Seen from the perspective of his psychological needs, Johnson's rhetorical use of Jacob's ladder takes on more importance than just a colorful picture of the democratic system. It represents the marriage of the two levels of his mind, the abstract and the real — the union of the two distinct elements that were the foundation of his own climb, the principles and rhetoric of Jacksonian Democracy and the realistic, personalized style of politics. Though he read Jefferson, came to worship Jackson, and learned to speak with the words of both, Johnson's understanding of democracy was essentially his own, forged by rugged experience.

When he delivered his Jacob's ladder speech, he had just been elected governor of Tennessee for the first time. The janitor's son had climbed the ladder himself, and, bent on climbing further, he merely paused for a moment to praise the ladder for being there and, by implication, Andrew Johnson for having the good sense to climb it. In spite of all his rhetoric, in the realm of ideas Johnson was no real radical — especially not a leveler. Nor was his brand of Jacksonian Democracy as unusual as he liked to think. It was basically the same call for equality of opportunity that has been a continual undertone in American history, seen from the perspective of an embittered East Tennessee tailor. His own position as a self-made man illustrated that the ladder could be climbed and therefore, if his own life was to have any meaning, the system had to be seen as basically just. To destroy it, whether by secession or by a radical change of the social structure, would destroy the meaning of all his victories. In this sense, the tailor-politician was profoundly conservative. He believed in, demanded, and perhaps even worshipped a society structured as a hierarchy containing class divisions. All his praise for those who worked with their hands, the mechanics, the mudsills of society, did not mean he actually wanted every man to be equal. The vicious attacks on entrenched privilege would lose their meaning if privilege ceased to exist — if there was nowhere to climb. He wanted a man to be judged by his works, his position in society determined by accomplishments, not birth.

Characteristically, Johnson's abstract mind turned his personal feelings and sense of justice into general principles. Democracy was a principle "inherent" in the nature of man:

In this principle, called Democracy, consists his capability of self-government. It is that which enables him to reason correctly, and to lift himself above all animal creation. It is this principle that constitutes the intelligence of man; or, in other words, it is that in Man, which partakes most highly of the nature and character of Him in whose image he is made—which I term the *Divinity of Man*. And in proportion as this Divinity is enlarged, the Man becomes more and more capable of self-government, and still more elevated in his character. I will also assume, what I know none will venture in reason to deny, that this *Divinity of Man can be enlarged*, and that man can become more God-like than he is. It is the business of the Democratic party to progress in the work of increasing this principle of Divinity, or Democracy, and thereby elevate and make man more perfect.[38]

When reading one of Johnson's homilies on the principles of democracy or the basic nature of mankind, it is always best to translate generalities into personal specifics. It was the way his mind worked, and it makes the real import of the statements clear. Democracy was the best system because it allowed mankind—translate Andrew Johnson—to rise, climbing that great ladder toward God. One's place on the ladder should be determined by "virtue and merit"—translate hard work and native ability—not social or educational advantage. The best indication of worth was success or, in the classic phrase of the self-made man, "the school of hard knocks." Johnson was a graduate with honors and, therefore, should be one of the true aristocracy. In other words, democracy was a great system because it allowed a tailor to join the "Grand Duke of Lick Creek" and other members of the Greeneville elite in their exalted position. It might even allow him eventually to look down on his former tormentors.

The supreme irony of his view of American democracy is obvious. No matter what Andrew Johnson did, he was not going to be socially acceptable to the upper classes. As a result, the driving force of his ambition would never release its pressure. A kind of Jacob's ladder did exist in nineteenth-century America, but it did not necessarily lead to social acceptance. A few men somehow found the right path, but Johnson never could, particularly given his style of politics. He never learned, or lacked the patience, to play the social game by the prescribed rules. Perhaps he was just too honest to play a role pretending to be something he was not. So Johnson worked harder and hated more.

The so-called aristocrats became his private enemies. They had been his bane in Greeneville and, as his horizons widened, he found them everywhere, most especially in his native South. To him the upper class of Dixie was

> an illegitimate, swaggering, bastard, scrub aristocracy, who assumed to know a good deal, but who, when the flimsy veil of pretension was torn off from it, was shown to possess neither talents, information, or a foundation on which you can rear a superstructure that would be useful.[39]

Johnson claimed to be happy that he was not a member of such a group. On the contrary, he was proud to be a mechanic, the class who represented the real aristocracy — "If this country is to have an aristocracy at all, I want that aristocracy to be an aristocracy of labor, an aristocracy of agriculturalists and mechanics."[40]

It was a familiar refrain, but the frequency of repetition raises suspicions. It is simply a case of protesting too much. Johnson was sincere in his conscious hatred, but the very extreme of his hostility was rooted in classic feelings of inferiority. From the first rebuffs, he never ceased to desire acceptance into the same class he professed to despise. One of the most ironic twists would come when the tailor finally reached the top rung of "Jacob's ladder" — president of the United States. The flowers of southern womanhood humbled themselves before the former mechanic to beg pardons for their rebel husbands, men Johnson had sworn to hang as traitors. It would be incorrect to assume that these entreaties were the sole reason for the president's pardoning policy. The pardons were granted with more complex motives. But the ladies had their effect, and the president enjoyed playing the great, magnanimous man of power.[41] Even in the end, he failed to realize that social acceptance was something the presidency itself could not buy.

When he returned to Greeneville in 1869, apparently defeated because he defended the South and, by a curious unintended twist of fate, her aristocracy, he was still applying for membership. In May of that year he sent a barrel of flour to Mrs. Clement C. Clay, belle of the Alabama aristocracy and wife of one of the pardoned "traitors." Perhaps the proud old plebeian thought the esteemed lady was now "his friend," or perhaps it was just a simple act of kindness. At any rate, when no acknowledgment of the gift was received after two months, the ancient bitterness (or, perhaps, it was solicitude) reasserted itself, and the ex-president fired off a wire inquiring from the railroad agent the whereabouts of the flour. It had arrived, and another snub joined the long list Johnson kept tucked away in his mind. Mrs. Clay was shown the wire by the railroad agent, and in July she wrote a letter to her "dear friend" apologizing and explaining the delay, which no doubt soothed the old man's feelings. But nothing could truly dampen the fire that had been burning for so many years. His last days would be spent fighting the "Bourbons" of Tennessee and, much more important in his eyes, fighting for his own vindication.[42]

This view of Andrew Johnson's character is not particularly flattering, but it is realistic. His perception of the world he lived in was not completely inaccurate. If it is only half true, as Abernethy maintains, that Andrew Johnson "was the only true and outstanding democrat produced by the Old South, for he never was absorbed into the privileged class. . . . he never erred from his purpose of improving the condition of the masses, politically, economically, and intellectually," then perhaps the source of motivation can be forgiven.[43] Opprobrium, if that is part of the historian's task, should be reserved for the hypocrisy of Jacksonian Democracy or the antebellum South, not its victims. Johnson's world was no place for the timid, and Jacob's ladder was not easy to climb. The way upward is never easy for the self-made man. Had Johnson been satisfied with himself and his society, he would have remained a Greeneville tailor. He would have had little effect on American history and, as a matter of course, on the black man.

Chapter 3

The Defender of Slavery

So far as I am concerned, if it suited him, and his inclination led him that way, I wish to God every head of a family in the United States had one to take the drudgery and menial service off his family.

Andrew Johnson on Slavery[1]

As a southerner, Andrew Johnson could never escape slavery. Shackles had been forged for a whole society long before his birth and few individuals, especially tailors, were consulted. To a person growing up in Raleigh or anywhere in the South, the peculiar institution was as much a part of nature as the wind and rain or, perhaps more appropriate since it involved a social relationship, the difference between men and women. It was typical for an apostle of democracy, "an angry young man" of nineteenth-century America, to wish for the extension of any benefit in the community to all *men* — including himself. The great evil to a mind steeped in the mythology of Jacksonian democracy was not the structure of American society but special privilege for the few. Privileges are always easier to extend than to take away.

Unfortunately for Johnson and Jacksonian America, human bondage is much more than an ideological system that can be explained in the abstract language of political theory. Most important in the American situation was, of course, racism. Slavery here can not be separated from race. The enslaved were black, their masters white. Whether racial antipathy preceded or emerged from slavery was basically immaterial to the nineteenth-century dilemma. It was there, and it was more difficult for Johnson and his fellow southerners to escape than it was for their servants to flee north.

Throughout most of his political life, the would-be statesman faced problems stemming from Negro slavery and, as a result, had ample opportunity to clarify and explain his own attitudes. However, public statements, especially of a politician, can seldom be accepted without qualifications. Behind each public face there is always a private man. In Johnson's case, getting at the private man presents the most difficulty. He left no diary, wrote no books and, in the few extant personal letters, was not in the habit of ruminating about the subject of race. Moreover, as pointed out earlier, he was deeply concerned with image, in an historical as well as a contemporary sense. Evidence that might reflect negatively, if any existed, would probably have fallen victim to selective editing either by him or by loyal descendants. By the same token, the intimate and most revealing relationships between a master and slave are not likely to be recorded in written documents. As a result, a portrayal of Johnson's race thinking is more like a collage than a detailed portrait. It must be pieced together from scraps of evidence whose edges seldom fit smoothly.

One of the most revealing private conversations Johnson ever had on the subject of race occurred in unusual circumstances. In the spring of 1861, prior to the clash at Fort Sumter, Senator Andrew Johnson boarded a train to Tennessee. The situation everywhere was tense, especially for a man like Johnson. A prominent leader from a border state, one likely to secede should war break out, the senator had already committed himself to the Union, publicly denouncing secessionists as "traitors." He was returning home to wage the most desperate battle of his career in a vain hope to keep his state loyal. He must have recognized that chances of winning were slim, and, if anything, the trip home should have reinforced doubt. Along the route at several points hostile crowds gathered when rumors of Johnson's presence were circulated. It was not the last time the senator would be threatened by his fellow southerners.[2]

Riding on the same train was another unionist. Thomas Shackelford made his living as a Mississippi cotton planter and owned a large number of slaves, yet he was also a staunch opponent of secession who would suffer considerably at the hands of rebels. As an admirer of Johnson's recent course, the Mississippian sought an introduction through a mutual acquaintance and, after making it clear that he personally abhorred the "heresy of secession," settled down for what turned out to be a long conversation. The senator was apparently in the mood to talk. Perhaps he needed a sympathetic listener to share his deep anger and frustration with the whole secession movement. The policy was nonsense. If the southerners had remained in their seats in Congress, he believed, they could have effectively blocked any radical moves attempted by Lincoln. In fact, Johnson claimed, "we could have had a frolic through Lincoln's administration & all the pretended fears of the South for the institution of slavery would have vanished at the Close of it."[3]

As Shackelford remembered the conversation years later, the Tennessean went on to explain his idea of the relationship of slavery and the black man to the terrible war both foresaw. People "would volunteer fast enough now (when they knew nothing of war) . . . they considered it fun.— but when the cold & bloody reality of it, were upon them — they would desert, and those who had no negroes would say 'it was a rich mans War & a poor mans fight'." Explaining further, the senator pointed out that there was a natural "antagonism between the Slave owner, and the poor." The "poor man disliked the negro and his prejudice extended to his Master—" Illustrating his thinking with an anecdote from his days as governor, Johnson described a member of the nonslaveholding class bursting into the executive office one morning demanding that he be given a gun from the state arsenal. The man's reason was simple. He wanted, "to shoot a d——d negro fellow, who had been stealing his turkies." Trying to calm the irate farmer, the governor asked if the Negro had actually been seen stealing the turkeys. Though the reply was negative, the farmer knew to whom the thief belonged, and the owner, much to the victim's disgust, had refused to punish his bondsman. Johnson advised his intruder to catch the slave in the act and then demand payment for his losses. He should forget about shooting anyone. But, payment alone could not satisfy. The poor white left the governor's office "breathing vengeance against the negro & his Master," furious at Johnson for not giving him the means to solve the problem in his own way.[4]

The substance of Johnson's tale is not nearly as significant as the image that lay behind it. The senator clearly believed that not all southerners were as happy with the peculiar institution as apologists maintained. Most important, the nonslaveholder harbored an intense prejudice against the Negro, which in the former tailor's estimation carried over to include the master class. Comparable views were not uncommon in the South. Edward Pollard, a Richmond editor, reveals a similar conception in his autobiographical *Black Diamonds Gathered in the Darkey Homes of the South* (1859). He empathized with the "working classes and the yeomanry," who were to be pitied because they were "deprived of all share in the benefits of the institution of slavery, condemned to poverty, and even forced to bear the airs of superiority in black and beastly slaves!" Pollard was particularly infuriated by impudent blacks:

> Of all things I cannot bear to see negro slaves affect superiority over the poor, needy, and unsophisticated whites who form a terribly large proportion of the population of the South. My blood boils when I recall how often I have seen some poor "cracker," dressed in striped cotton, and going through the streets of some of our Southern towns, gazing at the shop windows with scared curiosity, made sport of by the sleek dandified negroes who lounge on the streets, never unmindful, however, to touch their hats to the "gem'men" who are "stiff in their heels" [i.e., have money]. . . .[5]

Pollard's solution was simple — import more Africans, making them cheap and available to everyone. Though Johnson would never advocate such a course, at least publicly, the logic was similar to his factious wish that every man have a slave of his own.

Like most southerners, Johnson was not born a slaveowner. When he talked about the bitter hatred that nonslaveholders had for blacks, his appraisal is convincing. He spoke from experience. The former tailor had been poor much of his life, and he still considered himself the personal representative of the southern mechanic class in Washington. Growing up in Raleigh and as a struggling young tradesman in Greeneville, he must have felt the same bitterness toward impudent slaves that Pollard described. The black was a constant reminder — a symbol — of a poor man's lack of status, and, especially if the Negro appeared in any way better off than an observing white, he became the focal point for frustration. In Johnson's case, the very harshness of his rhetoric on the stump and in debate betrayed deep-seated feelings. He became incensed when the ideas of abolitionists seemed to "place every splay-footed, bandy-shanked, hump-backed, thick-lipped, flat-nosed, woolly-headed, ebon-colored negro in the country upon equality with the poor white man."[6]

Whether all nonslaveholders consciously projected hatred of the Negro to the master is unclear. Johnson certainly did and assumed that others of his class felt the same. This attitude, however, may have been as much a function of a unique personality as the product of a slave society. An ambitious, upwardly mobile individual like Johnson was apt to identify slaves as at least part of his problem. To a man trying desperately to climb the social ladder, any advantages possessed by those on the lofty heights above might well seem unfair — in Johnson's terms, undemocratic. Even as a loyal southern politician dutifully defending his section, he never publicly expressed anything but contempt for the slaveholding aristocracy and could even refer sarcastically to the hallowed position of "master" if the occasion demanded. Once during a debate in Congress Johnson lashed out at an opponent who was showing disapproval with facial expressions. "The gentleman's scowls or threats have no terrors for me. 'He may go show his slaves how choleric he is, and make his bondmen tremble.'"[7] Such a remark would have been more typical, if less justified, coming from a northern abolitionist.

Unlike Hinton Rowan Helper, however, who also hated the masters as well as the slaves, Johnson never really questioned the fundamental basis of slavery. To most southerners the institution was not only moral, it was necessary. The East Tennessean gave a clue to the depth of his own as well as the nonslaveholder's feelings in a Senate debate as late as 1860:

> I say that if the day ever does come when the effort is made to emancipate the slaves, to abolish slavery, and turn them loose on the country, the nonslaveholder of the South will be the first man to unite with the slaveholder to reduce them to subjugation again; and if one would be more ready to do so than the other, it would be the non-slaveholder. . . . if their resistance to subjugation were obstinate and stubborn, the non-slaveholder would unite with the slaveholder, and all this abolition philanthropy, all this abolition sympathy, when pressed to its ultimatum, would result in the extirpation of the negro race.[8]

The senator may have been, as he often did, allowing rhetoric to run away with meaning, but the import of his remarks is clear. Rather than allow the black to be free — there is no mention of equality — the poor white of the South was ready to commit a nineteenth-century version of genocide. Such a response from whites was a kind of self-defense. Anything approaching equality with blacks would destroy the meaning of white lives.

If extreme views of this kind were the only element of Johnson's race thinking, they could be easily understood. But in the East Tennessean's case, as with most other southerners, the concept of the Negro's "place" in society was much more complex. Only the fanatic always viewed the problem as total war between black and white. Most understood things with more shades of gray, even if their ideas were seldom verbalized. This other side is visible in the atmosphere of Johnson's early years. Those bygone days were recalled to mind when his stubborn resistance to secession attracted the attention of an old friend. John E. Patterson's letter to the senator praising him for his steadfast loyalty might have been just another missive from an acquaintance reminding a famous man of the good old days, save for the fact that the writer was black. Both had spent their childhoods in Raleigh at the same time, but their lives had taken very different paths. Patterson assumed that Johnson had forgotten him but that did not make him any less "proud" of his "friend's" success:

> . . . we was will [well] acquainted & play mates neighbors in your days of Boyhood[.] Many play of marbles & other amusements of youthful enjoyment we had in the yard of your mothers home — as we my mother — to yours was near neighbors — even for a time on the same lot. . . .⁹

The belligerent southern politician denouncing abolition or discussing the extermination of the black race and the white boy squatting in the dust of his mother's yard shooting marbles, apparently oblivious to the color of his playmate's skin, were the same person. White southerners of all classes lived among Negroes, and it was almost impossible to avoid personal relationships. In other words, the mental category "black," with all its negative connotations, often broke down where individuals were involved. The very young, of course, had not yet developed totally separate mental compartments for people of a different color, and the scenes of black and white children playing together were part of the normal southern landscape. Yet even after adulthood, with all its pressures helping to create a more rigid color line, most whites could not completely reject the blacks whom they lived with intimately. When Johnson and other southerners talked of "beastly slaves," they were speaking in the abstract; they were not talking about their own slaves, friends, playmates, and mistresses. In unusual circumstances, especially if the blacks themselves broke the fragile relationship by violating the southern concept of "place," a violent rejection might occur. Behind every black face lurked a potential enemy. But most of the time familiar Negroes do not seem to have been the object of extreme white hatred. The real enemy was a distant, unknown threat, more of a symbol than a person. The concept "good nigger" meant more than just an Uncle Tom; it also tended to mean "black person I know."

Familiarity, along with status security, formed the basic support for the fabled paternalism of the slaveowner so often praised by slavery apologists. The absence of familiarity might also help explain the apparent racial hostility of whites in regions with comparatively few slaves.

In Johnson's case, both factors became increasingly important as he ascended the ladder of success. In his conversation with Shackelford, the senator clearly spoke of the "poor whites" as if they were a group separate from him and his planter companion. He may have empathized with the nonslaveholder and often as a political device glorified his humble origin, but obviously the tailor-politician no longer belonged with the "mudsills" of society.[10]

Johnson acquired the necessary element for membership in the "master class" in 1842, with the purchase of a Negro girl called "Dolly." A short time later he bought her half-brother, Sam, who according to contemporary accounts became Johnson's favorite slave. The servants were procured for what might be best described as cosmetic purposes, since they were clearly not an essential part of the family's economic support.[11] In Johnson's world, success almost inevitably resulted in slaveholding, in the same manner that today surplus funds result in the purchase of a washing machine or a larger automobile. Not buying a slave "to take the drudgery" of household labor from his family, if one could afford it, would be unusual and probably require a conscious moral commitment against the institution. In addition, what better way could be found to illustrate a rise in class position than acquiring the chief badge of social distinction in the South?

Johnson would never own many slaves, but the exact number is surprisingly difficult to determine. According to the census figures, he possessed four slaves in 1850 and five in 1860, but the biographer Robert Winston, who probably has the most extensive description of Johnson's slaves, maintains that he owned eight. Unfortunately, Winston does not cite his source, and it is probable that the figure, like much of his work, comes from local lore. It is possible that Johnson did own more slaves than the census records show since other bondsmen may have been hired out at the time the census was taken or been living with one of Johnson's children. Johnson's own words, where available, only add to the confusion. In speeches during the war he maintained, at various times, that he owned seven, nine, or ten slaves. In reality the exact number is unimportant since it was never large enough to constitute anything on a significant scale beyond basic domestic slavery. As a mechanic and village dweller, Johnson had little need for field hands, though he possibly indulged in the practice of "hiring out" his slaves for profit. And unlike many lawyers and merchants in the plantation regions, the East Tennessean would never develop a financial dependence on the institution through dealings with planters.[12]

Engaged in domestic labor, Dolly, Sam, and their fellow servants enjoyed the "benefits" of close contact with the master's family. If the Johnson progeny are to be believed, the head of the household exhibited almost too much indulgence, especially of Sam. Mrs. Martha Patterson, Johnson's eldest daughter, claimed in what became a family joke that Sam was not a slave at all. "Sam did not belong to her father but her father belonged to Sam."[13] Johnson's favorite was apparently a neighborhood character, prone to be troublesome and proud of his favored position. His antics elicited a more serious complaint from Charles Johnson to his father in 1860:

> I will just make one suggestion,—I think were I in you[r] place I would sell *Sam*; it does not suit him to stay in this country; — a few days since Mother sent him word to cut wood at Pattersons,—he came up in the house and said, he would "be damed" if he wanted to cut wood there; and if you wanted to sell him you could just do so, just as soon as you pleased, he did not care a *dam*," you will see he is quite an independent gentleman and just to show his notions of himself and his rights, at another time he was asking Mother for his part of some money paid him for work[.] Mother remarked to him if he was as ready to pay others as he was to collect, he would do better; he replied that he did not get half enough no how; — that he ought to have *all* that he could make &c, well, it may be all right, but one thing is certain; I do not desire to own negroes; but if I did, they should know their place or I would not have them about me. do not understand me, as complaining at your course; not so; but it does seem the more attention, the more kindness you show a negrro, the less account he is; they seem to misconstrue it; — but after all the negro to be of any value, must be subjugated; and they are the fewest number of men that are fit to have negroes; this is especially the case in E Tennessee [.] the negro must have a Master; and those who, use them severly seem to have the best slavs; but more of this again[.][14]

The younger Johnson's letter illustrates more than the extent of his father's tolerance; it also says a great deal about the peculiar love-hate relationship between southern whites and their slaves. Sam obviously took liberties not normally expected of bondsmen, and the family, in the father's absence, probably threatened the slave with the classic punishment of being sold "down the river." Both knew such a sale was unlikely and the bickering between them was more of a family ritual than real hostility. The letter itself illustrates that Sam was given considerable latitude in his actions. He perhaps even hired himself out with the wages paid to his master, from which he received a share. While Sam was acting the "independent gentleman," a direct contrast to the picture of the perfect servant, Charles Johnson possibly felt restricted by his lot in life and very far from the ideal of the southern master. His advice on the subjugation of Negroes and his theoretical speculations on the virtue of extreme discipline must be seen as the ideas of a man who owned no slaves in his own right and, in fact, had no real status save through his father. It is never easy to be the son of a famous father, especially a father who has pulled himself up by his bootstraps and expects the same tireless labor and dedication from his sons. At this time in his life, the younger Johnson could only be characterized as a failure. Chronically addicted to alcohol, Charles was simply unable to find a niche for himself and must have been insecure in his own self-evaluation.[15] He was likely to feel resentment at impudence in any black, especially one who enjoyed a privileged position in his father's eyes.

The elder Johnson, though never secure in the perception of his own status, was at the height of his political career in 1860 and in a position to be more compassionate since he probably felt less of a symbolic threat from Sam and his kind. Coddling a slave was one of the recognized prerogatives of the master class. One was kind to "his people" because it was the thing to do if one wished acceptance, as Johnson did, in the polite, refined circles of the South. In spite of his harsh rhetoric about slaves and their masters, the former mechanic made no attempt to obscure his membership in the slaveholding class and, at times, seemed inordinately proud of the fact. He is even supposed to have taken a manservant with him on some of his political journeys. Such servants were a highly visible symbol of their owner's position. According to local folklore, Johnson's personal retainer slept in the same room on a pallet and bragged on returning home, "Old mas'r let dem po'white folks know de body servant's place was in the room with him."[16]

In a typical twist of Johnsonian logic, this self-appointed representative of the southern working man had a peculiar justification for his version of slaveholding. He deserved his slaves more because he "made them by the industry" of his own hands. "What I own cost me more labor and toil than some who own thousands, and got them because they were the sons of moneyed people." After the outbreak of the Civil War changed the public attitude toward slavery in unionist circles, his own paternalism was added as an explanation. His slaves were only purchased, he claimed, because they wished to belong to him, and he never sold one. In this case memory may have been deceiving Johnson.

One of the few documented records of his slaveholding is a bill of sale, dated 1857, for a thirteen-year-old boy called Henry. The name does not appear on the 1860 census, and it is possible only to speculate about what happened to Henry. Aside from death, prominent among the possibilities, would be a quick resale, though Johnson might also have simply given the slave to one of his children or been acting as an agent for someone else.[17]

Even if time and unionism exaggerated paternalisitic benevolence, there can be little doubt that Johnson did have genuine affection for at least some of his slaves. In a letter to his son Robert in 1854, the governor explained that he would be returning home soon and had sent some articles ahead for the family — "a basket and some other little notions for your little brothe[r] (Andrew Johnson, Jr., called Frank by the family) and a little chair for Liz & Florence. . . ." Liz and Florence were slave children apparently treated as special pets by the family. The only extant photograph of one of Johnson's female slaves is of this same Florence, taken in 1863 or 1864, probably in Nashville. She is posed along with Johnson's grandson, Andrew Johnson Stover. The picture shows a handsome young woman of very light color most tastefully dressed in a manner that appears quite expensive and not the sort of attire one would expect of a common servant.[18]

On the other hand, it would be incorrect to carry the meaning of Johnson's paternalism, or southern paternalism in general, too far. Kenneth Stampp makes some interesting observations on the phenomenon in his study of *The Peculiar Institution*, pointing out that "The most generous master, so long as he was determined to *be* master, could be paternal only toward a fawning dependent; for slavery, by its nature, could never be a relationship between equals." At its best the situation was one in which the owner became the parent and the slave a perpetual, if sometimes petulant, child. Putting it in the words of Professor Stampp, "The system was in its essence a process of infantilization — and the master used the most perfect products of the system to prove that the Negroes were a childlike race, needing guidance and protection but inviting paternal love as well."[19]

Even in a case like Johnson's Sam, where the slave appeared to have a mind of his own, there should be a legitimate question as to how much the "loyal" slave's personality was warped. It is quite possible to conceive of the twisted kindness of the master as having an equally damaging effect on personality development as harsh treatment. Sambo could be impudent as well as fawning. Permanent childhood was a terrible fate, whether faked to please the master or the product of a destroyed personality. It could also result from gentle chains or the lash.[20]

Whether or not there was a darker side to Johnson's relationship with his slaves remains a mystery. Like most slaveholders, Johnson would not have been anxious to have written records of harsh treatment survive for posterity. Much of the general evidence of this nature that exists is preserved in the writings of abolitionists who, on the other extreme, were seeking just such evidence for propaganda purposes and seldom singled out a particular individual. Moreover, any relationship of a sexual nature that Johnson might have had with his female slaves is hidden in the fog always surrounding that delicate subject. There is simply no conclusive evidence one way or the other. This is particularly regrettable because sex plays such an important part in racist mythology. If Dolly, for example, had been purchased for purposes other than domestic, it might clarify the nature of Johnson's personality as well as explain the kind treatment of her half-brother Sam or her children, Liz and Florence. If the converse is true, that Dolly and her counterparts, under the theoretically absolute power of the master, were not exploited in such a manner, it could possibly say a great deal about the strength of Johnson's personality and his feeling toward blacks.[21]

He clearly accepted or was at least aware of the sexual content implied in American racism and was not above using it as a political weapon. In 1848, in the House of Representatives during an exchange with John Gorham Palfrey, a Whig from Massachusetts, Johnson broached the subject, as he put it, "to test the sincerity of the gentleman. . . ." Palfrey had been attempting to illustrate that blacks would become "elevated in character" as their station in life improved. He made his point by citing the example of an "intellectual, interesting, and charming negro boy" who had attended school with his son. Johnson retorted with the ultimate question in a racist society: Would the gentleman consent to his daughter's accepting this "charming negro boy in wedlock as her companion through life?" It was the specter that most haunted white males — interracial sex involving a black man and a white woman, and interestingly Palfrey, the northern opponent of slavery, seemed to take the implication as a direct insult.[22]

Johnson brought up the subject again in an entirely different context to a very different audience. Speaking in Nashville in 1864 before an assembled group of blacks, he promised to see to it, personally, that slavery was ended in Tennessee and added a different twist to interracial sexual contact. Slaves became the victims, a point that gave the governor an opportunity to denounce secessionists and aristocrats with the same phrases:

> The representatives of this corrupt, (and if you will permit me almost to swear a little) this damnable aristocracy, taunt us with our desire to see justice done, and charge us with favoring negro equality. Of all living men they should be the last to mouth that phrase; and even when uttered in their hearing, it should cause their cheeks to tinge and burn with shame. Negro equality, indeed! Why pass, any day, along the sidewalks of High Street where these aristocrats more particularly dwell—these aristocrats, whose sons are now in the bands of guerillas and cutthroats who prowl and rob and murder around our city—pass by their dwellings, I say, and you will see as many mulatto as negro children, the former bearing an unmistakable resemblance to their aristocratic owners![23]

Publicly implying that sexual exploitation by the master class was common practice constituted the rankest form of heresy to the slave South and the fragile assemblage of myth and half-truth that made up its defense of the peculiar institution. One might whisper about such things on the backstairs of the manor or expect to hear similar charges from a northern abolitionist tugging at the heartstrings of sanctimonious old maids in remote, frigid New England, but on the streets of Nashville a southern white man simply did not make such statements, especially if his audience consisted of blacks, many of whom were still legally slaves. Demagoguery of this kind was certainly calculated to make Johnson's name more odious than it already was "along the sidewalks of High Street." But after all, it was wartime; excesses of rhetoric were common on both sides. More important for the moment than Johnson's apparent conversion to the antislavery cause was his concept of "equality." Ever a defender of white supremacy, the unionist was attacking his old enemies by making them advocates of equality, albeit in an oblique manner. It was as much the equality implied by interracial sex that made it evil as the obvious exploitation. The concept is particularly revealing. Johnson clearly recognized that access to black females, while denying the reverse privilege to black males, was a key symbol of white male superiority, which would have to be abandoned in the brave new world of postwar America. It degraded blacks as well as whites because it produced race mixture. The contact itself produced corruption:

Your wives and daughters shall no longer be dragged into concubinage, compared to which polygamy is a virtue, to satisfy the brutal lust of slaveholders and overseers! Henceforth the sanctity of God's holy law of marriage shall be respected in your persons, and the great State of Tennessee shall no more give her sanction to your degradation and your shame![24]

Blacks were being offered protection rather than equality. Physical separation freed them not from inferiority but from the "shame" brought about by unequal competition with their superiors. Such protection would also free whites from temptation — or possibly envy, if one were not in a position to be the exploiter. But perhaps most important, implied in Johnson's words was another kind of freedom for whites. They would no longer have to be reminded of the essential humanity of both races.

As a slaveholder (actually his own slaves were still legally his because of limitations in the Emancipation Proclamation), Johnson was in a position to know just how brutal the master's lust could be. This, of course, does not mean that the newly reformed slaveowner had exploited his female slaves. Quite the contrary: Johnson's words seem to indicate that he abhorred the practice. Still, he clearly linked white male sexual dominance with black inferiority, and it is probable that his horror at the resulting miscegenation was newly discovered. He had never given any indication of such an attitude before and, at least on one occasion, passed over the problem as unimportant. In 1843 while discussing the potential candidacy of Richard M. Johnson for vice-president, the aspiring young politician implied that the gentleman's well-known liaison with Julia Chinn was no real handicap — "Johnson's black children and all that kind of things, the people are perfectly familiar with it, . . ."[25]

The nuances of Johnson's private concept of race and any relationships he might have had with blacks of a personal nature, paternal or otherwise, help reveal one of the major difficulties in understanding antebellum race thinking, in addition to the obvious lack of hard evidence. Slavery and racism were interrelated, but the bond between the two was subtle and often variable. Any ratio formed between attitudes toward the socio-economic institution and personal feelings about blacks was not necessarily on a direct one-to-one basis. A person could be an extreme racist and not support slavery, or vice versa. Similarly, the actions one took in regard to slavery might not be directly connected to the content and depth of race hostility. Even visible expressions of paternalism or hatred are not to be trusted, since individual personality factors have such great bearing. Most people consider dogs inferior to humans, but some masters are kind and indulgent while others are openly sadistic.

Because a historical character like Johnson cannot be analyzed by a psychologist, nor his actions and personality controlled as a novelist does with a fictional character, the historian must look elsewhere for clues to his character. Here, there is a distinctive advantage in studying a politician. The balance struck between slavery and racism in public by almost all antebellum political figures reveals, in part, their deep-seated feelings and conceptions about race, even if the observer must often look between the lines. Rationalization in politics has to be based on a man's own thinking coupled with a perception of his constituency.

In Johnson's early career there is surprisingly little evidence concerning race thinking. The only question he faced as a city official involved the taxation of slaves, and there is no indication of Johnson's attitude in Greeneville's records. Apparently the presence of abolitionist sentiment in his area was of little concern to local government. Even when he moved to the wider realm of state politics, it was too late from the point of view of an historian of slavery. One year earlier the status of the Negro had undergone considerable discussion in the state constitutional convention of 1834, and during these debates the last real effort was made by a small group of East Tennesseans to bring about gradual emancipation. The antislavery forces had been soundly defeated by the slaveholding interests and, from this time until the southern rebellion, there would be no real political opposition to slavery as an institution in the state. Tennessee abolitionists, such as they were, had been driven underground.[26]

Johnson, however, did take several steps while in the state Senate that indicate a conflict of interest between the East Tennessee tailor and the large-scale slaveholder. The first involved the perennial fetish of East Tennesseans—a desire for separate statehood. On December 7, 1841, Johnson introduced a resolution intended to bring about the cession of the eastern grand division of the state to the federal government, presumably to form the nucleus of a new state of "Frankland." Though the movement seemed to have considerable support, the seriousness of its advocates in the General Assembly is questionable. They may have been simply raising the possibility to put pressure on representatives from the rest of the state who stood in the way of East Tennessee's desperate need for internal improvements. Interestingly, some of the impetus for the movement came from antislavery sentiment, but most such backers preferred to keep quiet because of the high feeling prevailing against abolitionists. One of these silent opponents of slavery wrote a friend, "Those who hope by this means to exterminate slavery in East Tennessee think it will be prudent to say but little on that subject or publickly on it untill the act of separation is determined. . . ." There is no evidence that Johnson was one of these clandestine abolitionists. His motives were based on state sectionalism. Like most of his constituents, he feared the growing power of the middle and western divisions of the state at the expense of the eastern one. However, sectional differences were plainly related to slavery, and, if successful, the move would have created a new state where the slaveholder had less influence.[27]

The sectional nature of attitudes toward slavery in Tennessee was made even more evident in another of Johnson's moves, which was closer to heresy in the minds of pro-slavery extremists. On October 4, 1843, Governor James C. Jones recommended that the Legislature divide Tennessee into new congressional districts. The action would result in a loss of political influence for the east because the other sections had increased in population, both slave and free. Johnson countered in the Senate by proposing two resolutions. The first would have divided the state into congressional districts "without any regard to the three-fifths of negro population"; the second reaffirmed the idea by requiring that the state's eleven congressional representatives be apportioned according to voters rather than total population.[28]

The resolutions, immediately tabled, could be viewed as an attack on the sacred, "three-fifths principle" and would haunt Johnson throughout the rest of his antebellum career. Tennessee Whigs, especially, would use the so-called white-basis stand as a focal point for attack, claiming that "in the Tennessee Legislature, he introduced and supported Abolitionism, thereby drawing down upon him the indignation of all parties." The charge was a deliberate exaggeration. "White basis" would have merely extended to the congressional districts the same system in use for apportioning the Legislature. Moreover, other southern states, even in the deep South, were having battles over their own version of the three-fifths principle.[29]

In spite of the obvious overstatement, being linked to abolitionism was not politically healthy, and Johnson felt that a defense was necessary. Characteristically, his explanation was more of a counterattack. He professed to be shocked. "It would require a man with a microscope to discover any abolitionism in either of these resolutions. . . ." Playing on the race hostility of poor whites, he reversed the Whig charge. The three-fifths ratio operating within a state was "well calculated to engender abolition. . . ." It made a nonslaveholder's vote count less than his more fortunate fellow citizen and degraded whites by making five Negroes equal to three white men. Still state sectionalism, not race, was the primary motivation as Johnson himself intimated; "Because I attempted to sustain the division of the State I had in part the honor to represent . . . I am denounced an abolitionist."[30]

When he moved from state to national politics, Johnson naturally had to extend his political horizon. Though at first he still represented East Tennessee, he would now be performing before a national audience and advancement would be possible only if he pleased most of Tennessee's and a good portion of the national Democratic Party. Moreover, his enemies were different. Along with the local Whigs sniping in the rear he had to face, directly, the Yankee abolitionist with his hateful attacks on the South and its institutions. Each attack required the obligatory reply from a "loyal" southerner. In response to his new role, there was an oblique change in Johnson's public posture on race and slavery. On questions that narrowly focused on the direct clash between slavery and abolition, the former tailor and self-proclaimed representative of the southern mechanic class became, on the surface at least, an ardent defender of the peculiar institution.

The new congressman's abstract mind was well suited for such debates, and he found little difficulty in wrapping slavery in the hallowed pages of the Constitution. In his maiden speech, which defended the notorious "gag rule," he argued against the introduction of abolition petitions because the Constitution itself recognized slaves as private property. Southerners would not stand idly by, he warned, but would turn "their faces toward heaven, and swearing, by their altars and their God, that they will all sink in the dust together before they will yield the great compromise contained in the constitution of their fathers." Later, in a speech in 1849, which he probably intended as a public explanation of his position on slavery, he expanded his constitutional argument. Slavery had its "foundation" in the Union, and the Union's survival depended on slavery's being left alone. The institution was beyond interference from the federal government; it was one of those sacred rights of the states and so much a part of the American system that it could not be abolished. "My position is that congress has no power to interfere with the subject of slavery, that it is an institution local in its character and peculiar to the States where it exists and no other power has the right to control it."[31]

Legalistic arguments, normal for a former admirer of John C. Calhoun, remained part of the Tennessean's repertoire until secession changed the rules of the game. Such arguments would have their counterparts in the Reconstruction period, but, like most southerners, Johnson could not let matters rest on legality alone. State rights may be a sincerely held belief, but it is so open to differing interpretation that it is usually buttressed by attitudes with far deeper roots. Furthermore, abstract legal theories seldom stir the souls of men — in a politician's language, attract votes. Like his colleagues on both sides of the Mason-Dixon line, Johnson almost always injected a strong dose of emotionalism into his "logic." In his gag rule speech, constitutionalism itself was given emotional content when he conjured up the image of southerners sinking in the dust to defend the revered document; and it was not the only vision invoked. The immediate antagonist was John Quincy Adams, elder statesman of the antislavery cause and opponent of the gag rule. In an earlier speech, Adams had compared emancipation with judgment day. Rather than the sound of Gabriel's horn in the former president's words, Johnson professed to hear the "evil genius" — Satan himself — hovering above the House "sending forth such unnatural sounds, predicting disunion, dissevered States, and the shedding of human blood! Frightful vision this!"

> Black he stands, as night:
> Fierce as ten furies; terrible as hell;
> And Shakes a dreadful dart.[32]

A few moments earlier, Johnson had betrayed the real source of his fear — men who were black, not demons. He did not need Milton's help to create the picture. Adams's ideas encouraged the "fiendish purpose" of the abolitionist and stimulated "the incendiary, who is standing with his torch ready lighted, prepared only for the destruction of the South. . . ." The ultimate end of abolition agitation was "servile war":

> Gracious God! are we prepared for scenes like these? are we prepared to surrender our homes and our firesides? are we prepared to see our fields, that now in due season yield luxurious crops, relapse into their original state, or be converted into fields of carnage? are we prepared to see the black hands of the negro wreaking in the blood of the white man? are we prepared

to see innocent women and children, virtue and beauty, all fall a helpless prey? are we prepared to see the land that gave a brother birth, drenched with a brother's blood? in fine, are we prepared to see peace, prosperity, contentment, and happiness, converted into discord, desolation, cries the most heartrending, lamentations (producing, to use the language of the poet) shrieks —

　— So wild, so loud, so clear,
　Even listening angels stooped from heaven to hear;

and yet be calm and deliberate?[33]

It is easy to dismiss such melodramatic language as an addiction to typical nineteenth-century hyperbole, but the assessment would be only half-true. By its very nature the problem evoked an emotional response. To a white southerner, regardless of social class, the fear of slave rebellion was omnipresent. This lingering anxiety provided a catalyst helping unite southern opinion concerning the essential need to maintain the system. The terrible consequences of a violent collapse, so easily imagined, insured that any response to abolitionist attacks would be couched in the most emphatic terms and that deviation, by a southerner, would be greeted with open hostility. Every slave-state politician had to keep this fact in mind if he wished elective office, and when complex problems disturbed surface unity making possible different interpretations, each point of view had to be reconciled as the most "loyal" to the South's socio-economic structure.

Throughout Johnson's antebellum career he remained a seemingly ardent if sometimes unorthodox defender of slavery. Any other course would have been, even in East Tennessee, political suicide. In Congress on direct questions of slavery versus abolition, he was often found in the company of the strongest pro-slavery extremists. His gag rule harangue made only the opening salvo of a bombardment that would continue on other bellwether issues. Even when supporting the general idea of the "Compromise of 1850," as did many other slave-state representatives, he voted against a key measure, the abolition of the slave trade in the District of Columbia. This kind of approach allowed him to defend his actions to all but the most extreme. He could claim to have voted for each bill in the series on its merits, not because it represented compromise in general.[34]

As the national situation became tense in the 1850s and vocal loyalty became even more necessary, the East Tennessean continued, perhaps with greater intensity, to follow the prescribed path. While governor of Tennessee and senator, he spoke vigorously in favor of the extreme southern position in the Kansas squabbles and used the vacillation of some Whigs on the question as a political cudgel. It was a typical Johnsonian tactic and illustrates how deeply he wished to identify himself and his party as the exclusive protectors of slavery. The target would be set up — perhaps a Millard Fillmore or an archenemy like John Bell — and his apostasy exposed by Johnson's battering "logic." The victim's votes and speeches would be juxtaposed with Johnson's loyal actions and words to "prove" beyond a shadow of doubt that the enemy was an advocate of abolition. It also proved, as a matter of course, that Andrew Johnson and the Democratic Party were sound on the slavery question. When the enemy was an avowed opponent of slavery rather than an imagined one, the response was automatic. John Brown's northern eulogists, for example, evoked a veritable flood of hostile rhetoric.[35]

In supporting sectionalism and southern rights, the East Tennessean could apparently be as zealous as any fire-eater. He seemed to genuinely mistrust northern motives, New England's in particular, and enjoyed rhetorical thrusts couched in sectional terms. The epithet "Boston codfish aristocrat," referring to Robert C. Winthrop, former Speaker of the House from New England, was one of his inventions. Even his rigid support for the national Democratic Party could be rationalized as support for the South should the occasion demand. In 1856, for example, Johnson stumped vigorously for James Buchanan, though he privately admitted the nomination "operated on a portion of the democrats like letting down an iceburg in their midst." He explained his position in terms of southern loyalty, arguing that Buchanan was the only feasible alternative to the Republicans, whose election would be a disaster for the South.[36]

Party loyalty based on sectionalism could be dangerous in the long run. Like many other southern Democrats, Johnson contributed to the division of his party by his strict insistence on southern rights and his refusal to compromise with the Douglas wing of the party in the northwest.[37] When Jefferson Davis introduced a series of resolutions in 1860 designed to embarrass Stephen A. Douglas and destroy his chances for the party's nomination, Johnson publicly supported the future president of the Confederacy, in spite of the fact that he hated Davis perhaps even more than he hated Douglas and felt that the resolutions were generally useless and divisive. For the moment, blocking Douglas was the primary concern. It could possibly enhance his own chances for the nomination and, most important, increase the likelihood of a southern nominee. As he explained to one supporter, he was satisfied in his mind "as to the propriety and Correctness of the South nominating a Candidate from a slave holding State . . . the South will lose nothing even in defeat, if She is only united. . . ."[38]

The high-water mark of Johnson's seemingly orthodox fidelity to southern sectionalism came with his "lukewarm" support of John C. Breckinridge following the division of the Democratic Party in 1860. O. P. Temple, a fellow unionist but scarcely an admirer, blamed this last act of collaboration with the future secessionists on pure self-interest. Johnson's fortunes were closely tied to the Democratic Party in Tennessee and, underestimating the possibility of secession, he simply had to remain in line with the majority of his party. Indeed, if viewed from a narrow perspective, self-interest does seem to explain Johnson's assertive southernism. As he advanced further in the Democratic ranks, he depended more and more on the support of slaveholders. In his two gubernatorial victories, for example, he failed to carry his own section of the state yet carried Middle Tennessee, where slavery was more important economically.[39] When this is tied to an increasing personal interest in the institution after becoming a slaveholder himself in 1842, his course would appear natural. Yet there always remained something hollow, something that rang false, in Johnson's pro-slavery rhetoric.

The dominant southern leadership, especially of the fire-eating variety, could never accept this self-proclaimed leader of the southern mechanic class as one of their own. Part of the problem was undoubtedly personality. Abrasive assaults on aristocrats would make few friends among men who professed to belong to just such a class. But, perhaps equally important, such men recognized that the former tailor, as an individual and as a representative of a social group, had no real economic interest in the maintenance of slavery. At the very least, any interest he might have would be of a different sort. To dispel these doubts, Johnson tried to deny the obvious:

> Pardon me if I am inclined to be egotistical. Though I may not own quite so many slaves as some other, though I may not have quite so deep an interest in the subject as some others when you measure by dollars and cents, yet I claim to understand the philosophy and the basis of the institution of slavery as well as, and I do not know that it would be very vain in me to say better than some who own their hundreds. My position is more defensible, if it required defense.[40]

Self-justifications of this kind may have satisfied the average voter who was also a nonslaveholder or a small-scale slaveholder, but they made little impression on the leadership of either party in the South. There was an obvious conflict of interest between upper and lower economic classes, and Johnson's own aggressive political rhetoric continually called attention to that fact. If the swaggering belligerent version of democracy had not been enough, the East Tennessean's positions on other issues where the clash between North and South was not readily apparent would provide ample excuse for alienation. Most symbolic was his longtime advocacy of the homestead principle. As an idea, the homestead never set well with the southern leadership. It smacked of agrarianism and promised through its operation to create more and more free states. Men with slaves were not likely to take advantage of the benefits of free land. By the same token, as the homestead idea rose in popularity in the North, becoming an eventual plank in the Black Republican platform, its fervid supporters became increasingly suspect. Johnson was especially sensitive to any attempt to associate the homestead with opposition to slavery and tried many times to dismiss such fears. He failed. Guilt by association alone was sufficient to convict in the minds of some. His ideas were too close to the thinking of Yankee radicals, like Horace Greely, and Johnson refused to repudiate completely such support.[41]

Perhaps what made the measure most galling was that it struck a responsive cord among the poor, even in the slave South. The East Tennessean's incessant agitation, joined with that of other southern sponsors, helped make the measure nationally popular. In the last vote on the question prior to Buchanan's veto, only seven slave-state senators voted in the negative.[42] The widespread acceptance, reluctantly by many southern leaders, illustrates that the solid phalanx of pro-slavery opinion was not the result of a united state of mind. The South was potentially infested with a respectable kind of "Helperism" of which Andrew Johnson was a striking and vocal example. At the very least, his positions revealed that though all southerners might support slavery, the primary motivation stemmed from different sources. A large block, probably even a majority, were not wedded unconditionally to the plantation system and all it stood for.

The idea that slavery was a necessary evil that would eventually die out had always been part of American thinking and had been commonly accepted by southern leadership in the early days of the republic. But for southern Democrats in Johnson's day, it was no longer a fashionable assumption. At least, one did not discuss such things publicly. In response to a hostile world opinion and the increasingly shrill voice of abolition, slavery had become in the minds of some southerners the only basis of civilized society. The most extreme no longer wished to imagine the South without slavery. To an East Tennessee tailor, the idea held no comparable horror. He made this aspect of his thinking plain while a young congressman. The subject involved was the annexation of Texas, which provided an opportunity to launch a standard barrage cataloguing the benefits of slavery. His speech, however, contained an unusual passage. Directing his remarks toward the unbelievers in the free states, Johnson pointed out that Texas would, in fact, increase the profits of slave labor,

> . . . thereby enabling the master to clothe and feed that portion of our population, softtening and alleviating their condition, and in the end, when it shall please Him who works out all great events by general laws, prove to be the gate-way out of which the sable sons of Africa are to pass from bondage to freedom, where they can become merged in a population congenial with themselves, who know and feel no distinction in consequence of the various hues of skin or crosses of blood.[43]

Even this rhetorical flourish, perhaps only half-serious, would raise eyebrows in some circles. As slavery had become a "positive good" in the minds of many of its ardent defenders, any emancipation, no matter what the conditions, would be unacceptable. If asked directly, Johnson would have probably claimed that slavery was a positive good, but he was clearly able to conceive of eventual freedom for blacks. However, he was also careful to point out that such a "great" event could occur only if Negroes were no longer living in the same physical space as whites.

The conception was not unpopular in the South, especially in the border-state regions, and found its expression in support for the colonization movement, which in southern eyes provided the additional advantage of removing that unpleasant and unnecessary element — the free Negro. The Tennessee General Assembly gave its approval to the approach on February 24, 1854, with a measure entitled "An act to regulate the emancipation of slaves and to provide for the transportation of Free persons of Color to the Western coast of Africa." Johnson, then governor, seems to have supported the movement. Required by law to handle the removals, he corresponded freely with William Mc-

Lain, president of the American Colonization Society, and his letters indicate that he was not averse to the idea. He claimed in one case to be willing personally to contribute financial aid in sending a particular black family "if my pecuniary affairs would admit of it but they will not." On another occasion, he noted that the slaves being sent "will be good emigrants, and I think a valuable acquisition to the new colony."[44]

It is tempting to dismiss the popularity of colonization in the South as the rankest form of hypocrisy, as did the radical abolitionists. Many obviously believed it was a means to strengthen, not weaken, slavery. Moreover, the idea implies an extreme form of racism. Freedom for Negroes must be accompanied by banishment, a view with appeal to the prejudice of the nonslaveholder. In most cases, and certainly in Johnson's, these attitudes played their part, conceivably even a lead role, but like so many elements of southern race thinking, the concept of black removal had a dual — almost schizophrenic — nature. It provided another means by which a pro-slavery man could illustrate to the world and, perhaps most important, to himself the extent of his kindness — his paternalism. In writing to McLain, the governor was careful to point out that he would not give his consent to the separation of families in the process of transportation.[45] Such concerns were a continual reminder, at least in the mind of a slaveholder, that his own actions were based on justice and not any desire to mistreat blacks. Such southerners may have been hypocrites but, like so many of their kind, their blindness was a necessary element in their adjustment to the world they lived in.

This mental dualism would be a continual element in Johnson's conception of race. It emerges again in relation to colonization after he had advanced to the United States Senate. As in other parts of the South, hostility toward free blacks had increased in Tennessee, perhaps in response to the escalating national crisis, and on October 6, 1859, a bill was introduced in the Legislature providing for the expulsion of free blacks. The measure went through several versions, including one in which violators would have been auctioned into slavery. After an amendment was added requiring that free blacks who refused to leave be hired out until earning enough to pay their passage to Liberia, Robert Johnson, who served in the Legislature, wrote his father in Washington asking advice. The amendment convinced the senator, since it "puts the measure in a pretty good form and relieves it from anything like oppression or inhumanity to the free Colored man. . . ." He advised his son to support the bill.[46]

In Johnson's view the amendment changed the bill materially. The free blacks would still be removed, which was desirable, but the deed would be accomplished in a manner that would not reflect badly on Tennessee — and by implication its senator. This was not simply political cant. There seems to have been no conception in Johnson's mind that removal itself might be inhuman. It was perfectly acceptable to tear a man from his home and force him to emigrate to a totally strange environment simply because his skin was black. Of course, one must not separate him from his family in the process or return him to slavery if he refused to leave or provide the expenses for his own transportation — that would be "inhumanity." Such logic is almost inevitable with an institution like slavery. Johnson and most other slaveowners were not naturally evil or any more prone to cruelty than normal men. They had to erect a partition in their minds that hid reality and created a separate code of conduct involving blacks. The partition was necessary for all southerners, but it was most important for those like Johnson who were most concerned with social justice.

Another influence on this nineteenth-century southern version of George Orwell's double-think is visible in the reaction to that most terrible of all specters — slave rebellion. Though always unlikely in the antebellum South, the lingering phobia, used by Johnson himself as one justification for slavery, became a real possibility — or, at least, what seemed to be a real possibility — while he was governor. The violent rhetoric of the election of 1856, which Johnson joined in creating, apparently stirred emotions in Tennessee, resulting in a flood of rumors about slave plots. Typically the conspiracies were supposed to be the work of "recreant abolition emissaries, who are using their utmost to incite our slaves to the murder of their benefactors." Whether these rumors represent reality or were ultimately the product of overactive imaginations is unclear. The consequences for blacks, however, were immediate and disastrous. The white hysteria resulted in numerous lynchings and what must have been a reign of terror in some counties.[47]

Through all the excitement the governor remained aloof and made no official statements. It was not the business of the state government to protect blacks except as property. His only official act involved providing state arms for one panic-stricken community that felt itself in imminent danger. To have refused to provide state aid on such a touchy matter would have been politically dangerous. However, there is no real evidence that the governor took the rumor seriously. Perhaps he had too much simple good sense. Outside the inflated rhetoric of stump speeches, he seldom referred to a fear of rebellion and never mentioned any of the events of 1856 in his extant correspondence. Also, he seems to have acted unofficially to calm fears. A nearby ironworks had been one of the supposed centers of the insurrection. As the rumor died down, Johnson personally led the owner "back to the Works" to protect him and his Negroes from a local mob of poor whites. On another occasion, possibly during the same disturbances, Mrs. Lizinka Campbell Brown, one of Johnson's close social acquaintances in Nashville, rushed to the governor, who at the time was standing in front of the state capitol, with a horrifying tale. She had been told by a friend of a Negro plot to rise on Christmas morning and murder all the whites in their beds. She feared such a thing might happen unless the governor could be convinced "to have cannon fired over the town on Christmas eve in order to intimidate the black conspirators." The governor listened to the tale and then looked out over a quiet city. "Where is the evidence of disturbance Mrs. Brown? Upon whom am I to fire?"[48]

Johnson's sober reply to the excitable Mrs. Brown illustrates far more than the fact that the governor was of sound mind. He had come a long way. Though still willing to use extreme rhetoric about any subject for political advantage and simply because he loved playing the demagogue, he was no longer the enthusiastic young congressman invoking the image of Satan to prove his point. He was not quite as concerned with "proving" himself. In private with no audience requiring a performance, he was not as apt to overreact to something like rumors of a slave rebellion. He naturally preferred to calm rather than frighten hysterical ladies. Success in politics had granted a certain, if fragile, security and separated his life from those who had little stability or personal confidence, such as the poor whites with whom he identified politically. The tailor had become a "master"—a paternal one at that. Still, it was clear that he did not belong to the planter class and had very little in common with that new power in southern politics—the fire-eater. Moreover, his career was not built on the defense of the peculiar institution as were the careers of some southern Democrats.

How well Johnson actually understood the distinction between him and his ultra-southern colleagues is by no means clear. It is possible that both sides perceived the origin of their mutual hostility on an unconscious level without ever understanding the actual source. Real conflicts of interest were easily transformed into personal aversion. It was characteristic of Johnson to see things as clashes of personality, but, no matter how sincerely the personal insults flung in both directions were meant, they reveal a deeper division. To the southern extremist, the key element in society was slavery. Loyalty was focused on the maintenance of an economic system that created the southern society. Any other alternative was unacceptable. To Johnson and men of his stamp, slavery could never be such a dominant force. Society was simply defined differently. Support for the institution came not because of its economic aspects but in spite of them. Unlike the planter, Johnson would lose very little in an economic sense if slavery disappeared and had nothing to fear if the people enslaved also vanished.

Though the Tennessean often advocated, as he put it, taking "high ground on the slavery question" for political advantage, it was not the issue that most occupied his mind.[49] In the last days of the slavery crisis, he revealed his exasperation in a speech in the Senate defending his precious Homestead Bill:

> We have been driven round and round upon the slavery question; round and round the giddy circle of slavery agitation we have gone, until our heads are reeling and our stomachs are sick, and almost heaving. . . . It really seems to me that if some member of this body was to introduce the ten commandments for consideration, and they were to receive consideration, somebody would find a negro in them somewhere, . . . Is it not time that the legislation of the country was directed to something else, and that some other things were considered? I do believe that the country, North and South, is becoming sick and tired of the constant agitation of the slavery question, to the exclusion of all others; and I do trust and hope, in God's holy name, that there is a public judgement and public spirit in the country that will rise above this agitation, and the purposes for which it has been kept up.[50]

Johnson's disgust with radicals of both sides was genuine and deeply rooted. He had made similar statements earlier in private correspondence. These feelings are another indication that the tailor-politician, though claiming to abhor conservatism, had a mind that worked differently from contemporary extremists in either camp. The contrast with the abolitionist is most apparent. The William Lloyd Garrisons and Theodore Dwight Welds of nineteenth-century America saw the world in black-and-white terms, as Johnson often did, but their point of reference was not the same. An abolitionist, whatever his approach, was basically a humanitarian — a moralist and reformer. Johnson clearly was not. Besides being a man of practical politics, his radicalism was directed, in the abstract, at the structure of society rather than cruelty or inhumanity. He spoke of justice — each man receiving from society what he deserved. The abolitionist was more comfortable with words like "sin" and less concerned with the forms of society than its "purity." Slavery was opposed because it was evil; as a moral wrong, it could not be tolerated.[51]

This differing view of mankind may well have been related to class differences. Some historians have maintained that the abolitionist-reformers were essentially middle-class intellectuals — a displaced elite — trying to recapture moral leadership and thereby replace the political leadership they had lost in the rising tide of Jacksonian America.[52] Johnson was part of that rising tide and, as such, would have been operating from an entirely different position. He was a man fighting to enter and become part of the existing social structure. Basically satisfied with existing institutions, he wished to work within, not outside of, them. Change could be brought about by slight changes in the political structure, which made it more democratic.

The divergent world view is also visible in separate concepts of religion. Many antislavery advocates came, even when they later embraced other ideas, from a strongly religious background. Johnson, in contrast, had almost no religious training in his early years and during his life exhibited little attachment to any church. Parson Brownlow even went so far as to call his old enemy an "infidel." As usual, the good parson was probably exaggerating, but clearly Johnson was little influenced by religious thought. It is probably accurate to say that he was close to a free-thinker or perhaps a deist. At any rate, he never belonged to an organized denomination and attended church meetings only rarely. When he did, it probably had a political purpose, just as his claim to Christianity in reply to Brownlow's charges was a political necessity.[53]

Unlike Johnson, the abolitionist had a concept of right and wrong supposedly based outside man and his institutions — determined by otherworldly and absolute truth. Basic Christianity also holds an ideal concept of perfection — God — that man because of his corrupt nature can never achieve but must keep striving to attain. Johnson's ideas of right and wrong came not from outside but from inside man's society. They were forged through his own experience and personal sense of justice created by the hard, never-ending climb up "Jacob's ladder." He may have been, as he asserted, a man of principle, but his principles were almost totally related to the structure of the existing social order. If society were fair — right — democratic — then man (Andrew Johnson) could reach perfection (achieve status and recognition). He had only to use the machinery of Jacksonian society. With it, he could travel those converging lines — democracy and religion — and eventually reach God.[54]

The conflict in world view bomes even stronger when the influence of Transcendentalism is added to the abolitionist side of the equation. All abolitionists were not, of course, Transcendentalists, but almost all Transcendentalists were antislavery, which made them abolitionists from the southern viewpoint. Also, the philosophical approach to life, if it may be called that, had a clear influence on abolitionist thinking. Like Johnson, the Transcendentalist saw the possibility of perfectibility in man, rejecting the older, bleaker view of life at the core of Calvinist doctrine — yet the path to perfection was very different. The Transcendentalist was an ultra-individualist. He lived, ideally, outside ordinary, corrupt society, rejecting its institutions. He could, therefore, like the Christian-abolitionist, embrace the famous "higher law" principle. On the contrary, though often chafing under restraints Johnson accepted, perhaps even worshipped, institutions, particularly government. Moreover, to Johnson there was something almost holy about the idea of a majority — public approval. The phrase "the people" was always on his lips. American institutions would work if only the people were heard — the *voice of the people is the voice of God.*"[55] To the Transcendentalists, a majority meant little; one's own concept of morality, everything. Thoreau, the Transcendentalist, would go to jail rather than pay taxes to support what he saw as an unjust, if popular, war. Garrison, the radical abolitionist, could burn a copy of the Constitution as a gesture because it recognized slavery. Johnson revered the Constitution as a symbol of justice. At his most radical he could only propose amendments. Later, when the crunch came, he proved incapable of rejecting that chief symbol of American institutions to join his own state and party in secession. If there was a higher law for Andrew Johnson, it had become the *structure* of American government itself — the Constitution, the Union — which he always conveniently assumed to equal the will of "the people."

The same kind of conflicting perspective separated the former tailor from his pseudo-aristocratic adversary in the South — the fire-eater. Both professed to be strict constructionists supporting state rights, yet they often seemed to be talking about a different Constitution, governing a different sort of human being. The fire-eater was certainly not a Transcendentalist, but his mind worked in a strikingly similar fashion. He created his own version of "higher law" most visible in the ideas of the extreme pro-slavery propagandists like George Fitzhugh. Slavery, a single economic institution, assumed a character that carried it far beyond the normal meaning of the word "institution." It became the basic foundation of a good society, necessary because man was basically evil. He needed a rigid system of masters and slaves to absorb the perpetual conflict and prevent the collapse of civilization. In Fitzhugh's twisted mind, racial difference became, in fact, relatively unimportant. Slavery was just because it allowed the superior man to dominate and control lesser orders of humanity, whatever their color. This does not mean that Fitzhugh was not a racist; as his post-war career would indicate, he clearly was. It means that in his obsession with slavery everything else became subordinate. No institution — including the Union itself — could be tolerated if it interfered with what he believed to be the moral foundation of society.[56]

The contrast with Andrew Johnson could not be more apparent. As a firm believer in democracy, the East Tennessean could never accept Fitzhugh's conception of mankind. Though Johnson was also attached to a rigid, institutionalized social order, that attachment was based on a directly contradictory understanding of the function of society. He saw the structure of the American system, which he called democracy, as the means of freeing mankind, destroying entrenched privilege, and, ultimately through its operation and improvement, creating a just society — Johnson's version of utopia or, as he put it in his Jacob's ladder speech, that great day when government will cease to exist and "Theocracy begin."[57] Both Fitzhugh and the Transcendentalist-abolitionist saw slavery as a limiting factor. To the former, it was the last bastion of civilization against barbarism; to the latter, it was the major impediment on the path of human perfectibility. Either concept was foreign to Johnson. To be acceptable in his understanding, an institution like slavery had to become a positive factor contributing to the advancement of mankind within the democratic system.

Given the situation in which Johnson found himself, that of a southern politician, it was almost inevitable that he become a staunch defender of the peculiar institution. Any other course would have required an almost revolutionary personality. Johnson was no revolutionary, and his personal craving for acceptance would preclude any action that actually threatened the southern social structure. All his radicalism was designed only to open the system for him and others like him, not change its basic design. Moreover, the mythology of his society provided a convenient means of avoiding the central question of morality.

The American system had been spawned by a revolution that had done little to alter the status of the slave in the South, and Johnson's own patron saints, Jefferson and Jackson, had been large-scale slaveowners. If American society was the best in the world, and Johnson never assumed anything else, then slavery had to be at least an acceptable if not a positive good.

The operation of a person's mind is never as simple as explanations of his thought make it seem. Ideas, attitudes, and a general outlook on life come from a long process of social conditioning, random certainly but still beyond an individual's control. When this is coupled with unconscious psychological motivation, to a large extent still mysterious, it is apparent that complicated reasoning is often arrived at after the fact. Most individuals are prone to rationalize the society in which they live before ever questioning it. The tendency is particularly important when trying to understand a subject like Negro slavery. To a nineteenth-century southerner, the institution was so ingrained that it would require a considerable counter-force to alter a general acceptance. Such forces are always present within an individual's own mind and within society, but how and upon whom they work vary greatly. Moreover, what would seem a counter-force to the existing order may well be twisted by the social system or individual thinking to produce exactly the opposite effect.

From the modern viewpoint it would appear obvious that slavery and racism are incompatible with the principles of democracy. If all men have the right to participate in government, a rough approximation of equality, at least before the law, must exist. Such a political ideology should, theoretically, provide the strongest possible counter-force to slavery. Yet, in nineteenth-century America, this was simply not the case. Democracy, especially of the Jacksonian variety, became one of the institution's strongest supports.[58] This twisted perception is perhaps in the long run the most significant result of the peculiar institution and is clearly visible within the mind of a man like Andrew Johnson as he wrestled with the agents of abolition. His elaborate system of defense was obviously most effective when heard by fellow southerners; but, since it was based on preconceptions shared by many Americans, his argument had an appeal north of the Mason-Dixon line, especially to followers of Jackson. In the end, most northerners might not have agreed with Johnson about the institution of slavery, but ideas concerning the nature of blacks were a different matter.

As was pointed out earlier, there was a clear separation between slavery as an institution and personal attitudes toward black people. Johnson had to create two distinct modes of rationalization, one based on the economic value of slavery and the other based on the social necessity of racial separation. For a man like Johnson, the former argument was by far the more difficult and in the long run much weaker and less significant, especially outside the South. Thinkers like George Fitzhugh, of course, had no real problem. Not committed to democracy, they did not have to sell their ideas to the general populace. Johnson, on the other hand, had to find some explanation of the benefits of the institution for the mechanic class that he claimed to represent. It was not enough to see slavery as simply a limiting factor, protecting the upper classes. It had to be instrumental in advancing opportunity for all *men.*

In his 1849 speech at Evans' Crossroads, Johnson advanced a unique theory that became a common refrain in his defense of slavery. Unlike Fitzhugh and others who saw a natural alliance between the slaveowner and the northern capitalist, the mechanic representative professed to believe that the slaveholder was actually a staunch supporter of labor and a natural ally of working men everywhere. The concept was based on a peculiar interpretation of economics that was almost a direct inversion of Fitzhugh's logic:

> The institution of slavery in the United States might be considered in another point of view and I think well founded in true philosophy — labor needs advocates, it must have talent to defend and watch its interests. The twelve hundred million of dollars vested in slave labor in the United States is a powerful auxiliary on the side of high prices for labor — the Southern man is the true and interested advocate of high prices for labor — his capital consists in labor and the more labor brings the more he makes.[59]

The image of the planter aristocracy marching in the vanguard of a sort of pro-labor movement is almost ludicrous beyond belief. It obviously could not come from reading the same kind of propaganda that had become the staple of a fire-eater's diet. The *Charleston Courier*, for example, observed that the use of slaves as mechanics "is our bulwark against extortion and our safeguard against the turbulence of white mechanics, as seen in the great strikes, both in England and the North, and is the only protection we have in any possible struggles between capital and white labor." Johnson's mental gymnastics also illustrate the clear separation between his ideas and those of Hinton Rowan Helper, who hated slavery precisely because he believed it was a handicap to the southern working classes.[60] But, most important, Johnson was plainly contradicting the basic tenor of his own beliefs. Throughout his career he recognized the natural conflict between the planter and the mechanic class and made such a conflict an integral part of his political appeal. Yet somehow he could also imagine the slaveowner as an advocate of labor.

It is tempting to write off such ideas as another example of demagoguery since political expediency obviously had a role in this kind of argument, but to do so ignores the most important element in Johnson's convoluted reasoning: he actually believed what he was saying. The need to defend the social order in which he lived, for both political and psychological reasons, created a situation that destroyed any real hope of a rational perception of society. The facts and statistical evidence marshaled to justify these positions were in reality immaterial. Whatever they were, Johnson would have used them to support preconceived notions. Southerners of all classes tried to argue and probably believed that slavery was an economic benefit to the whole nation, and whether their arguments were accurate makes no real difference. Men who assumed to belong to the planter aristocracy naturally saw what they considered their counterpart in the North, the capitalist, as a fellow beneficiary of the peculiar institution. A southern mechanic who also supported his section might well have the opposite perception. The northern working classes, his natural allies, were the people who really benefited. Only a Helper, a real outsider who as a social, economic, and political failure owed nothing to the system, could overcome mental barriers and view slavery as inimical to his interests. Even in this case, the rejection was perhaps more of an excuse for failure than any real understanding of society.[61]

The blinders worn by most southerners when dealing with subjects involving blacks and slavery were the products of an extreme form of racism. Of course, such an assumption is not new. Many historians have pointed out that race control and white supremacy were probably more important in the defense of slavery than was economics, particularly in the mind of the nonslaveholder. Yet calling it "extreme" provides only a hint to the depth and meaning of southern racism. In Johnson's mind and the minds of many of his contemporaries, white supremacy had a unique result closely related to its operation within a supposedly democratic system. In fact, racism became an important factor in the evolution of Jacksonian Democracy as it was understood in the South. The odd twist of ideology is visible as part of the second pillar in the East Tennessean's personal defense of the peculiar institution. These ideas were the real basis of his support for slavery and were rooted in assumptions concerning the biological or inherent inferiority of the black man. He plainly believed that the Negro was something less than a white man — something not quite human. The attitude was made clear in the young representative's first speech before the House:

> . . . he had no hesitancy in bringing his mind to a conclusion upon the subject, believing and knowing, as he did, that the black race of Africa were inferior to the white man in point of intellect — better calculated in physical structure to undergo drudgery and hardship — standing, as they do, many degrees lower in the scale of gradation that expresses the relative relation between God and all that he has created than the white man: hence the conclusion against the black man and in favor of the white man.[62]

On one level such an attitude does much to explain the nature and content of racist mythology in America. The Negro, as Johnson and most southerners saw him, occupied a position much closer to the concept "animal" than did a real human being. This animalization provided the foundation of most racist myths. For example, since sex was considered an animal-like function, the Negroes would obviously be sexually overactive and, as "beasts," a threat to the purity of white womanhood. Similarly, animals would be incapable of real rationality and prone to violent or unpredictable acts. The list is nearly endless and is familiar in racist thought with different variations depending on the society and the people involved. Yet in a mind like Johnson's, these myths received an added impetus on another level. When the East Tennessean spoke of black inferiority, he was careful to point out that a "conclusion" was implicit — "against the black man and in favor of the white man." The implied relationship between two such groups was inherent in the nature of society. Mankind was always divided into "superiors and inferiors," and "the existence of civilization was dependent on this state of things."

> If we survey the earth geologically and penetrate its surface and keeping down through the rind and the successive strata beneath, we shall find, as in cutting an onion, *it may* be a strata of sandstone, a strata of clay, a strata of another rock, and so on, passing through the globe. . . .
> Now, my illustration is this: What is this thing you call Society? We find some occupying the upper positions, and others the lower positions — composing in the whole and making up what men call Society. . . . We find also this institution of slavery (whether white or black) incorporate into this so-

cial condition of man. . . . Thus the institution of slavery exists, and so long as one man grows with more physical or intellectual power than another, so long there will be grades in society.[63]

Such a concept of social structure might seem more at home in the mind of a self-proclaimed aristocrat like Fitzhugh than in the mind of a supposedly "egalitarian" democrat. But Johnson's rationale twisted the meaning of equality and democracy to fit the society in which he lived. When Jefferson wrote "all men are created equal," he did not mean Negroes, as Johnson himself pointed out.[64] To both men such an assumption was ridiculous. On the other hand both, especially Johnson, did sincerely believe that all *men* should be treated as equals. Blacks were just not *men* in the full meaning of the word; they were something else.

This belief made an important contribution to the development of the democratic system in America. When Andrew Johnson and many of his contemporaries spoke of democracy, they did not mean to imply that everyone within the system was actually equal. Such an assumption would have required another revolution and social changes that were simply beyond possibility. Society remained a hierarchy. Nowhere could this be more evident than in Johnson's Jacob's ladder concept. In order to climb, to improve one's status, there had to be superiors and inferiors. This kind of division provided a part of the drive present in men like Johnson, who sought to "raise" themselves. In the older aristocratic world of Europe, such divisions were dependent to a large extent on one's birth. A peasant would always remain a peasant. In America, especially in the South, the presence of an inferior species, which could never produce members of society in the proper meaning of the word, added a different element to the social equation. All white men were automatically elevated to a kind of psychological aristocracy within which competition was fair. To be sure, the upper classes might not willingly accept such an implication, but to those in the lower ranks it was an important factor giving meaning to their lives. In other words, the presence of the black man, a nonhuman, provided a symbol illustrating the basic equality and brotherhood of all *men* — real humans. Blacks helped make it possible for a tailor or any other member of the lower orders of society to consider himself as good as the most established aristocrat, in spite of obvious social and economic differences, and insist on the maintenance of social equality, at least in theory.

Looking at Johnson's ideas in this way does much to explain the contradictory nature of his beliefs and actions. Since blacks were conceived as a kind of animal, it is easy to see how a man could be paternal and kind on the one hand and harbor intense fear and loathing on the other. Few things evoke such strong feelings as an animal that turns on its master—for example, the concept "mad dog." Of course, the idea of including such creatures in a society as equals would be ridiculous. Moreover, in a democratic system where each member, theoretically, has power and the right to compete, it would be positively dangerous. Not only would equality for inferiors hamper the operation of the system, but it would also automatically diminish the status of every other member.

Such an understanding lay behind Johnson's and most poor whites' support for the peculiar institution. Negro slavery helped each white man understand the meaning of his own freedom and equality, giving each an added psychological lift into the upper class within which democracy could be practiced. White supremacy was the element that united all southerners in opposition to abolition, even if their own economic interest would have been served. This manner of thinking, however, also provided the most important chink in the southern armor. It was not slavery, the institution, that held the loyalty of the majority in the South but its companion, racism. The nonslaveholder would support slavery only so long as he could not conceive of any other means of protecting white supremacy.

Chapter 4

The Reluctant Liberator

Colored Men of Nashville: You have all heard of the President's Proclamation, by which he announces to the world that the slaves in a large portion of the seceded States were thenceforth and forever free. For certain reasons, which seemed wise to the President, the benefits of that Proclamation did not extend to you or to your native State. Many of you consequently were left in bondage. The taskmaster's scourge was not yet broken, and fetters still galled your limbs. Gradually this iniquity has been passing away; but the hour has come when the last vestiges of it must be removed. Consequently, I, too, without reference to the President or any other person, have a proclamation to make; and, standing here upon the steps of the Capitol, with the past history of the State to witness, the present condition to guide, and its future to encourage me, I, Andrew Johnson, do hereby proclaim freedom, full, broad, and unconditional, to every man in Tennessee.

Andrew Johnson
October 24, 1864[1]

There is no evidence that Sam or any of the governor's other slaves were present on that night in late October 1864 to hear their master's proclamation of freedom "full, broad, and unconditional, to every man in Tennessee." If the Johnson servants were there, one can only regret the failure to record their impressions. Certainly old friends of a lighter hue must have suffered considerable shock. The voters of Tennessee were often the targets of similar seizures of grandiloquence, but they had never been subjected to a speech quite like this one, especially from this man. Not only did his words apparently reverse positions doggedly held throughout a long political career, but they were also delivered to a gathering the likes of which Tennessee had seldom seen.

The night had been a strange one in Nashville. Beginning with a torchlight parade in support of the Union Party ticket, it finished with the Union Party candidate for vice-president standing on the steps of the state capitol addressing a crowd of Negroes, many of whom were still technically slaves. That the members of the audience could not vote was apparently no deterrent to either their enthusiasm or the ardor of their speaker. In his vivid description of the scene, Clifton R. Hall, the usually benevolent interpreter of Johnson's years as military governor, fails to hide his disgust at the former tailor's obvious surrender to the temptations of demagoguery. In Hall's estimation, the performance suggests that "his too constant friend, the whiskey bottle," was the real "inspiration of his unfortunate diatribe."[2]

Drunk or sober, with this vow to the blacks of Nashville, Johnson clearly began one of the most unusual speeches of his long career. Before finishing he had thoroughly scourged the "iniquitous system" of slavery, assaulted more harshly than usual the "damnable aristocracy" (even to the extent of mentioning several of Nashville's elite by name), and promised that black women would no longer be victims of the slave master's "brutal lusts." Flushed with excitement near the end of his tirade, he called for a "Moses" to lead the freedmen "safely to their promised land of freedom and happiness." He had confidence, he claimed, that such a savior — God's chosen "instrument" — would surely "be revealed." When a few in the crowd responded to the obvious hint and shouted their own personal nomination for the honor, the self-anointed liberator submitted to the will of "the people" with an obligatory show of reluctance:

> Well, then . . . humble and unworthy as I am, if no other better shall be found, I will indeed be your Moses, and lead you through the Red Sea of war and bondage, to a fairer future of liberty and peace. I speak now as one who feels the world his country, and all who love equal rights his friends.[3]

Viewed either from the perspective of Johnson's antebellum career or his stormy residence in the White House, this profession of love for "equal rights" appears the sheerest form of hypocrisy or, even less charitably, a conscious attempt to deceive. Certainly nothing in his staunch defense of slavery foreshadowed the metamorphosis into liberator, and most modern Reconstruction scholars blame his adamant opposition to the federal enforcement of "minimum civil equality for the Negro" as, at the very least, an important element in the struggle over Reconstruction. Yet to simply write off Johnson's words as gross hypocrisy or the product of overindulgence in alcohol (either charge may or may not be partially true) is to oversimplify a highly complex individual caught up in a situation over which he had little control. More important, it would obscure the operation of his own racial attitudes on both personality and career. Four years of civil strife had wrought fundamental changes in the East Tennessean's world, and Johnson could hardly avoid being influenced by those changes.[4]

Secession and war had been a personal as well as national tragedy for Andrew Johnson. In his eyes, the years immediately preceding the Democratic Convention of 1860 were, on the whole, good ones. He consolidated his hold on the state's Democratic Party, was elected governor and senator, and had the goal most coveted by his driving ambition dangled just before his fingertips when the Tennessee Democrats selected him as their favorite son candidate. In addition, at least one of his pet projects at last appeared within his grasp. In late 1860, both houses of Congress seemed willing to pass a homestead bill — Johnson's personal panacea that he claimed would solve many of the country's problems and inaugurate a "new era." Even his family life gave the impression of a brighter future. One of his wayward sons, Robert, had taken himself in hand, presumably with the intention of making a useful career. A member of the state legislature, the younger Johnson attended the Charleston convention as his father's most loyal advocate.[5]

Yet for Andrew Johnson, as for many other Americans, that convention marked the apparent end of cherished dreams and a secure future. Not only did his long-shot bid for a place on the ticket fall short but, more important, his ill-concealed hopes for the nomination at a subsequent convention were also smashed beyond redemption with the division of the Democratic Party and the rapid slide toward secession. His eventual "lukewarm" support of the Breckinridge ticket seemed more reflex than an expression of will. In addition to the national crisis, unsettling enough in itself, he soon suffered a grievous personal defeat when President Buchanan vetoed the Homestead Bill and was sustained by southern Democratic votes. Even Johnson's family contributed to his anxiety. While Robert temporarily continued to behave, Charles, the eldest son, had used his trip to Charleston as another excuse for a drunken "spree."[6]

To Johnson it must have appeared as if the whole country were indulging in a drunken spree. In part, his bitter condemnation of secession should be seen as a response to a deep sense of personal loss. This is not meant to imply that his often-professed loyalty to the Union as an idea was not sincere, but that the concept of Union had come to represent something more to him than just an abstract principle of government — something more personal. His long climb through the ranks, which gave him whatever real self-esteem he had, had not been the result of economic success or achieved with the help of his section's wealthy leadership, the real beneficiaries of the threatened institution of slavery. Johnson was the product of the American political system — as he would have called it, democracy. He owed everything to that system, embodied in the national government, and he repaid the system with all the strength of his unyielding personality. Of course, he was also aware that he could never have fared so well in a government dominated by Jefferson Davis and his ilk; no man with Johnson's aggressive sense of class was likely to be president in an "aristocratic" southern Confederacy. Such awareness could only reinforce his loyalty to the Union and increase his hatred of "traitors."[7]

The very depth of devotion to the national system, coupled with his own rigidity of thought, was probably responsible for a tendency to underestimate initially the real danger of secession. It was never easy for Johnson's closed mind to see another point of view; actually breaking up the government, for any reason, was simply beyond his understanding. Problems were worked out and injustice removed by "fighting" within the system, not running away. This self-induced blindness helps explain his own guiltless spasms of pro-southern rhetoric and his capacity to ignore the need for measures encouraging sectional harmony. As late as 1859, he took time out in a Senate speech to chastise those who were continually tying the Union to every little bill brought before Congress. So much verbiage professing loyalty was unnecessary. It had been done so often that it became "entirely a business transaction." Loyalty to the Union was not merely a matter of practicality, and, besides, he claimed that he had "never considered the Union yet in danger."[8]

Such confidence was exaggerated. Johnson did not wish to admit publicly, and probably in some measure to himself, how severe the situation had become. When the days following the Charleston debacle saw his fanciful image of the world slowly crumble before the reality of disunion, his stifled pessimism intensified until it could no longer be ignored. Still, the imagined threats to the South were never serious enough either to warrant revolution, in his estimation the real meaning of secession, or to shake his basic attachment to the national system. As the worried senator wrote one supporter in July 1860: "While my hopes are Strong that there is no party that is in favor of dissolving the Union *my fears are great* that it is So— For my part I intend to [keep] fighting in the Union not outside of it—"⁹

The idea of "fighting" within the government was an essential element in Johnson's conception of loyalty, especially as it related to slavery and racism. He always tended to view the democratic system as a field of battle in which men of justice, as he imagined himself, confronted the forces of injustice, anyone who disagreed with him. Secession was unnecessary. The legitimate weapons were words and political maneuvers, not guns. In his first great speech against secession in the Senate, he made it clear that his section and her peculiar institution could best be defended by staying within the system and that, by opposing secession, he was trying "to accomplish the same end" as other southerners. The struggle to protect slavery should be fought "not outside, but inside of the Union and upon the battlement of the Constitution itself."¹⁰

Though his attacks on the South Carolina heresy would soon become more strident, they did not at first result in a lessening of publicly expressed hostility toward abolitionism. In fact, by using a typical twist of Johnsonian "logic," he developed an argument—a kind of twin devil theory—that would reappear during Reconstruction with far more damaging consequences. Secessionists and abolitionists were really allies—cut from the same cloth, to use a tailor's metaphor. They were both "bad men" desiring destruction of the government for selfish ends— the government that Andrew Johnson and "the people," by implication all the good people, loved:

> Sir, the Abolitionists and the distinguished Senator from Mississippi and his party both stand in the same attitude, to attain the same end, a dissolution of this Union; the one party believing that it will result in their own aggrandizement South, and the other believing that it will result in the overthrow of the institution of slavery.

Secession became in Johnson's mind a kind of conspiracy in which southern extremists—"red-hot disunionists"—were aided and abetted by northern extremists—"run mad Abolitionists"—or vice versa, depending on which group happened to be in his sights at the time.¹¹

This conception of the root cause of the Civil War was, in part, the natural product of that peculiar division in Tennessee that pitted the mountain region of the east against planting and slaveholding interests in the middle and western sections of the state. To be sure, abolitionists were not popular in East Tennessee, and few in the area had any wish to see blacks free. On the other hand, at loggerheads politically for years with planters, East Tennesseans could find little community of interest with the leaders of secession and certainly had no wish to be part of a government totally dominated by slaveholders. In a sense, Johnson's home region was a no man's land caught between two irreconcilable forces and, understandably, felt hostility toward both sides.

In the former tailor's individual case, hostility toward the planter aristocracy was even greater because of his obsessive hatred toward those occupying higher rungs of the social ladder than he. Now these old antagonists were attacking the element in American society that granted Andrew Johnson the means to *act* as their equal—the national political system. In 1861, the angry senator wrote his old confidant, Sam Milligan:

> My dear f[r]iend, you now see that it is not guara[n]tees in reference to slavery they want: it is a go[vern]ment South so that they Can have the absolute Control of it in their own hands—And would erect today a monarchy if they had in their power— I know what I say— It is not the free men of the north they are fearing most: but the free men South and now desire to have a goment so organized as to put the institution of Slavry beyond the reach or vote of the nonslave holder at the ballot box. The people of Tennessee in all matters of Legislation would differ as much with the Gulf States as they do with the northern states and would be more difficult to agree in regard to the organic law than they would with the north. The north in my opinion will give the middle states a[n]y reasonable guarantee they desire which would make us much more Secure in Slave property than if they were a separate hostile power.[12]

Neither Johnson nor other Tennessee unionists were ready to abandon slavery; they simply placed it lower in importance than they did the national government. During the crisis, the senator made every effort possible under the circumstances to save the institution. He supported efforts at compromise that would protect slavery and even introduced his own measures.[13] Most important, after war had broken out he used his considerable power and influence to limit the actions of the government to suppressing rebellion and to prevent the war from becoming a crusade against slavery. His position was clearly stated in his war aims resolution passed by Congress and supported by such an antislavery luminary as Charles Sumner:

... this war is not prosecuted upon our part on any spirit of oppression, nor for any purpose of conquest or subjugation, nor for the purpose of overthrowing or interfering with the rights or established institutions of those States, but to defend and maintain the supremacy of the Constitution and all the laws made in pursuance thereof, and to preserve the Union, with all the dignity, equality, and rights of the several States unimpaired; that as soon as these objects are accomplished the war ought to cease.[14]

Acquiescence to such an approach toward the war was necessary from the Republican perspective to insure the loyalty of the slaveholding border states—something Lincoln himself justifiably considered a prime object of governmental policy. In the unlikely occurrence that abolition had initially been adopted as a northern goal, it is doubtful that even the staunch loyalty of Andrew Johnson could have survived the shock. For a time during the crisis, he at least toyed with the idea of a middle-states confederacy that would have eliminated both the abolitionist and the fire-eater, and the idea would always remain a remote possibility should the government fail.[15] Most significant to Johnson, however, immediate emancipation would constitute a challenge as severe as secession itself to his understanding of American democracy. The political system may have provided the necessary framework for a "plebeian" like Johnson to advance—climb up Jacob's ladder and act as if he were equal to the loftiest patrician—but white supremacy was a part, perhaps even a necessary part, of that framework. Certainly its contribution went far beyond the economic structure produced by slavery.

For southerners like Johnson the plantation system meant next to nothing. In fact it is not hard to imagine Johnson cheering if the great planters were stripped of their economic power. Yet slavery had created a permanent under class, a group who for biological reasons could never be equal to real men. Their very existence allowed Johnson and other poor whites to *feel* equal even when the reality of social discrimination told them otherwise. The visible symbol of white skin contrasted with black illustrated the essential kinship of white "men" as nothing else could. Moreover, since the Negro was inferior to the point of being nonhuman, to make him a free "man" would pervert the meaning of Johnson's radical democracy and actually threaten the "equality" of white Americans.

Though they initially agreed on the purpose of the war, the majority of Republicans did not see the situation from the same perspective. Certainly most held views that deserve the terminology "racist," but the average Republican, with the exception of a few in the Northwest, did not give white supremacy as prominent a place in his conception of society as did Johnson. Blacks as individuals were not that important; Republicans were more concerned with the abstract question of slavery. In this sense there is a different "quality" inherent in the two forms of racism. Part of the difference is probably attributable to the fact that Republicans and northerners in general had long been subjected to the rigidly moralistic propaganda of radical abolitionism, which simply had not penetrated the closed southern mind after 1830, except in the sense of being a rejected heresy. The humanitarianism of the abolitionist had at least helped many in the North accept the essential "humanness" of the Negro, if not his equality. But far more important, because most northerners lived in areas with only small black populations, they were not forced to face the real implications of emancipation. Further, as few Republicans held the extreme egalitarian philosophy that was an integral part of Johnson's variant of Jacksonian democracy, they would never have been as concerned with the result of including inferiors in a supposedly democratic system. If one did not truly believe that all white men were or should be "equal," then inferiors were already part of the system. There was no place, as yet, in Johnson's world for inferior "humans" or a permanent lower class, except slavery.

One of the best illustrations of this basic difference is the contrast between the attitudes toward race and slavery of Abraham Lincoln, remembered and almost worshipped as the "great emancipator," and his more reluctant successor. Like Johnson, Lincoln, the antebellum politician, clearly believed the Negro inferior and made political speeches that could only be termed racist. Debating Stephen Douglas in Charleston, Illinois, on September 18, 1858, Lincoln made one of his strongest declarations against human equality:

> I will say then that I am not, nor ever have been in favor of bringing about in any way the social and political equality of the white and black races, (applause) — that I am not nor ever have been in favor of making voters or jurors of Negroes, nor of qualifying them to hold office, nor to intermarry with white people; and I will say in addition to this that there is a physical difference between the white and black races which I believe will forever forbid the two races living together on terms of social and political equality. And inasmuch as they cannot so live, while they do remain together there must be the position of superior and inferior, and I as much as any other man am in favor of having the superior position assigned to the white race.[16]

One could hardly ask for a clearer statement of racism. In addition, throughout the war Lincoln flirted with various schemes of colonization, which he hoped would solve America's racial dilemma by removing the discordant element. This approach had been accurately branded by abolitionists as anti-Negro years earlier. Yet there was also in Lincoln's career a consistent opposition to the institution of slavery and a vague uneasiness about the injustice present in the American system. One of the clearest expressions of this attitude came in an 1855 letter to Joshua Speed, an old friend who had settled in Kentucky and come to differ with Lincoln on the slavery question. Lincoln described a trip taken down the Ohio fourteen years earlier. At that time he had been repelled by the visible cruelty of slavery, which he described as a "continual torment" every time he touched the border of slave territory. In defending his position he complained to Speed, "It is hardly fair for you to assume that I have no interest in a thing which has, and continually exercises, the power of making me miserable."[17]

There is no evidence that slavery ever made Andrew Johnson miserable, except possibly for the fact that he could not own more slaves than he did. By the same token, one looks in vain among the words of the former tailor, spoken or written, for hints of the kind of compassion so prominent in Lincoln. Even in his most extreme expression of paternalism the East Tennessean never, before the war at any rate, questioned the ultimate justice of enslavement, and his kindness, when present, was more on the order of that extended to pets than people. Paternalism is usually directed toward an individual or individuals, not a whole group. The recipient benefits because of the superior's supposed kindness, not because just treatment is his simple right as a human being.

The basic injustice of the institution of slavery was always on Lincoln's mind, and though he was a politician from the old Whig tradition who never accepted the extreme egalitarian rhetoric tossed about so freely by Jacksonians, he could not reconcile the institution with his understanding of the American system. In another of his debates with Douglas, Lincoln declared to his audience, "I hate it because of the monstrous injustice of slavery itself. . . . I hate it because it deprives our republican example of its just influence in the world — enables the enemies of free institutions, with plausibility, to taunt us as hypocrites. . . ."[18] Johnson, on the other hand, since he never saw blacks as "people," remained oblivious to the contradiction and, in fact, had accepted white supremacy as an integral part of a social and political system he revered, a system, in Johnson's mind at least, that had a far more radical emphasis on "equality."

Perhaps the best way to understand the basic difference between these two forms of thinking about slavery and race would be to measure the sum of guilt in some way. Lincoln, who never owned a slave and had always opposed slavery, felt a deep sense of personal anguish because blacks — people — were deprived of freedom. Johnson, though he at times seemed to feel that slavery was less than a positive benefit, neither questioned the institution because of what it did to blacks nor left any evidence of a conscious sense of guilt. On the contrary, slavery and white supremacy were transformed by Johnsonian logic into elements that contributed to "democracy" by providing increased opportunity for men like him.

This conflicting perspective on race reveals a basic, if subtle, division between the allies fighting secession at least partially obscured from the immediate participants by the extreme nature of the crisis. In fact, "allies" is probably not the best word to describe Johnson's relationship with Lincoln and the Republicans. A better term would be that used by the United States government in World War I to describe its relationship to the countries fighting Germany — "associated power." The enemy was certainly the same and the immediate goal, in this case saving the Union, was also the same, but the long-range views were very different. No matter how pious Republican declarations to the contrary in the heat of the moment, they clearly believed slavery would and should eventually die out if the policies of their party were followed. Johnson claimed to see and certainly hoped that the Union was the best means of defending slavery, not destroying it.

There is another element in the East Tennessean's "association" with the Republicans that must be considered if his transformation into "Moses" for the freedmen is to be understood. When Johnson committed himself irrevocably to the Union and against secession, which he did very early in his usual violent style of rhetoric, it was what might be called a "gut" reaction. He automatically cut himself off from many of his old allies — especially his power base in Tennessee's Democratic Party. Granted, many East Tennessee Democrats remained loyal to their leader, which was perhaps as much an indication of Johnson's personal popularity as basic unionism, but the majority of his new associates in Tennessee politics were Whigs, men who for years had been the targets of Johnson's none-too-gentle political invective. In addition, a large segment of the northern Democratic Party, though not secessionist, soon adopted a position advocating conciliation that was clearly unacceptable to extreme southern loyalists.[19] Compromise of any sort with the South on the question of secession would have left unionists in seceding states — especially a renegade Democrat — in an intolerable political position. As a result, Johnson became an unwilling dependent of northern Republicans — particularly the Lincoln administration — for immediate political survival.

This new association was not without its immediate advantages. Johnson's stand made him a kind of folk hero in the North as well as among loyal southerners, and his papers are filled with letters of praise from correspondents at all levels of society, including prominent northern leaders. Salmon P. Chase, for example, wrote asking for a copy of one of Johnson's speeches and included a statement comparing Johnson to the Tennessean's avowed idol, Andrew Jackson. Such letters could only have inflated a never inconsiderable ego and helped confirm his determination. Moreover, association with the Republicans in power had more tangible rewards. Lincoln moved immediately to cement Johnson's loyalty to the Union, and at the same time to himself, by placing Tennessee's patronage in the Democrat's hands rather than in the hands of a Republican's more natural Tennessee allies, former Whigs such as John Bell. In addition, Johnson found himself, by default, the loyal South's most important spokesman in Congress as most other southern leaders, one by one, followed their states out of the Union. In this position, Johnson could exert considerable influence and was even given a place on the influential Committee on the Conduct of the War, where his hatred for the southern aristocracy allowed him to make common cause with some of the most radical Republicans.[20]

The advantages of Johnson's stand were obviously reciprocal. His loyalty was a considerable embarrassment to southern Democrats and helped the Republicans illustrate, both at home and abroad, that the war was not purely sectional. Johnson's contacts in the national Democratic Party as well as the South were also potentially important, even after Tennessee seceded, and many times Republicans sought his aid, especially in states where the political ratio was nearly equal. Schuyler Colfax, for example, wrote in 1862 requesting that Johnson "redeem" his "promise" to assist in the Indiana canvass, claiming that "a few lines" from the popular War Democrat "would be of great value in swelling my vote." Even Lincoln himself, often the victim of severe criticism within his own party, at times welcomed the Tennessean's support, and

Johnson did not hesitate to give it where possible.[21] Yet in this unnatural association Johnson always remained the junior partner. Should the renegade southern Democrat abandon the administration it would be painful, but the loss would not be fatal. To Johnson, once the decision was made to support the Union, any course other than steadfast loyalty would have been political suicide. To a man of Johnson's driving ambition, that was a matter of no small consequence.

Lincoln made this political dependence even stronger when he appointed the East Tennessean military governor. Though it appears natural, the choice was not universally popular, and whatever Lincoln's motivation, the nature of the office made Johnson, heretofore a powerful and independent-minded senator, directly subject to the will of the president, even to the symbolic military subordination of a novice general to the commander in chief. Interpreters of Johnson's years as war governor have traditionally stressed the fact that Lincoln and his secretary of war, Stanton, usually seemed to defer to the wishes of the hot-tempered southerner.[22] Certainly the assessment is accurate, but it does not mean that Johnson was actually in control of the situation. Lincoln deferred to Johnson only when the Tennessean's desires coincided with his own or did no immediate violence to the president's conception of the war effort. Moreover, it is a tribute to Lincoln's political aptitude that he was able to handle the sometimes difficult ex-tailor with proverbial "kid gloves," always willing to bring Johnson slowly to the support of presidential policies, never demanding immediate and unconditional acceptance. It was political wisdom to leave "associates" with room to maneuver. As a result, the president seldom directly *ordered* the governor to do anything, even when the Tennessean seemed particularly obstinate. Rather, with his unique political approach, Lincoln would simply suggest a course of action and present it in such a manner that Johnson was left with little alternative but compliance.

A typical example of such manipulation occurred following one of Johnson's many disputes with local military authorities. Concerned essentially with political goals and often viewing the situation from the perspective of Nashville, Johnson was bound to disagree with commanders on the scene. The problem was made even worse by the confused lines of authority and Johnson's own naturally contentious personality. Lincoln usually supported his appointee because the governor's adversaries were seldom in the president's good graces. Unsuccessful generals were not popular in Washington. Yet when Johnson's demands became too extreme, the president had his way, albeit gently. After one particularly ludicrous request from Nashville, Lincoln sent the following wire:

> Yours of yesterday is received[.] Do you not my good friend percieve [*sic*] that what you ask is simply to put you in Command in the west. I do not suppose you desire this.
>
> You only wish to Control in your own localities, but this you must know may derange all other parts[.]
>
> Can you not & *will* you not have a full Conference with Maj. Gen'l H. W. Halleck [?]
>
> Telegraph him & meet him at such place as he & you can agree upon. I telegraph him to meet you & confer fully with you — [23]

The dispute in question is not actually important in this context. What is significant is that Lincoln's "good friend" was not a political novice. He had the simple good sense to recognize that in his unique predicament a gentle request from the president, though easier to swallow, had as much impact as a direct order. He may not have liked the state of affairs, but having few alternatives the governor reacted to presidential suggestions with uncharacteristic flexibility. The same process was at work in the realm of general politics. Johnson's precarious political situation, his overwhelming desire to crush secession, and the simple development of events forced the stubborn East Tennessean to move gradually to positions that would have been unthinkable only a few years earlier. The process would be slow, but it paralleled to a great extent Lincoln's own thinking and would be guided by the president's gentle prodding.

In a sense, this process also worked in reverse. Johnson was apparently successful in convincing Lincoln of his ability and loyalty. Several times in the early years of the war, the president expressed confidence in his military governor. Schuyler Colfax, for example, wrote Johnson that the president had twice in his presence compared the Tennessean favorably with other military governors and said that "'Andy Johnson' had never embarrassed him in the slightest degree." This failure to embarrass the president would have momentous consequences in 1864 with the selection of Lincoln's running mate.[24]

The people of Tennessee were not nearly as concerned with the sensibilities of their new leader as Johnson was with the attitude of his commander in chief. When the governor arrived in the conquered capital of Tennessee, he had been warned by General Don Carlos Buell to enter the city without fanfare because of local hostility. Johnson accepted the advice, but he still brought with him high hopes. His seemingly un-shakable faith in "the people" helped convince him that a majority of southerners, especially those in Tennessee, had been duped by a cor-rupt and mendacious leadership bent on personal profit. All that was really needed was for Andrew Johnson to return bearing the flag and truth; Tennessee would then return to loyalty. This totally unjustified optimism was partly responsible for his administration's relatively leni-ent course during the spring and early summer of 1862. As he told the somewhat sullen citizens of Nashville in the first of what turned out to be many lectures on loyalty, "I come with the olive branch in one hand and the Constitution in the other, to render you whatever aid may be in my power, in re-erecting, upon her rightful domain of Ten-nessee, the Star Spangled Banner — . . ."[25]

The idea of returning Tennessee to the "Constitution" had another implication in Johnson's mind when related to the institution of slavery. He told his listeners in the same speech that the rebels were only pre-tending that secession came about because of a desire to protect slav-ery, and that "it was clear to every candid mind that the only protection to slavery was in the Constitution of the United States." The same argu-ment was repeated a week later in an official "Appeal to the People of Tennessee," and he quoted from the war aims resolution to illustrate that the government had no intention of attacking the institutions of the South. This theme provided the core of his public approach to the question of slavery throughout the spring of 1862, and he hammered away on the argument in almost every speech. However, the former mechanic also added an interesting corollary obliquely tying slavery with opposition to democracy. He pointed out to several audiences that in South Carolina, the heart of secession, a man like him (and by im-plication most Tennesseans) could not even hold a seat in the state leg-islature because he did not own enough slaves to meet the property qualifications. In Johnson's mind, such a barrier revealed the true na-ture of the Confederacy.[26]

The view of secession as an antidemocratic movement provided Johnson with part of the rationale for his first significant public change of position on the slavery question. The occasion was a Fourth of July speech in Nashville, and the ample content was the harshest yet. "The Southern chivalry," the governor claimed, "have been the greatest rob-bers and enemies of the rights of the people, that the country has ever seen." If the war goes on "slavery is at an end." It had no protection outside the Union. Then after repeating his timeworn twin-devil thesis scourging both abolitionists and rebels and praising that "great middle party between these two extremes who must maintain the government," he made a statement that for Andrew Johnson was revolutionary:

> I am for this Government above all earthly possessions, and if it perish, I do not wish to survive it. I am for it, though slavery should be struck from existence and Africa be swept from the balance of the world. I believe indeed that the Union is the only protection of slavery—its sole guarantee; but if you persist in forcing the issue of slavery against the Government, I say in the face of Heaven, Give me my Government, and let the negroes go![27]

For the first time the former defender of slavery was publicly expressing a willingness, however grudgingly, to give up slavery if necessary to save the Union. To be sure, his words indicated no change in feeling toward the Negro, but the timing of the statement illustrates that he was not completely isolated in remote Nashville. No politician as experienced as Johnson could ignore the obvious change in Republican sentiment. Abolitionists had been unceasing in their pressure since the war began, and there were clear signs, in early 1862, that their appeals were being heard. Slavery had been abolished in the District of Columbia in April, and on May 26 the House defeated by only four votes a bill providing for the confiscation and emancipation of all slaves belonging to rebels. A similar bill would actually pass in July. Moreover, Johnson was receiving information through letters and private conversations reinforcing the considerable public evidence of slavery's bleak future. Postmaster General Montgomery Blair, hardly a friend of the black man, wrote the war governor after receiving a report of some of Charles Sumner's more extreme statements and warned that abolitionists "want the South to be disloyal." The southern people must be told by men like Johnson that their actions were aiding the opponents of slavery.[28]

In a very real sense, Blair's attitude provided another element in the rationale that made it possible for Johnson and other southern unionists with a similar frame of mind to abandon slavery. Emancipation would not be their fault but would be the direct responsibility of those foolish enough to support secession. Johnson hinted at this argument in his speeches, and the careful actions of the president seemed to give the view credence. With the advantage of hindsight, it is obvious that Lincoln, along with a majority of the Republican Party, was moving toward some kind of emancipation policy, but he was doing so slowly in a manner calculated to avoid offending the tender sensibilities of border-state unionists. Throughout the spring and summer of 1862, he had been trying to encourage gradual and compensated emancipation in the loyal slave states, always careful to stress his hope for the success of some sort of colonization scheme. But most important, he publicly refused to go along with extreme abolitionists and quashed the actions of overzealous subordinates who moved precipitously against slavery.[29]

On April 25 General David Hunter, commander of the Department of the South consisting of the coastal districts in South Carolina, Georgia, and Florida held by the Union, issued a proclamation of martial law. The proclamation provided an excuse for a second order, on May 9, which declared that "Slavery and martial law in a free country are altogether incompatible," and therefore all slaves in the affected states were "forever free." The edict was not published in the northern press until May 16, when it was immediately hailed by abolitionists who assumed it had been authorized by the president. Lincoln was not pleased; in fact, he was incensed that a military commander would take such a step totally without authorization. In spite of opposition in his own cabinet, including Chase and Stanton who argued that nine-tenths of the Republican Party approved Hunter's action, Lincoln issued a proclamation of his own on May 19, revoking the order and stating clearly that decisions of so momentous a nature were reserved to the commander in chief only.[30]

Lincoln's concern about the impact of Hunter's move and the quick reversal did not go unnoticed in Nashville. On May 22 Johnson sent the president a wire thanking him for his proclamation, adding that "It gives great satisfaction here." Conversely, Johnson's response and his refusal to interfere with slavery in his jurisdiction "gave satisfaction" in Washington. Horace Maynard, one of the governor's closest contacts left in the capital, wrote his fellow Tennessean on June 7 that all, "with the possible exception of a few extreme men," approved of Johnson's course. The president, in particular, was pleased and "expresses himself gratified in the highest degree that you do not let them raise any 'nigger' issues to bother him."[31]

Seeming to have a life of their own, those troublesome "nigger issues" would not die and, as Lincoln began to take more definite steps toward the Emancipation Proclamation, Johnson and the other southern unionists either had to move with him or be left behind. It is an almost too remarkable coincidence that in the same month Johnson first expressed a willingness to give up slavery to save the Union, Lincoln began working on a draft of the proclamation itself. As a last-ditch effort, the president summoned representatives from the border states to his office on July 12 to press once more for some sort of compensated emancipation scheme. "If the war continues long, as it must," he warned, "the institution in your states will be extinguished by mere friction and abrasion — by the mere incidents of the war."[32] In spite of the reasonable nature of the argument, it made little impression on his listeners, with one notable exception. The Tennessean, Horace Maynard, was the only man out of the twenty-nine present to give unqualified approval to the president's plan. In his solo minority report, he illustrated considerable sympathy with Lincoln's dilemma:

> Your whole administration gives the highest assurance that you are moved, not so much from a desire to see all men everywhere made free, as from a desire to preserve free institutions for the benefit of men already free; not to make slaves of freemen, but to prevent freemen from being made slaves, not to destroy an institution which a portion of us only consider bad, but to save institutions which we all consider good.[33]

There is no direct evidence that Johnson had a hand in Maynard's report, but it is quite likely that the governor was close to endorsing such a view privately if maintaining silence publicly. Certainly he had to be aware that emancipation in some form was becoming more and more possible. The proclamation for which he had thanked Lincoln only a few months earlier had contained, along with its reversal of Hunter's action, a plea for gradual, compensated emancipation, and he made no objection to the idea at the time.

Any influence he might have exerted to prevent the administration's endorsement of emancipation became a moot point less than two weeks later. On July 22 the president revealed a rough draft of the Emancipation Proclamation to the cabinet. The proposal would not be made public for political reasons until September 22, and, since the measure would obviously be controversial, the need for secrecy probably prevented any exchange of views between Lincoln and supporters like Johnson outside Washington. It is, of course, conceivable that some unofficial contact was made through written material not preserved or through intermediaries such as Maynard, but it is doubtful that any man's opinion would have deterred Lincoln once the decision was made.[34]

Certainly both Lincoln and Johnson were aware that such a move would change forever the political climate in a place like Nashville. Given the immediate task, local political considerations had to remain the primary concern for the Tennessean, and there is a good chance that his views toward the institution of slavery would have undergone an evolutionary change even without direct pressure from Washington. Desiring above all a victory over secession and suffering the same disappointments felt by Lincoln over the agonizingly slow progress of the Union war effort, Johnson was probably drawing similar conclusions albeit with more reluctance. In Lincoln's words, the "mere friction and abrasion" of war were taking their toll on many former advocates of slavery. A good part of the irritation came, in the governor's case, from the people of Tennessee in whom he had placed so much faith. Their initial response to his "olive branch" and "Star-Spangled Banner" had been less than enthusiastic.

The vain hopes of bringing his home state back into the fold and his own rabid unionism had blinded Johnson to the real extent of loyalty to the Confederate cause in Middle and West Tennessee. His first glowing reports had assured his superiors that loyalty would be quickly reestablished. He was simply wrong. Acquiescence to federal rule could come only with military conquest, and following the bloody victory at Shiloh, complete success eluded the Union Army. In fact, it would not be an exaggeration to say that Johnson's first year in office was spent under a state of siege. Even when major Confederate units were not threatening Nashville, raiders like Nathan Bedford Forrest and John Hunt Morgan harassed the northern forces and made the lives of Tennessee unionists miserable. The continued possibility of ultimate victory was bound to bolster the spirits of southern sympathizers.[35]

Moreover, many citizens of Nashville, rather than cooperating with the military governor, actively resisted or at least ignored his efforts. This obstinancy went from the ridiculous extreme of women, presumed ladies, holding their noses as they passed Union officers to far more serious offenses, such as espionage. Most aggravating to Johnson was the citizens' failure to respond positively to attempts at establishing a loyal civil government. Barely two months after arriving, Johnson held an election to fill the position of judge of the ninth circuit, which included Nashville. The candidates were Mason M. Brien, "a thorough and straightout loyalist," and Turner S. Foster, a "fierce and intolerable Rebel." Johnson tried to avoid interfering with the election, and the result was disaster. Foster won. The somewhat embarrassed governor had to arrest the new judge for disloyalty rather than allow him to occupy the post. He appointed Brien in his place.[36]

Such events were bound to have an effect on a man of Johnson's temperament, not to mention ambition. His personal attitude toward people he considered traitors had never been gentle, and failure in Tennessee would not make him look good in Washington. In the hostile atmosphere of Nashville, everything else soon became secondary in his mind to crushing the rebellion. In light of his frustration, the Fourth of July speech becomes more understandable. The change of position toward slavery was only part of a generally more repressive administration in Nashville less tolerant of those with southern sympathies. "Leniency," he pointed out in a letter to General George H. Thomas, "is construed into timidity, compromising to concession, which inspires them with confidence & keeps alive the fell spirit of Rebellion."[37]

While punitive measures toward the recalcitrant may have seemed justified, they placed considerable strain on the loyalty of many unionists and threatened to split the supposedly united forces against secession in Tennessee. As the symbolic leader of the state's loyalists, Johnson was naturally concerned with maintaining unity, but when the administration finally issued the Emancipation Proclamation on September 22, his task became truly formidable. As always, he could ill afford a break with Washington. The governor was currently involved in a power struggle with local military authorities over policy in Tennessee, which would not end until General Buell's removal in October.[38] It is doubtful that the administration would have taken the side of an official who publicly repudiated a decision as important as emancipation.

Unconcerned with Johnson's administrative problems and uninterested in the ultimate outcome of his political career, other unionists could afford the luxury of a less calculated response. Lincoln's apparent conversion to abolitionism was a shock to many of the faithful and provided an excuse for the wavering to transfer their allegiance to the rebellion. T. A. R. Nelson, for example, the most notable Tennessee unionist who remained behind Confederate lines, seized the opportunity to announce his conversion to the secessionist cause, and the Richmond government was quick to circulate a printed copy of his declaration in East Tennessee. But men within the clutches of the enemy were clearly of less concern than the supposed loyalists within the governor's personal dominion.[39]

Fortunately, the president left his southern associates with room to maneuver. The official proclamation of freedom would apply only to those areas still in rebellion as of January 1, 1863. Lincoln hoped that reorganization might be hastened in states like Louisiana, Arkansas, and Tennessee by the threat of general emancipation, and he reinforced his hopes by sending commissioners to encourage popular support for holding elections and securing valid representation in the federal government. Such a course, he theorized, would make it possible for loyal southerners to "avoid the unsatisfactory prospect before them."[40]

Well-acquainted with the futility of elections under the circumstances, Johnson was undoubtedly less sanguine than the president about the opportunity. However, he eventually authorized a congressional election to be held in the two West Tennessee districts on December 29. Because public opinion in the area, even among staunch unionists, was strongly opposed to the new departure on emancipation, it is fortunate that Confederate military activity intervened to make balloting impossible. The results would have been a considerable embarrassment for the Union cause.[41]

To Johnson, Lincoln's general flexibility and the loopholes built into the Emancipation Proclamation were most important, for the moment, in his local sphere of influence. He could remain publicly silent concerning the new policy, which so many of his immediate allies felt was "unconstitutional and inexpedient," and try to maintain the leadership of at least the simulant of a united party in Tennessee. In fact he actually joined efforts, quietly to be sure, to have Tennessee exempted from the proclamation. The most visible opposition gambit was led by William B. Campbell, who wrote Johnson early in November about the "very injurious" effect of the proclamation and by the end of the month had obtained the governor's signature on a petition to the president. Supported by a number of the state's prominent unionists, this document asserted that, since Confederate activity prevented the loyal majority from holding fair elections, the whole of Tennessee should be exempted from the effects of the proclamation.[42]

How much influence Campbell's petition actually had on Lincoln's final decision is unclear. Certainly Tennessee unionists in Washington, such as Maynard, let their views in favor of exemption be known, and there is a good chance that Johnson found other means with which to communicate his opinion. James G. Blaine, for example, maintains in his memoirs that the state was excluded at Johnson's insistence.[43] Once Tennessee became the only seceding state totally omitted from the impact of the final document issued on January 1, 1863, Johnson certainly lost no time in congratulating the president and sent a wire that might be taken as a hint of some sort of prior consultation:

Your proclamation of the 1st excepting Tennessee has disappointed & disarmed many who were complaining & denouncing it as unjust & unwise.

> I think the Exception in favor of Tennessee will be worth much to us Especially when we can get to discuss it before the people.[44]

Even though Johnson may have had serious reservations about emancipation and complained to at least one supporter in early 1863 that "the Administration made a sad mistake" because of the policy's impact in the border states, he was astute enough to recognize that the institution of slavery was living on borrowed time even if "the people" were not.[45] Convincing them that its ultimate demise was necessary to preserve the Union had to be one of his goals if he hoped for political survival. For the present, since Lincoln did not expect, or probably even desire, an immediate public statement and since Johnson's eventual endorsement would have some propaganda value, it was simple political wisdom, on his part, to find out what his support was worth by remaining silent.

The men who would soon form the nucleus of unionist opposition to Johnson in Tennessee were in very different positions. Emerson Etheridge, Baile Peyton, and William B. Campbell, the most noted leaders of the conservative unionists, were former Whigs and supporters of John Bell. They were not directly dependent on the Lincoln administration and, since the majority of Tennessee unionists were old Whigs, probably had more residual strength outside East Tennessee than a renegade Democrat. It was also possible that being from different sections of the state, Middle and West Tennessee, they were more closely connected with the planter class and had a deeper personal commitment to slavery as an economic institution than did a former mechanic. At any rate, the Emancipation Proclamation provided a convenient excuse for a reaction against the Lincoln administration and their old enemy in Nashville.[46]

The timing of individual decisions and the relationship between Johnson and the conservatives are not completely clear. As late as mid-January Johnson was still pressing the administration about a military command for Campbell, and he probably still hoped to bring Campbell and some of the others to his point of view. With the advantage of hindsight, however, the eventual split in Tennessee unionism seems inevitable. Once Johnson refused to denounce openly the president's proclamation, real hope for holding the support of conservatives was lost. The break, which soon became more open, further weakened Johnson at home and made him more than ever dependent on Lincoln and the Republicans in Washington, as well as a growing group of younger Tennessee radicals who were often less sensitive to the subject of emancipation than their titular leader and many of the older, more established leaders.[47]

Johnson quite probably made his private decision to support what he understood as Lincoln's position in the winter of 1862. On December 3 the *Daily Union*, at that time supporting Governor Johnson, came out in favor of a limited emancipation policy. After all, with Tennessee's exemption from the final proclamation, little violence would be done to Johnson's original position, and there was even a certain consistency. Slavery would still exist in Tennessee, technically unmolested, and unionists like Johnson could temporarily take the credit. On the other hand the *Daily Union*, in 1862 and early 1863, often seemed a little in advance of the governor on questions involving blacks. Perhaps Johnson, not sure in his own mind, was simply content to allow the administration newspaper to sample the troubled waters of public opinion.[48]

Johnson's grudging conversion to the antislavery cause gradually became visible during 1863. Early in the year the embattled war governor left Nashville for a speaking tour of the North, including stops in Indiana, Ohio, Pennsylvania, New Jersey, New York, Maryland, and finally Washington. To be sure, his was no pleasure junket; the Lincoln administration needed help. In several midwestern states anti-war forces had gained enough strength to cause considerable embarrassment. In Indiana, always a refuge for copperheads, the Legislature had even passed resolutions opposing the president's schemes for gradual emancipation, requesting a withdrawal of the Emancipation Proclamation and denouncing any use of blacks in the military. From a northern Republican's point of view, a loyal voice from the South, especially one belonging to a Democrat, might do a great deal to deflate the movement for conciliation. As a southern unionist, Johnson was just as interested in blocking compromise, and such a tour could only enhance an ambitious politician's national image.[49]

As always the former tailor's speeches were delivered in a style typical of the stump speaker infected with demagoguery. Yet the haphazard, seemingly extemporaneous approach to public speaking should not obscure the fact that, as usual, the crafty politician knew exactly what he was saying, especially in relation to delicate questions involving slavery and emancipation. The tone and basic content of his vivid addresses were established early and varied little throughout the tour. His primary concern was repudiating the idea of compromise, and most of his time was spent damning rebels and denouncing copper-heads. But given the political situation, slavery could not be ignored. When he mentioned the institution he simply carried the positions already established in Tennessee a little further, placing more emphasis on the threatened end of slavery. It, like all other institutions, was subservient to the Constitution. Any institution that assumed itself more important than the government would be put down. "Has slavery a right to agitate the government and shake it to its center, and then deny the government the privilege to agitate slavery?" Still, this growing hostility did not mask his reluctance to embrace the moral principle behind the Emancipation Proclamation or take any responsibility for emancipation in his own state. In Ohio he made the following statement:

> But about the President's Proclamation: as for its effect, I care not the snap of my fingers for it; because the laws derived from the nature of things are at work that will work out the same results, whether right or wrong. . . . These the Proclamation cannot affect, one way or the other. And let me tell you, my friends, that to continue this war is to work the end of slavery. (Immense cheering.)[50]

The cheers greeting Johnson's perfunctory benediction for the peculiar institution were not likely to come from the throats of blacks or any of their extreme allies who took the time to listen carefully to his words. Johnson made it clear, with phrases stuck in between his violent indictments of rebeldom, that he was no friend of the Negro. His harshest invective was directed toward the slaveowning rebels, and curiously, in his rhetorical imagery, blacks were often spoken of as if they were allies of their masters rather than unwilling victims. At one point in his Indiana speech, he used a very appropriate metaphor: "If the negro gets in the way of the car of state, let him be crushed; If not let him remain where he is."[51] The former tailor had apparently managed to transform his own intense race hostility into an important element in his growing opposition to slavery. Such an approach would be familiar and appeal very nicely to former advocates of the free-soil doctrine in the Northwest.

Throughout his tour, Johnson probably assumed he was speaking for the president, and Lincoln's actions certainly allowed just that interpretation. But there remained a clear difference in the basic approach of the two leaders. The variance is best illustrated by one point where there was substantial if muted disagreement. Following the Emancipation Proclamation, Lincoln moved rapidly toward the use of black troops. Johnson could not have been unaware of the considerable sympathy for such a course in the North, but he probably did not realize the extent of the president's own growing commitment. In his first speech in Indiana, according to at least one report, the military governor made plain his opposition to the use of blacks in the army. The subject was not an important element in the rhetorical baggage he carried in his northern trek, and there is no record of any reference to his opposition in later speeches.[52] Perhaps the initial response from his northern friends had caused Johnson to modify his ideas before he arrived in Washington. His hesitancy concerning the subject had not gone unnoticed in the capital. While still visiting that seat of political power he received another of Lincoln's gentle hints in the form of a "*Private*" note:

> I am told you have at least *thought* of raising a negro military force. In my opinion the country now needs no specific thing so much as some man of your ability, and position, to go to this work. When I speak of your position, I mean that of an eminent citizen of a slave-state, and himself a slave-holder. The colored population is the great *available*, and yet unavailed of, force, for restoring the Union. The bare sight of fifty thousand armed, and drilled black soldiers upon the banks of the Mississippi, would end the rebellion at once. And who doubts that we can present that sight, if we but take hold in earnest? If you *have* been thinking of it do not dismiss the thought.[53]

Lincoln was not alone in disturbing the consistency of Johnson's "thoughts." While the governor was absent from the state, Tennessee's union volunteers in General Rosecrans' army held a meeting. According to reports, possibly exaggerated, fifteen thousand attended, and a long list of resolutions was passed affirming loyalty and denouncing compromise. Significantly, on the question of slavery and the black man, the East Tennessee soldiers went a little further than the governor had in his recent speeches. Not only were they in favor of "subjugation, emancipation, extermination, and colonization," or anything else that might end the rebellion, but they also "heartily" endorsed Lincoln's Emancipation Proclamation and specifically approved "the employment of slaves and persons of African descent, in the Government service, to aid in suppressing the rebellion."[54]

Johnson was again under pressure, subtle and perhaps unintentional, from both the president and more radical Tennesseans. Once more he would have to shift slightly leftward on the Negro question to maintain his position as leader of Tennessee unionists and to keep the firm support of the administration. And once again timing made that support seem even more crucial for Johnson. One of his personal reasons for visiting Washington was to lobby for increased military action in East Tennessee. There is little question that Johnson was genuinely concerned with the harsh fate of his own home section. He had been harping on the subject since the war began, and the volume of his appeals had not diminished. While in Washington he even wrote his wife that he intended "to appropriate the remainder of my life to the redemption" of East Tennessee. This emotional commitment was reinforced by urgent political considerations. With the mountain regions firmly in Union hands, it would be easier to reorganize the state with himself firmly in control. His personal following was always stronger in the east and could counter the growing strength of conservative unionists in Middle and West Tennessee. The day following his chief's pointed suggestions about black troops, he sent a copy of the soldier's resolutions to the president as an argument for the liberation of East Tennessee; it is not likely that either man overlooked the fact that Tennessee's military men were closer to Lincoln's present position than Johnson.[55]

It is of course possible that the war governor had become more radical in private. Surely when he returned to Nashville from the heady atmosphere of Washington, any hope that lingered for preserving slavery, even on a limited scale, must have disappeared. The question now was one of timing. The Nashville Union Club, formed in January 1863 with a primary goal of supporting the governor's administration, provided an excellent vehicle for testing public reaction prior to a total commitment on his part. On April 23, soon after Johnson's return to Nashville, the club published a declaration of principles. In addition to the usual attacks on rebels and copperheads, the document contained a radical statement on slavery:

> We do most solemnly affirm, as the result of our life-long acquaintance, and our intimate familiarity with all its workings, that the institution of slavery tends to dishonor labor and smother enterprise; is incompatible with an intelligent public policy, sound morality, the safety and permanency of the Republic, the development of the resources of the state; that it roots out the industrious, and has the effect of lessening the free population of the country.

For these reasons the group advocated abolition as early as possible consistent with "safety to the slaves and justice to the loyal owners."[56]

This attitude was a clear departure from the governor's public stance. Slavery was to be ended because it was an evil in itself, not solely because it constituted a threat to the government. Once again radical Tennesseans may have been placing gentle pressure on their leader, or, quite possibly, Johnson's own hand lay behind this declaration. Whatever the actual origin of the statement, there was no real need at the time for Johnson's open endorsement of the view. As the year wore on, however, events made some visible change on his part seem expedient. The impetus came from two directions: a bold offensive launched by the conservative unionists and the success of the Union armies in East Tennessee. Both events provided a challenge to Johnson's position as Tennessee's principal loyalist and required some kind of response.

According to the state constitution, August 4, 1863 was designated as the date to elect a new governor to replace Isham G. Harris, who had long since fled with the Confederate army. The possibility of holding constitutionally sanctioned elections was naturally attractive to all unionists, and the call for a convention to meet in Nashville on July 1 was circulated under the signature of numerous unionist leaders, including such stalwarts as Horace Maynard and William G. Brownlow. The assembly, far from united on particulars, was obviously controlled by forces loyal to Johnson. As a result, no election date was set. Having been burned once too often, the governor no doubt wished to avoid holding any election until East Tennessee was liberated and her loyal voters added to counter the growing copperhead strength among unionists in Middle and West Tennessee. The meeting did, however, appoint a state executive committee consisting of men of undoubted loyalty to watch the situation and call another convention if it seemed feasible.[57]

Men of more uncertain loyalty, the conservative unionists, were far from satisfied. Led by Emerson Etheridge, they decided to hold their own election on the required date, totally without authority from the military government. Balloting actually took place only in Shelby and Bedford counties, and even there the returns were dubious. Unperturbed, the conservatives declared William B. Campbell, now firmly one of their number, elected governor. Johnson naturally ignored such nonsense, but Etheridge, ever determined, journeyed to Washington to seek Lincoln's support. After receiving a presidential cold shoulder, he remained there as a persistent if minor irritation to the administration.[58]

This abortive "coup" and the ill-humored opposition of men like Etheridge must have been a source of considerable embarrassment and probably destroyed completely any residue of hope left in Johnson's mind for a united front in Tennessee. He was now totally dependent on the support of men with more radical opinions just at the moment when the long-awaited victory at last appeared. The Union armies of Generals Rosecrans and Burnside were driving the Confederates from Tennessee during the late summer and fall.[59] It would now be theoretically possible to reorganize a "loyal" state government. Political action became imperative.

On August 22, 1863 the governor and his ancient adversary—now compatriot—Parson Brownlow traveled to Franklin to address what was described by the loyal press as an "immense Union meeting." The subject was "restoration," and Johnson made his view clear. He wanted to dispel the "shallow humbuggery and deception" circulated by some of the cunningly disloyal that the North would prevent the southern states' return to the Union. Tennessee had never been out of the Union, and therefore no objection could be made to her returning. The state government merely lay "dormant." As military governor, he was sent under the authority of the Constitution itself to act as agent of the federal government to aid in this simple process. As for the question of slavery, he was "for a white man's government, and for a free, intelligent, white constituency, instead of a negro aristocracy." The South had been ruled long enough by "cotton and negroes," and the people were tired of a government based on "Slave property, where no more whites are wanted than are necessary to form *a negro police.*" For years there had been no free discussion of the subject in Tennessee. In other words, the liberty of whites had been destroyed by slavery. He concluded with a timeworn pronouncement. He was for his government with or without slavery even if it meant "seeing Africa itself swept beyond the line where gravitation ceases to act."[60]

Only a few days later in Nashville, Andrew Johnson, slaveholder and defender of the peculiar institution, illustrated how far he was willing to go to achieve a "white man's government" under loyal control. It required the reversal of a lifelong belief. The occasion was an "impromptu outpouring" of loyal citizens gathered at the state capitol to celebrate the fall of Fort Sumter. The *Nashville Daily Union* reported the governor's address a few days later:

> Governor Johnson said that the heart of the masses of the people beat strongly for freedom, that the system of negro slavery had proved baleful to the nation by arraying itself against the institutions and interests of the people, and that the time had clearly come when means should be devised for its

total eradication from Tennessee. Slavery was a cancer on our society and the scalpel of the statesman should be used not simply to pare away the exterior and leave the roots to propagate the disease anew, but to remove it altogether. Let us destroy the cause of our domestic dissensions and the bloody Civil War. It is neither wise nor just to compromise with an evil so gigantic.[61]

He was not mincing words. In the short space of a few days Johnson had become a public advocate of "immediate emancipation, if he could get it[;] if this could not be obtained he was for gradual emancipation; but emancipation at all events." The new doctrine was a radical departure. The former bane of abolitionists was in favor of abolition not simply as a war measure or because slavery supported an aristocracy but because "slavery was a curse." Its disappearance would make Tennessee "stronger, richer, happier, and more prosperous."[62]

Once the decision was made, the belated "abolitionist" was not reluctant to spread the news of his "moral" commitment outside Tennessee. A little over a week later in a candid conversation with Charles A. Dana, he assured the special representative from the War Department that slavery was in fact destroyed by the war in Tennessee, and all that remained necessary was legal abolition. He was personally in favor of "immediate emancipation because it was a matter of moral right and . . . an indispensable condition of the large immigration of industrious freemen which he thought necessary to repeople and regenerate the State." Dana would, of course, carry such information to Washington, but in reality there was no need for a private emissary. The pages of the *Nashville Daily Union* broadcast his message beyond the borders of the state and the implication was understood. The day before his interview with Dana, one of Johnson's old congressional colleagues in faraway Boston was busily writing to congratulate and thank the southerner for his new moral stand on slavery in Tennessee.[63]

It is quite possible that the most important target of Johnson's message was not in Tennessee or Boston but in Washington. On September 11, less than two weeks after Johnson's speech, the president sent a private letter to Nashville. Since the state was clear of armed insurrectionists, now was the "nick of time for re-inaugurating a loyal State government." But such a government would not be acceptable if "Gov. Johnson is put down, and Gov. Harris is put up." Because no one could be sure who would be the next president, Lincoln warned, Reconstruction should be the work of loyal men only with all others excluded.

The president then added words which indicated not only that he had been following Johnson's course carefully but also that the presidential definition of loyalty had been further restricted to include emancipation. "I see that you have declared in favor of emancipation in Tennessee, for which, may God bless you. Get emancipation into your new State Government — Constitution — and there will be no such word as fail in your case." Almost as an afterthought the president concluded, "The raising of colored troops I think will greatly help in every way."[64]

Encouraged by the commander in chief's expression of confidence, Johnson answered the letter by dispatch. He agreed that now was the time to reorganize the state government. The authority could come directly from the president, "authorizing the military govt to exercise all power necessary & proper to secure to the people of Tennessee a republican form of gov't[.]" He made it clear that he recognized the importance of abolition and reaffirmed his new position. "I have taken decided ground for Emancipation for immediate emancipation from gradual emancipation[.]"[65]

From this time until he became president, the former slaveowner would work hard to bring about the end of slavery in Tennessee and, in fact, in the whole nation. Opposition to the peculiar institution had been forced from the beleaguered unionist by the ceaseless logic of events, and given his addiction to extreme rhetoric, the leap from advocate of "immediate emancipation" to "Moses" was not too far. Unfortunately, this reluctant conversion, which was limited in nature and so clearly the product of political necessity, could be easily misunderstood.

The failure of contemporaries to appreciate the limits of Johnson's new departure was related to the generally muddled state of affairs concerning the treatment of slaves during the early phase of the war and the sheer magnitude of the problem posed by the collapse of the institution that had so long tortured the national psyche. The chaotic situation in Nashville was certainly no exception. From the perspective of a man in the governor's position, no other difficulty was quite so bothersome as the hundreds of minor incidents stemming from the nebulous status of the freedmen. Slaveowners wrote letters and sought interviews demanding that lost slaves be found and returned or asking advice about what to do with their charges. Blacks free and otherwise wrote begging the governor's help because of mistreatment at the hands of whites, both northern and southern. Northern philanthropists flocked to the captured Confederate state capital and demanded support for their schemes. And, of course, there were the inevitable clashes between races unsure of changing status relationships. Johnson, like others in similar positions, undoubtedly wished the whole problem would simply disappear.[66]

The actual reception accorded the freedmen in Nashville reflected the complexity of the situation and the lack of clear guidelines. As a result, some of the contemporary judgments made concerning Johnson's role sound as if they were describing different men. In early 1865, for example, after the Tennessean had been elected to higher office, a young antislavery journalist, John A. Martin, penned a flattering assessment of the new vice-president that stopped just short of beatification. According to this account published in the radical *Nashville Times and True Union*, from the very first Johnson was the freedmen's staunchest friend:

> Thousands of times we have seen him surrounded by a crowd of these poor, ignorant, helpless people — his earnest, manly, intelligent, and usually stern face lightened and softened with divine pity for their woes and suffering; his clear, brilliant eye occasionally flashing his hearty indignation at some story of deeds meaner and more ignoble than common; and his kindly voice giving counsel and instruction with a touching cheerfulness that came from a heart in the right place; . . .[67]

This sort of image, which would certainly be useful in corralling the votes of Massachusetts' abolitionists, would seem effusive nonsense to an observer like John Eaton, who found Johnson's heart in another place entirely. Eaton served with Grant's army in Tennessee and later as assistant commissioner of the Freedmen's Bureau. Years later he recalled a private meeting with the famous southern unionist during the war. The young officer, "filled with enthusiasm" for work among the freedmen, immediately launched into a recitation of ideas for improving their lot. The obvious lack of concern on the part of the Tennessean came as a shock:

> Johnson, it will be remembered, was fond of referring to himself as the "Tribune of the people," but when I spoke of the opportunity for establishing schools and organizing new industries for farmers and mechanics, he was quite obviously bored, and all that might have been said on the subject had no more inclination to stay by him than has water to stay on a duck's back.[68]

The apparently cold attitude toward an idealistic youth with bright ideas like Eaton is perhaps understandable. Johnson undoubtedly heard many such proposals from enthusiastic northerners who were unconcerned with his difficult political position or his personal future. In John Martin's case, on the other side, there is reason to suspect that the young newspaperman might have been seeking his own advancement by flattering the newly elected vice-president. But to dismiss these contrasting assessments with the simple explanation may be missing the most important point. Neither man was consciously lying or attempting to deceive. Both were reporting what they believed to be true. Their disagreement stems from conflicting perspectives.

When viewing the actions of a man like Johnson with regard to a subject like race, contemporaries, and too often historians, see only part of the picture colored by their own preconceptions. Martin, who served as provost marshal in Nashville for a brief time, may well have witnessed the governor behaving in a paternalistic manner toward freedmen.[69] There is no record that Johnson was ever overtly cruel to blacks and, like most slaveowners, he tried to appear the benevolent master. To a northern observer unfamiliar with southern social custom and immersed in the hostile atmosphere of disloyal Nashville, such actions might appear to indicate enormous goodwill, especially if the individual wished to find such goodwill among loyal unionists. Eaton, in contrast, had the advantage of hindsight in framing his description. The events of Reconstruction would distort the memories of many who lived through the experience. Moreover, a personal rejection of one's youthful idealism by a practical-minded politician might seem more revealing than it actually was.

Views like that of Eaton would probably have been more common among friends of the freedmen during the first eighteen months of military occupation in Nashville. The city was not a good place for black people. The governor and other military authorities seemed to regard any black man, including the slaves still held by many citizens of Middle Tennessee, as basically an exploitable source of labor for the Union army. Negroes were the subjects of wholesale impressments into the federal service. The work was menial and the pay, if any, none too certain. Those attempting to escape could be shot. Apparently little control was exerted over the system, and abuses of power by white officials were common. One officer reported that when he first arrived in Nashville, blacks were "treated like brutes; any officer who wants them, I am told, impresses on his own authority and it is seldom they are paid." Difficulties of this kind might be understandable under the demands of military necessity, but city officials, whose needs had little to do with the war effort, were allowed to impress "vagrant negroes" into service for "performing scavenger duty" as long as it did not interfere with military requirements.[70]

It is safe to assume that in the early years of the war such abuse of contrabands was not limited to Tennessee. To be fair, the situation may not have been amenable to control by a military governor even if he were a man of goodwill who wished only to help blacks. The disordered conditions of wartime meant that military commanders directly involved in a particular situation were often of greater influence than a quasi-political officer whose primary consideration was restoring loyalty among whites, few of whom wished to see blacks in any condition other than slavery. Most important, of course, was the simple fact that slavery was still technically legal, and the military government was obliged to protect the institution long after its Confederate defenders had fled south.

Once emancipation became an acknowledged part of the Union war aims, the situation obviously changed, and conditions gradually improved for blacks in Tennessee as well as in other Union-held areas. While a turnabout hardly signaled the beginning of a utopian existence for blacks, it must have created a sense of optimism among those committed to improving life for the Negro. Schools were established for freedmen by northern philanthropists; contraband camps were set up to provide for refugees; and dedicated antislavery northerners began to have influence even in the military government.[71]

Ironically, though there is no evidence that Johnson played a significant part in initiating the transformation, he may have been one of the real beneficiaries. His public declaration in favor of immediate abolition coincided with the positive shift, and his image in the eyes of northern antislavery forces may have received an undeserved boost. Given his position, he had to respond actively to the altered state of affairs. For example, in September 1864, after it became apparent that the old slave code was no longer enforceable, he personally suspended all such codes in Tennessee and ordered state courts to treat slaves as free blacks.[72]

Actions of this sort combined with his traditional paternalism, his public advocacy of emancipation, and his well-advertised hatred of southern "traitors" might well be misunderstood and make it appear to many in the North, who did not know him well, that a remarkable change of heart had occurred. Actually the former defender of slavery remained surprisingly consistent in his basic attitude toward black people, in spite of his apparent conversion to abolitionism. A better indication of his actual state of mind is visible in his response to a problem that came to a head about the same time as his public declaration for immediate emancipation and perhaps even influenced that decision.

In March 1863, when Lincoln wrote Johnson his cryptic note during the latter's visit to Washington, the president made it clear in his oblique fashion that Johnson should begin recruiting black troops as soon as possible. There is no record of an immediate direct response from the Tennessean, but certainly his efforts in the summer of 1863 could hardly be considered satisfactory to a government now firmly committed to black recruitment in the border states regardless of local objections. When the president congratulated Johnson in September for his new public stand on emancipation, he pointedly renewed his suggestion about black troops. The truth of the matter was that the administration had already taken further action to influence the situation in Tennessee apparently without consulting the governor. In mid-August, Major George L. Stearns was ordered to Nashville to organize black units. Stearns, a Boston merchant, was an abolitionist of the extreme variety who had actually supported John Brown financially in the 1850s. He was pleased with his assignment and wrote, "I have determined either to burn slavery out, or be burnt by it myself. . . . this war was a *civilizer* not a *barbarism*. The use of the musket was the first step in the education of the black man."[73]

Johnson had never been particularly concerned with educating or civilizing blacks, and it was certainly asking a great deal to expect him to work harmoniously with a former supporter of John Brown intent on giving freedmen "muskets." On September 17, the same day that he personally informed Lincoln of his new commitment to emancipation, the governor sent an angry telegram to Secretary of War Stanton complaining about Stearns' mission. He claimed a practical motive for his objections. More laborers were needed than were available. "Maj. Stearns proposes to organize & place them in Camp where they in fact remain idle[.] . . . all the Negroes will quit work when they Can go into Camp & do nothing." In his opinion there were too many people running about Tennessee trying to organize Negro regiments "without regard to the Condition of the Negro or the suppression of the rebellion." Major Stearns' mission "with his notions" could give no aid at all. If necessary there were enough men in Tennessee to raise the regiments and lead them into battle. Johnson requested that his complaint be shown to the president and, clearly concerned, also sent a similar wire to General Rosecrans.[74]

Typically, Stanton replied with haste, deferring to the governor's wishes and assuring him that he could dismiss the major at any time if he proved to be of no aid or "his presence is obnoxious." In Tennessee, Stanton pledged, the administration relied on Johnson's judgment in all matters relating to "the people whether white or Black bond or free."[75] On the same day, however, President Lincoln also sent a telegram, ostensibly a reply to the governor's dispatch concerning the restoration of state government. It was a typical Lincoln "message." He informed Johnson of the receipt of the dispatch, which he promised to study, and added:

> In the meantime let me urge that you do your utmost to get every man you can black and white under arms at the very earliest moment, to guard Roads bridges and trains allowing all the better trained soldiers to go forward to Genl. Rosecrans. Of course I mean for you to act in cooperation with and not independently of the military authorities.[76]

Again the stubborn Tennessean would have to bend because of pressure from the Lincoln administration. He could directly oppose the use of black troops and face the possibility that men like Stearns, with all their foreign "notions," would actually control the process in Johnson's own bailiwick. Or, he could become involved in the recruitment of black troops himself. Naturally Johnson chose the latter. At first working with Stearns proved difficult, but the archradical soon left for other climes because of a disagreement with the War Department. Then, working through men like Reuben D. Mussey, almost as dedicated as Stearns but more easily controlled, Johnson saw to it that Lincoln's wishes were acted on. By acquiescing rather than resisting, the governor even managed to alter particulars, making the whole process more politically acceptable in Tennessee. For example, he convinced the administration to pay three hundred dollars in addition to the present bounty paid to "Loyal Masters" who allowed their slaves to enter the federal army.[77]

Johnson's opposition, however, was deeper than his obvious desire to control political affairs in Tennessee. A gulf still existed between his attitudes toward the use of freedmen and that of men like Stearns and even Lincoln. These northerners (outsiders) saw blacks as potential soldiers—men; the East Tennessean, who had experience in dealing with *slaves*, could see them only as tools, potentially dangerous ones at that. They were obviously not fit to be soldiers. As he explained to Stanton, the freedmen in a military camp would idle away their time. The Negro, as all southerners knew, would not work, much less expose himself to danger, without being forced. Yankees, with their peculiar notions, could not understand the real condition of the former slaves. Johnson and his fellow southerners were sure that they could.

The governor had the opportunity in late November 1863 to enlighten his northern associates concerning this matter. The American Freedmen's Inquiry Commission, appointed by the secretary of war with the task of studying the condition of southern blacks and recommending a program, interviewed the Tennessee leader along with other interested parties in Nashville. In view of the commission's membership, which included known humanitarian radicals like Col. James McKaye and Robert Dale Owen, Johnson was not likely to make statements overtly hostile to the freedmen. However, his testimony made it clear that he did not think they could make up for the disadvantages caused by slavery or take care of themselves without outside help. He still opposed the idea of contraband camps, which gathered "only the dross." Nor was he happy about blacks being made soldiers, "because a soldier's life is a lazy one." Of course, he had to admit that he was "very agreeably disappointed" by their performance so far, but even this strangely phrased compliment was qualified by a stereotyped explanation. The black soldiers took "discipline easier than white men," and there was "more imitation about them than about white men." If the Negro had "white men to stand by him and give him encouragement. . . . after a little while, he will fight."[78]

Though in some of his more radical-sounding speeches the governor had seemed to endorse some form of land confiscation, he made it clear to the commission that he opposed such action at this time, especially if it involved placing Negroes on the land. Too many whites were already destitute and the government had not given them special help. His solution was simple: It was "better to leave things as they are than to commence the other system." Blacks could simply be hired by their former owners and paid wages:

> My idea is, that with proper management, free labor can be made more profitable than slave, in a very few years. This will place the negroes upon & within the great Democratic rule; it will unfetter industry, & if they have the talents and enterprise in them to rise, let them come. In adjusting this

thing, the object is, to make them take the best and most beneficial relation to society.[79]

This statement clearly did not mean that blacks were to occupy the same position in society as white men. He noted that states had laws establishing "orphan asylums & similar institutions" which might be altered to apply to destitute blacks. There must also be "vagrant laws" and "laws to prevent their congregating in improper assemblies." In fact, he objected to "massing the colored people together." They "should be scattered as much as possible among the whites, because the influence of the whites upon them is beneficial, whereas the influences that surround them when congregated together are not calculated to elevate or improve them."[80]

Basically Johnson was responding to a difficult situation in a characteristic manner, and his solution became the dogma of his concept of "restoration." Problems that arose concerning the black man, or anything else for that matter, could best be solved by his old standby, democracy. The almost fanatical commitment to his version of Jacksonian ideology had not been weakened by the war and secession; if anything it had grown stronger under fire. He had few worries about the future so long as "democracy" prevailed. Solutions to most problems were still simple once true loyalty was restored. "The people"—in the immediate case a new loyal government of Tennessee—would make the right decisions when given the opportunity to express their will freely without the influence of a traitorous aristocracy. To be sure, when he spoke of "the people" he meant the white people, and certainly, as he made clear in his speeches, the new state government was to be a "white man's government."[81]

As a matter of necessity much that Johnson did as military governor seemed a direct violation of his own democratic creed, but as he explained to unionists whose constitutional scruples had suffered under his demand for a state convention to restore a loyal government, "sometimes we may do irregular things for the sake of returning law and order."[82] Emancipation was the most "irregular" of all the necessary changes. His own decision had obviously been made as a matter of practicality, yet it received emotional reinforcement when he convinced himself and tried to convince others that slavery was the root of the nation's troubles and, most important, a threat to the democratic system. Even here, the old Jacksonian was uncomfortable until "the people" had spoken.

In his almost frantic attempts to restore a functioning state government in 1864 and early 1865, Johnson used his considerable power to
ensure that slavery would be abolished forever in Tennessee and stressed
again to his supporters the need to include emancipation as part of the
new government.[83] This was not only a political move that would help
eliminate the conservative unionists' single most important issue; it
was also, as the fanatical democrat saw it, a kind of personal vindication. He desperately wanted "the people," even if his voting restrictions
stacked the deck, to ratify his course as a loyal unionist and, more important symbolically, his reluctant commitment to emancipation. The
same desire for popular approval spilled over into national politics and
helped motivate, along with political considerations, his support for
the proposed thirteenth amendment. The Emancipation Proclamation,
a presidential edict, was not enough. Johnson demanded an expression
of the "people's will." As he explained to the Union Party in his letter
accepting the nomination for vice-president,

> The mode by which this great change — the emancipation of the slave —
> can be effected, is properly found in the power to amend the Constitution
> of the United States. This plan is effectual, and of no doubtful authority;
> and while it does not contravene the timely exercise of the War Power by
> the President in his Emancipation Proclamation, it comes stamped with the
> authority of the people themselves, acting in accordance with the written
> rule of the supreme law of the land, and must therefore give more general
> satisfaction and quietude to the distracted public mind.[84]

Not surprisingly there were other considerations behind Johnson's
strong public support of emancipation. He was well aware that not all
of his wartime "associates" in the Republican Party shared his faith in
democracy, as he defined it, or believed in the basic loyalty of the southern people. Charles Sumner and other radical leaders had been flirting
with plans for a long time which actually assumed, in one form or other,
that the seceding states had destroyed their relationship with the national government. In November 1863 the worried Tennessean sent a
confidential telegram to his good friend in the cabinet, Montgomery
Blair, obviously implying that the postmaster general should use his
influence against such schemes. "I hope the Prest will not be committed
[to] the proposition of states relapsing into Territories & sold as such."
In Johnson's opinion, the president's reelection was sure as long as "he
steers Clear of this extreme." After all, he pointedly reminded Blair,

"The institution of slavery is gone & there is no good reason now for destroying the States to bring about the destruction of slavery[.]"[85]

To accept the idea that the states were out of the Union would invalidate the argument Johnson used to explain his own staunch unionism. In speech after speech during the war, he had hammered away on the same basic theme—separation was constitutionally impossible. It is not likely that a man whose personality was rigid enough to put so much emphasis on this argument in the first place would abandon it easily. He always liked to keep his ideas simple, and, to his way of thinking, nothing could be simpler than his conception of "restoration." Once true loyalty was restored, which as events proved in Tennessee was no easy task, the *only* real condition necessary to return the normal operation of government was emancipation. In fact, he probably made his reluctant conversion with exactly that simple condition in mind.

Like most constitutional arguments, Johnson's formula for restoration was clearly based on something far deeper than abstract legal theory. After all, he had abandoned slavery in violation of his original "principles" for political advantage. Why not his rigid interpretation of the Constitution? Moreover, the methods used to create a loyal government in Tennessee could hardly be considered normal constitutional procedure. Yet Johnson chose to ignore the precedent of temporary surrenders to expediency in developing his explanation of restoration. On the surface, Lincoln's own approach could certainly be interpreted in this manner but, more important, governments produced by this proposed system would likely fit his own personal desires, especially in relation to the future place of blacks. They would be controlled by southerners, "the people" who understood the problem as he did, not by northerners, such as Stearns or Lincoln, with their foreign "notions."

It was no accident that those Republican associates who disagreed with his simple solution for restoring government in the newly conquered areas were closely identified with the old abolitionist movement and the new, growing concern for the welfare of black men. To leave the fate of the freedmen in the hands of "democratically" elected southern governments—no matter how sincerely loyal to the Union—would not likely result in real freedom or even basic justice for the former slaves.

The experience of Tennessee's restoration under Andrew Johnson's control clearly illustrated what could be expected in such cases. In October 1863 the governor wrote General J. A. Hurlbut, commander at Memphis, "Practically I look upon the Emancipation of negroes in this state as having taken place, and the main thing now is to what status they shall occupy."[86] In spite of his claims that difficult questions could best be answered by "a fair and full reflection of the popular sentiment," he obviously had his own opinions. He explained some of his ideas to a mass meeting of unionists in January 1864. Personally he preferred that the Negro "be transferred to Mexico, or some other country congenial to his nature, where there is not that difference in class or distinction, in reference to blood or color." But if such an exodus were not possible, the people of the South had no reason for alarm. The Negro would be thrown upon society and forced to compete like everyone else:

> Political freedom means the liberty to work, and at the same time enjoy the product of one's labor, be he white or black, blue or grey, red or green, [laughter] and if he can rise by his own energies, in the name of God let him rise. In saying this, I do not argue that the negro race is equal to the Anglo-Saxon — not at all. There are degrees among white men; some are capable, others are not; some are industrious, others are not; but because we find inferiors among ourselves, shall every inferior man be assigned to slavery? If the negro is better fitted for the inferior condition of society, the laws of nature will assign him there. My own conviction is, that in less than five years after this question is settled upon the principle of hired labor, the negro's labor will be more productive than it ever was.[87]

In Johnson's mind, the eventual outcome of "free" competition within society was a foregone conclusion. As he explained to a friend in 1865, everyone "must admit that the white race was superior to the black, and that while we ought to do our best to bring them up to our present level, that in doing so we should, at the same time raise our own intellectual status so that the relative position of the two races would be the same. . . ."[88]

Such a conception was deceptively logical and even seemed to indicate a relatively benevolent attitude toward blacks. The former slaveowner, it should be remembered once again, liked to think of himself as a "kind" master. Later as president he would actually tell a delegation of black leaders that the "feelings of my heart" had always been "for the colored man" without being conscious of his own hypocrisy. After all, had he not sincerely volunteered to be the black man's "Moses"? But the real implication of Johnson's ideas is clear, especially when viewed within the context of his own rabid version of democracy. The

Negro would always be inferior — occupying permanently the bottom rung of "Jacob's ladder" — and nothing anyone might do could alter the verdict of nature. Since this was the case, it would be sheer folly to include blacks as an actual part of "the people" who must, in a just society, govern. Permanent inferiors could never be allowed to join the open hierarchy that Johnson saw as America's democratic society. It would not be fair to them and would destroy the real meaning of equality. Emancipation was not important because it freed blacks but because it freed whites; it lifted the millstone of slavery from the necks of poor white men. He supported freedom not because of his "devotion to the black man alone" but because of "a greater devotion to the white men and the amelioration of their condition."[89]

When the long-awaited convention that would restore Tennessee as a loyal state finally met, it illustrated the political result of these ideas. Some extreme radicals in the convention were in favor of granting suffrage to loyal "colored citizens," and a majority bloc of radicals backed a proposed amendment that, in effect, would give the vote to black soldiers. There was, naturally, violent debate on such questions until the military governor intervened, ostensibly on the side of the radicals. He recommended the amendment guaranteeing emancipation, certainly, but questions such as suffrage could be decided by the new legislature. Best forget divisive issues for the present and make no more amendments than necessary. The important objective was restoring a loyal state government, not a change of status for the black man. Johnson's timely intervention meant that Tennessee would return to the Union without slavery, but aside from this measure, as undeniably important as it was, the real "status" of the black man remained practically the same. In fact, legally the position of the freedmen would be the same as the free Negro before the war.[90]

Johnson and those who thought as he did were not unaware of the likely future of blacks under the democratic rule of "the people" of the South. Sam Milligan, Johnson's closest prewar confidant and adviser, gave a prophetic view in a letter to the governor. It was late October 1863; East Tennessee had just been liberated by Union troops. Milligan, who had remained at home under Confederate rule, seized the first opportunity to write his old friend. He admitted that some of his prewar ideas about government had "under gone a change." His time had not been wasted in the past few years; it had been spent studying the institution of slavery from Abraham down to Jeff Davis. The conclusion was inescapable: slavery could not be a permanent institution. Therefore, why not "assist the Almight[y]" and forever remove the cause of this terrible war? Freedom was "the true theory of government" and "individual liberty" the normal state of man. "The negro will be the greatest sufferer. They like the Indian must was[t]e away, or sink into a state of miserable serfdom, attached to the soil upon which they are found. The white race are and will continue masters of this Country."[91]

If Johnson had spoken in such terms publicly, perhaps some of his Republican associates would have been less than enthusiastic about his presence on the Union ticket in 1864. A good number, especially of the more radical variety, were in favor of some form of black suffrage by the end of the war, and most would have probably been uncomfortable with the idea of the Negro "wasting away."[92] But Johnson was a politician, and a good one; he was not likely to make public statements that would alienate support, even of a temporary nature, especially when something as important as the preservation of the government itself created convenient blinders for him and his associates. Moreover, a man claiming to be and perhaps believing himself the black man's "Moses" would hesitate to use publicly exactly the same phrases that Milligan had used privately.

The lack of absolute candor on Johnson's part, however, was clearly not the most important factor in what soon became one of the most significant "misunderstandings" in American history. After all, Johnson had been relatively honest about his feelings toward Negroes, even if when speaking in the North his views were often buried under a barrage denouncing southern traitors. Certainly the Tennessee unionist convention that nominated him for vice-president and carried its nomination to the national convention made no secret of its goal for the future. It passed a resolution, which was possibly authored by Johnson himself, stating that "the government of the United States and the governments of the states erected under the constitution thereof are governments of free white men, to be controlled and administered by him and the negro must assume that status to which the laws of an enligtened, moral and high-toned civilization shall assign him."[93]

The real problem was a failure to both understand the meaning of racism and appreciate the importance of that unanswered question—the future "status" of the freedmen. Except for a few extreme cases most Republicans, like Johnson, still personally assumed the Negro inferior and were not eager, even when they favored black suffrage, to carry such an issue to the voters in their own states. They often made statements and used political rhetoric similar to that of their southern associate. Neither side recognized the extent of the gulf that had separated them from the beginning of the war and still existed. The Republicans, even of the most moderate persuasion, had been basically antislavery from the beginning and were not reluctant converts. Most important, they had never been as deeply concerned with the purely "racial" aspects of the whole question as was a representative of lower-class white southerners. To northerners living apart from blacks, white supremacy had never been as crucial.

This difference was aggravated by conflicting views of politics still held on both sides. Though Johnson and the Republicans often spoke the same language during the war when praising the American system, their understanding of that system was very different. Most Republicans were never overly committed to Johnson's extreme Jacksonian version of human equality. Like their view of race, their conception of equality was simply different. Certainly as almost a reflex for American politicians they would have agreed with the general concept, but it was not for them, as it was for Andrew Johnson, the key element in a rigid ideology or a vital element in their own personal self-esteem. A few black inferiors joining the political system did not pose a threat in the mind of the average Republican. To Johnson the idea was *personally* repugnant and a serious challenge to democracy.

Had he remained vice-president in a position of relatively little power, these differences might have remained hidden. The Tennessean had compromised before for political expediency, or perhaps better, survival, and he might have done so again. However, once the gentle hand of Abraham Lincoln was removed and the threat of secession ended, the situation changed materially. It placed in the most powerful position in the government a man whose personal conception of black people was different from the majority of the party that had elected him. Perhaps most important, the elements which had converted that man from a slaveowner to an advocate of freedom were now missing. Unimagined by either side, a clash between Johnson and his former associates was almost unavoidable. Unfortunately it had to occur exactly at the moment when the future of millions of freedmen was to be determined.

Chapter 5

A Promise Betrayed

As for myself, my convictions in politics are things that I cannot change
to suit the expediencies of this or any other moment. They have grown
with my growth, they have strengthened with my strength, and they are
to me only less sacred, and as much to be preserved, as my religious
faith. Attempts are made to make it appear that my words at different
times have been inconsistent; but were not the circumstances inconsistent, under which the apparently contradictory words were spoken, or
opinions given?

Andrew Johnson
February 21, 1867[1]

If Andrew Johnson actually had a "religious faith," it was based
on the art of politics revealed in the canons of his personal version of
Jacksonian democracy rather than Christian theology. The complexity
of the political situation facing him as president was well suited to test
the strength of that faith, just as secession had tested his commitment
to the national government; and, certainly, his policies would leave little doubt as to the intensity with which his "convictions" were held.
Johnson's obstinate insistence on his own peculiar interpretation of
"right" was instrumental in determining the shape of Reconstruction.
His actions and the beliefs that influenced them helped transform an
already difficult political problem into an irreconcilable clash of "principle," which in the long run served no one very well, least of all black
Americans.

When the southern unionist took office as president, most Republicans shared an optimistic assessment of the future from the perspective of party as well as nation. Even Lincoln's assassination had not
shaken the basic confidence of the North in the completeness of its victory or submerged, for too long, the general public joy at peace. Al-

most everyone in the triumphant Union Party had his own private conception of what victory would mean, and with the possible exception of the most "radical," deeply committed to ideas like black suffrage, few were overly concerned about the form of Reconstruction. There were many theories, but all remained in the realm of conjecture.[2]

Ironically, from the vantage point of the group perhaps most interested in the direction the process might take, the radical Republicans, even the assassination was interpreted as a blessing in disguise. The harsh and often vindictive public statements of the vice-president appeared much more in tune with the radical approach than had the words of his apparently magnanimous chief, and on the surface there was little reason to imagine that such a rabid advocate of Union would toss away the fruits of victory that had required so much personal sacrifice. In a few short months, however, this loyal defender of the faith would succeed in alienating most of the party that had elected him, throwing the government into confusion and hardening the nebulous theories of Reconstruction into inflexible "principle."[3]

Perhaps the ultimate beneficiary of this schism among victors and the ensuing war between the legislative and executive branches of government has been the historical profession. Few periods in American history have been quite so attractive or controversial. The events — assassination, race riots, impeachment, three constitutional amendments, all embellished by violent passion — are exciting and challenging enough in themselves, but the ultimate outcome had influence far beyond immediate issues. Reconstruction strained the American system to the breaking point, testing the tenuous separation-of-powers doctrine and revealing the weakness inherent in the concept of a "limited" democracy. The solutions, if they can be called that, determined many of the basic elements of national life for the next century.

According to the president, his dispute with the Republicans in Congress found its roots in a controversy over the nature of government itself. They wished to destroy democracy; he wished to preserve it. This simplistic definition of the problem has traditionally been attractive to historians. It not only creates an opportunity to examine the theoretical basis of the American constitutional system, but it also has a ready-made cache of source material in the myriad of abstract theories antagonists threw at each other as if they were bricks. Equally important, a black-and-white conception of Reconstruction provides a convincing and easily understood argument pitting the "good guys" against the "bad guys." In the first half of the present century such an approach fitted well, apparently explaining for most historians what was then perceived as the unjustly harsh treatment of the South.[4]

Recent historians have generally been more skeptical, searching elsewhere for the "key" explaining the development of Reconstruction as well as the policies of Andrew Johnson. In the present era, with so much attention focused on human rights, the subtle dilemma of racism has become central to many interpretations. This approach is explained in its most radical form by Hans L. Trefousse. The "biased attitude of the President of the United States made it impossible for Johnson to sympathize in any way with policies furthering racial equality." Because Republicans, either for political or ideological reasons, favored measures that envisioned, in at least some degree, the integration of blacks into American life and politics, the struggle between the president and Congress becomes a natural battle over a *moral* principle.[5]

In its own way the modern rendition emphasizing racism can be as oversimplified as the older view based on constitutional theory. "Good guys" are still doing battle with "bad guys"; the moral roles are simply reversed. By no means do all modern scholars accept the implications of this argument unadorned. Even if one considers the obvious fact that Johnson was generally hostile toward Negroes, it does not necessarily follow that racism was the most important factor in his decision-making. Eric L. McKitrick, the writer perhaps most responsible for inaugurating the current reinterpretation of Johnson's role, finds his "key" in the nature of the president's one-dimensional personality. He argues, supported by considerable evidence, that the tailor-politician was a perennial "outsider" whose inability to work within the system, or perhaps more bluntly his political ineptitude, prevented him from working harmoniously with Congress. Another astute scholar, Michael Les Benedict, provides an even more telling objection to what he sees as an overemphasis of the East Tennessean's "Negrophobia" as the primary motive for his actions. "Certainly Andrew Johnson was a racist," he points out, "but so were many radicals. If both antagonists were racists and race the key issue, there is no reason to assume that their policies would have differed so widely."[6]

The debate among modern Reconstruction scholars is not so much over the substantive issues or the events themselves as it is a difference in concentration and perspective. Central to the confusion is the failure to come to grips with the *operation* of racism on the minds of the actual participants, such as President Johnson. Moreover most historians, including recent scholars, tend to examine the problem from the perspective of the seemingly endless Reconstruction squabbles, placing little emphasis on the actual roots of postwar racial attitudes—the much earlier clash over slavery itself. To view racism in this manner can create a false impression: in the latter case an exaggeration of the similarity between Johnson and the majority of his Republican foes, in the former a failure to appreciate the influence of racial attitudes on actual decisions.

Racism and slavery had been problems throughout the lives of all Americans in the 1860s. Attitudes and beliefs were formed long before anyone had to face the staggering problem of four million freedmen suddenly thrust upon society. The conflict between Johnson and his former "associates" lay in the past at a level of the mind of which neither was consciously aware. Both may have been racists, but they were racists of a very different sort.

Historians are obviously not the only ones who failed to understand the essential difference between Republicans, radical or moderately conservative, and their eventual bane in the White House. When the Tennessee unionist was selected as a vice-presidential candidate, whether at the insistence of Lincoln or with his tacit neutrality, the move was political in nature.[7] In a peculiar way, Johnson pleased all segments of the Union Party. Obviously the War Democrats supported the nomination of one of their number, and extreme Republican conservatives, like the Blair family, who represented a Jacksonian influence countering the Whiggish majority within the party, had a long-standing community of interest with Johnson.[8] Moreover, most radicals were also pleased. The military governor's intense unionism and his bitter denunciation of secession convinced many in the North that he thought as they did. Not privy to the inner workings of his mind, few realized that the former slaveowner's support for war measures like emancipation and the use of black troops came largely from the demands of political necessity rather than any sincere commitment. It was easy to accept at face value the master stump speaker's explanations of his conversion couched typically in the language of high principle. Johnson, it should be remembered, always liked to appear the man of principle. Only Thaddeus Stevens, possibly the most perceptive of the extreme radicals, had the foresight to complain to the supporters of Johnson, "Can't you get a candidate for vice-president without going down into a damned rebel province for one!"[9]

In taking exception to Johnson's sectional origin, Pennsylvania's Caliban was getting at the essence of future problems. Perhaps because of his natural cynicism, Stevens viewed southern loyalists with more skepticism than some of his fellow radicals whose humanitarianism was often undiluted. In this particular case, there was also personal mistrust; when the subject of the Tennessean on the ticket had first been broached in his presence, Stevens had warned Lincoln, "Mr. President, Andrew Johnson is a rank demagogue, and I suspect at heart a damned scoundrel." Yet neither Lincoln nor other Republicans of a more radical inclination ever understood the nature of Stevens' apparently instinctive clairvoyance. The process by which they deceived themselves, with Johnson's aid of course, is clearly illustrated in the example of George Luther Stearns.[10]

As was pointed out earlier, Stearns, a radical abolitionist and noted philanthropist, had been sent to Nashville in August 1863 to organize the enlistment of black troops. In his fifties he had been a longtime associate of northern abolitionists and radical politicians, including Wendell Phillips, Charles Sumner, and William Lloyd Garrison. It might seem that such a man, certainly no novice in politics, would have been a hard man to mislead, yet he may well have been an easy mark. Stearns, a humanitarian first, had never been a follower of "practical" politics and was probably incapable of understanding those who were. Andrew Johnson could be a very practical politician when the need arose.

On September 5, after arriving in Tennessee, Stearns wrote:

> Left Louisville on Friday morning and arrived here at 6:30 P.M. Have seen Governor Andy Johnson. He is well disposed, understands the subject, and will be very valuable. From him and others I got the following information. For years a large number of persons in this state, many of them wealthy slaveholders, have entertained feelings hostile to slavery, but did not dare to share their thoughts with any man. Many were afraid to think on the subject.
>
> September 6, 1863. I had a long talk with several influential men here last evening — I think it will result in an effort on their part to destroy slavery in Tennessee. They are in terrible earnest.

Actually, the war governor never worked "in terrible earnest" to destroy slavery until he had no other feasible choice, and he was certainly never "well disposed" to the use of black troops. Even the seemingly naive Stearns could not avoid detecting some hesitation on Johnson's part in accepting the *spirit* of abolitionism and wrote five days later:

Governor Johnson is afraid of me (or rather was) and opposed to my work, and I have been laboring to bring him over to the faith, and I think I have succeeded, but can't tell yet. If I do it will be a great gain, for then we will try to settle the slavery question at Washington before Congress meets.

The Governor showed me recent letters from Lincoln and Chase that were very encouraging, Lincoln looking to Tennessee for the key-note of his policy for bringing back the slave states; and I should not be surprised if I was to shape that policy, and the whole affair be settled before it was thought of at the North.[11]

The process at work creating Stearn's optimism, as well as the overestimation of his own influence, was subtle. When Johnson and Stearns discussed slavery and Negroes, they used the same words but meant very different things. They lacked a common vocabulary to deal with the subject. To Stearns, blacks were people; to Johnson they were something very different—certainly not "the people" in his often-abused meaning of the word. Moreover the East Tennessean, always a politician, would not be eager to alienate potentially influential men in the North. He and other southern unionists needed men like Stearns. A wise man would not use terms or express the same ideas he might in talking to a fellow southerner who "understood" the Negro problem as he did. Such ideas might offend the tender sensibilities of a northern reformer.

Little did Stearns realize how far Johnson was from being brought "over to the faith." Only a week after supposedly being converted, Johnson was writing to Lincoln, Stanton, and Rosecrans complaining about Stearns and his foreign "notions." It would be Lincoln's gentle hints and Johnson's weak position, not the missionary work of any abolitionist, that finally brought the governor to accept the use of black troops in Tennessee. Ironically, Tennessee was shaping the eventual policy of Reconstruction, as Stearns hoped, but not in the manner he imagined.[12]

The old abolitionist left Tennessee blind to the personal ill-feeling with which Johnson viewed his ideas. In fact, Stearns had become an enthusiastic Johnson advocate, never realizing how far the southern Democrat was from sharing his fervor for the antislavery cause. In September 1864 he even sent the slaveowning governor a circular with an invitation to join in forming a society or league "of Radical Anti-Slavery men . . . for mutual aid, encouragement and information." Johnson, naturally, did not respond, but Stearns was unperturbed.[13]

Earlier, when word of the East Tennessean's nomination as vice-presidential candidate reached him, Stearns wrote his "friend" in Tennessee: "If any thing can reconcile me to the renomination of Abraham Lincoln, it is the association of your name on the same ticket. Indeed I should have been much better pleased if your name had been placed by the Convention before our people, for the Presidency." Stearns claimed that he had been deeply impressed by Johnson in their early interviews and "subsequent intercourse confirmed the impression." Sure of a Republican victory, he trusted that the new vice-president, when in power, would "be able to carry out those plans for the regeneration of the south so freely canvassed by us in Nashville, in which you may safely count on the co-operation of myself and those working with me[.]"[14]

Stearns finally got his wish. Andrew Johnson became president. Like many other radicals the Massachusetts abolitionist was optimistic. His greatest fear seems to have been that conservative Republicans would be able to force through a version of Reconstruction without the essential element of Negro suffrage. The initial word from Washington, however, was reassuring. In the spring and early summer of 1865 Charles Sumner, beau ideal of the doctrinaire radicals, wrote several letters to Stearns. Sumner was confident that he had Johnson's ear, and, certainly, he assured Stearns, "*In the question of colored suffrage the President is with us.*"[15]

It did not take Johnson long to change Sumner's mind. As the administration's policies began to unfold most radicals reacted with shock and anger, but not yet the loyal Stearns. He felt that men like Sumner, with their puritanical New England personalities, had perhaps alienated the rough-hewn Tennessean. Apparently forgetting that he was also from New England and to a southerner just as foreign as Charles Sumner, if more congenial personally, Stearns assumed that he could do better and sought an interview with the president. The two wartime "friends" had a pleasant chat. Johnson assured his visitor that he had not abandoned the Republican Party. His objection to the present proposals for Negro suffrage came not from any basic animosity to the idea but because the federal government lacked the constitutional authority to determine the qualifications for voting in any state. If he were in Tennessee he would "try to introduce negro suffrage gradually; first those who served in the army; those who could read and write; and perhaps a property qualification for others, say $200 or $250." Of course, the president failed to mention that under such terms very few blacks would actually be allowed to vote, nor did he bother to explain why earlier, when he had the opportunity to force a minimum degree of black suffrage in Tennessee, he had neglected to make the effort. Moreover, the president added a peculiar statement. "This government is the freest and best on the earth, and I feel sure is destined to last, but to secure this, we must elevate and purify the ballot."[16]

Such a statement from a "radical" democrat should have been a clear indication that something was amiss. Johnson was talking about what amounted to a restricted ballot for freedmen. Such a measure would be an anomaly in his version of democracy. If the rabid Jacksonian ever achieved his utopian desire to have a "vast amphitheater" in which all "the people" could be gathered to decide fundamental legislation, did he contemplate a special restricted section for blacks? Why would any restriction ever be necessary? He was even talking about purifying the ballot—a strange phrase for an ideologue who usually advocated extending rather than diminishing democracy. Did he really mean that the black man would somehow soil the "pure" white democracy that he believed was, in its present form, already the best government on earth?[17]

Questions of this nature simply did not occur to Stearns. He had no real conception of the meaning of race or democracy to a man like Johnson. He left the meeting less than satisfied because the president had not given an unqualified endorsement of black suffrage, but sure the indication of support for a limited approach was a positive sign. With the approval of the president and over the objections of some of his more radical friends who had already come to the reasonable conclusion that Johnson was a lost cause, Stearns published an account of the interview. He hoped it would disarm the Democrats, who by this time were claiming the president as one of their own. It was the last time Johnson made any public statement endorsing even qualified black suffrage, and when the hard truth finally forced its way into Stearns' mind, the disappointment was acute. He could only explain his bewildering misjudgment by maintaining that there were "two Andrew Johnsons." One was the loyal military governor who had fought the righteous battle against traitors in Tennessee; the other was the beleaguered president surrounded and misled by "rebels and other enemies of the Republic."[18] Stearns was never able to understand one Andrew Johnson, much less two.

If the radicals experienced shock and anger as the actual direction of the president's policies became clear, the impact on more moderate Republicans must have been just as severe with perhaps an even greater admixture of surprise. The racial attitudes held by most of the less radical members of the party gave the appearance, at least, of being similar to those of their new titular leader. Moreover, moderates and conservatives, unlike many radicals, were less apt to have been extreme abolitionists or to be committed to other humanitarian reforms. They were practical men, usually willing to compromise and, like Johnson, were often professional politicians eager to return to normal political life. The type of rhetoric used by these center-to right-wing Republicans and the president concerning racial matters was often the same. Both initially expressed some kind of favorable attitude toward a *limited* form of black suffrage but had serious reservations about various schemes that seemed to promote racial equality. In fact, many conservatives had been free with counsel, advising the president to reject the more radical approach.[19] Yet there remained a basic difference between Johnson and the mainstream of the Republican Party, and that difference would continue to exist in spite of the Tennessean's reluctant and, as it turned out, temporary surrender to expediency.

Like Lincoln, moderate and conservative Republicans might have been described as racists. They undoubtedly shared the generally held assumption that blacks were naturally inferior to whites. Still, the majority of Republican leaders also came from some kind of antislavery tradition, and with the exception of the most reactionary usually accepted blacks as members of the human race. This simple acceptance could result, and often did in the North, in the belief that Negroes, even if inferior, retained certain basic "natural" rights within society as fellow human beings. Under a republican system, the government would invariably be called upon to protect such rights.[20]

The best description of the moderate-conservative approach to Reconstruction as it related to the freedmen would be the establishment of a kind of "second class" or perhaps "apprentice" citizenship, if necessary recognized and protected by the federal government. Since they controlled a probable majority of the party and counted on administration support, it was reasonable for moderates to assume that such would be the eventual outcome whatever the basic format.[21] However, few in the North understood or had reckoned on the racial views of Andrew Johnson.

The Republican conception of race usually contained a good portion of "guilt" associated with the idea of slavery. Even when these beliefs were strongly anti-Negro, as in the old free-soil movement, slavery was also seen as evil in itself because of what it did to black people. Since blacks had little real political power in the North and their numbers were too small to envision such power, party propaganda usually stressed the negative aspects of slavery for whites, but no Republican would have ever defended slavery as a positive "good" for blacks or anyone else.

Johnson, on the other hand, had done exactly that throughout most of his political career. He constructed an elaborate rationalization arguing that slavery was a positive good for both blacks and whites and necessary for the maintenance of civilization. Somehow this self-proclaimed scourge of the southern aristocracy had not identified slavery as the creator of that aristocracy until after secession. Moreover, as a former slaveowner himself, he never gave any evidence of a sense of guilt because he had personally held people in bondage. After the belated, war-inspired conclusion that slavery was "morally" unacceptable, he neither indicated a feeling of responsibility nor made any admission that he had been wrong. Even to northern audiences the staunch unionist was careful never to intimate that slavery had been an evil because of what it did to Negroes. In his letter accepting the vice-presidential nomination, for example, he informed the Party that as long as slavery remained "subordinate to the Constitution . . . I yielded to it my support." He opposed it now only because it "attempted to rise above the Government." Later, in his message opening Congress in 1865, actually ghostwritten by the historian George Bancroft, he explained that slavery was "evil" because it "was essentially a monopoly of labor."[22]

Andrew Johnson, in short, had come to terms with his racist beliefs, both morally and philosophically, long before Reconstruction. The injustice done black people was simply not the problem. They were not human beings in the normal meaning of the word and were certainly not "the people" who should rule in society. Perhaps most important, when this psychological expulsion from the human race was mixed with Johnson's strict version of democratic ideology and the volatile issues of Reconstruction politics, the division between him and his Republican associates would be exaggerated. There was simply no logical place in Johnson's amphitheater of democracy for second-class tickets.

The process of disillusionment suffered by moderates was similar to, if less rapid than, that of radicals like Stearns. The gradual alienation of Lyman Trumbull is one of the most important as well as typical examples of this process. The powerful senator from Illinois was chairman of the judiciary committee and later one of the "recusant" seven Republican senators voting "not guilty" on the articles of impeachment. No single Republican in the Senate exercised as much influence over

Reconstruction legislation and policy. He personally steered fourteen Reconstruction-related bills through Congress, while the most any other senator had to his credit was two. Trumbull's ideas were consistently conservative on matters of race, and he usually opposed radical legislation, especially measures calling for black suffrage. In fact, during the war he had been vocal in his opposition. In the 1864 debate over whether to include black suffrage in the bill organizing the Montana territory, he warned his fellow Republicans of dire consequences:

> The tendency is to alienate and divide loyal men and to help the rebellion. You give men who are really opposed to the government something to go to the people upon, and to get up divisions and distractions, when we want no divisions . . . the effect of such a proposition is evil, and only evil.

Trumbull, not Johnson, was initially considered the enemy by radicals like Stearns who, in the spring of 1865 wrote Sumner, "You I understand are to have a 'fight' with Trumbull and Co. next winter."[23]

"Trumbull and Co." should have been harder to mislead than the less pragmatic radicals. Not only was the Illinois senator an experienced politician, having served in the upper House since 1855, but he had also crossed swords with Johnson on the race question prior to the war. The general subject then had been John Brown's raid on Harper's Ferry. Three days before Congress convened, in December 1859, Brown was executed. On the first day of the new session, Senator James Mason of Virginia introduced a resolution calling for an investigation into Brown's foray. Trumbull countered in the name of Republicanism by offering a resolution calling for an investigation of a raid upon the federal arsenal at Liberty, Missouri, by pro-slavery forces in December 1855. Given the charged atmosphere, such resolutions provided an opportunity for the distinguished gentlemen on both sides of the aisle to insult each other while ostensibly debating the issue.[24]

In defending his resolution, the Illinois Republican took advantage of the opportunity to discuss the justice of his party's position on slavery in the territories. He cited as an example a plank in the Republican platform of 1856 that used the Declaration of Independence as its basis: "We hold it to be a self-evident truth that all men are endowed with the inalienable right of life, liberty, and the pursuit of happiness, and that the primary object and ulterior design of our Federal Government is to grant these rights to all persons under its exclusive jurisdiction." Later in the same speech, he argued that though he did not assume it a crime "under all circumstances to hold a negro in slavery," he believed "that the negro has the same natural rights that I have."[25]

Connecting Thomas Jefferson, one of radical democracy's patron saints, to racial equality was a challenge that could hardly be ignored. Andrew Johnson, then a freshman senator from Tennessee, accepted the gauntlet. The idea that Jefferson was an advocate of Negro equality was ridiculous in his estimation. "There is not a man of respectable intelligence who will hazard his reputation upon such an assertion." The aroused defender of southern honor explained his statement by developing an interesting argument comparing the position of the slave in the South with the free black in Trumbull's home state. What was the real meaning of the senator's "clamor . . . about all men being created equal?" The citizens of Illinois had shown that they agreed with Johnson about the natural inferiority of the black. There a Negro could not vote, testify as a competent witness against a white man in court, intermarry, serve in the state militia, or even remain in the state without giving security that he would not become a public charge.

> What, then, does constitute a freeman? Oh, yes, I suppose he enjoys liberty. Liberty! Deprived of every privilege, he yet enjoys liberty! He is a freeman, and yet can exercise no franchise that pertains to a freeman! He is a worse slave, in fact, than the African who is in the South and in bondage; a great deal worse, for by these restraints and restrictions he is made a slave; he enjoys the shadow and the name of being a freeman, but is stripped of all the franchises that constitute a freeman. He is a slave, in fact, without a master; and I think his is a great deal worse condition than that of a slave who has a master.[26]

Johnson turned to his adversary and posed a direct question. How could the distinguished senator, as a truly free man in Illinois, assume that the Negro had the same rights as he? Trumbull tried to clarify his position by making a distinction between what he considered "natural rights" and "political rights." While it was true, in the abstract, that all men were created equal, society in its political structure could justifiably discriminate among men. Such a distinction did not make sense to an extreme Jacksonian Democrat like Johnson, and he pressed his northern rival further. Suppose, given the Republican interpretation of the sovereignty of the federal government in the territories, that the party had to deal with a community made up entirely of Negroes; did that mean the government could make Negroes equal to white men in

such a place? Did Trumbull propose to admit a territory made up entirely of a free colored population as a state in the Union?[27]

Obviously aware that Johnson was deliberately missing the point,
Trumbull clarified his position on political participation by blacks with
an eye toward partisan expediency. He explained that "under ordinary
circumstances" he would not grant "the same political rights either to
females or negroes" that he would "to the white male population." Nor
would he accept a community of blacks or Indians as a state. Personally he preferred a separation of the races when the Negro eventually
became free.[28]

Johnson, of course, was not worried about the Negro becoming
"free," and Trumbull's attitude, in his opinion, illustrated the hypocrisy of the Republican view. He thanked the senator for his admission
"that the Creator himself has made a difference between the black and
white race." Trumbull objected, trying to interject his concept of "natural rights," but the Tennessean refused to listen. "The Senator, in his
last explanation, has conceded the whole ground; and all this clamor
and claptrap about liberty, and men being created equal, falls to the
ground."[29]

To a remarkable extent, this prewar debate parallels the eventual
clash between Trumbull and the president during Reconstruction, even
to the interpretations of the role of the federal government. Trumbull
was initially unwilling to grant political equality to the freedmen, but
he conceded the abstract equality of the races. In his mind, blacks had
"natural rights" that society—in this case the federal government—
should protect. To Johnson such an argument was ridiculous. His extreme democratic ideology made no distinction between natural and
political rights. A man was either equal, and thereby a politically functioning member of society, or he was not. Because most people, even
Trumbull, assumed that the Negro was inferior, society was not ob-
ligated to grant any "rights" at all. In fact, to do so would be interfering
with the natural development of society, giving unfair advantage to a
group that did not deserve special treatment.

Trumbull, however, overlooked these prewar differences and initially
provided strong support for the President's Reconstruction policies. In
the early summer when other Republicans, including some conservatives, were becoming alarmed about the development of the administration's program, Trumbull remained loyal. As late as June 24, 1865, he
confided to Gideon Welles, the archconservative secretary of the Navy
who would obviously inform Johnson, that he, Trumbull, was a "John-

sonian." However, even this self-proclaimed Johnsonian began to have second thoughts in the fall as southern governments established by the president made transparent their lack of concern about protecting the "natural rights" of freedmen or accepting southern unionists as political leaders. It was hard to ignore the warnings of loyalists like R. King Cutler, Louisiana's senator-elect, who initially worked closely with Trumbull and other conservatives battling the more radical Republicans. Cutler changed his mind and now warned Trumbull early in December that rebels "reign supreme" in Louisiana because of the president's policies. Congress, in his opinion, needed to assert control over the franchise, assuring the vote to blacks as well as loyal whites.[30]

Still, Trumbull did not want to consider himself an opponent of the president or become attached to a politically dangerous proposal like black suffrage. In December and January he worked hard on two pieces of legislation that, in his estimation, would solve the problems: the Freedman's Bureau Bill and the Civil Rights Bill, both reported out of committee on January 12. The measures, as he later explained, were in response to the president's own call in his annual message for some kind of protection for freedmen. Trumbull hoped that national action guaranteeing protection would defuse politically volatile issues, like black suffrage and the flagrant disloyalty of the southern governments, before they could become critical. "One great cause of apprehension on the part of loyal men of the country would be removed, and I believed the work of restoration would go on." Trumbull also assumed that he had done everything necessary to secure administration support, visiting the White House several times and leaving with the impression that he had received presidential approval.[31]

Aside from the expected Democratic opposition, the most serious reservations concerning these bills came from radicals who wanted strong measures. Thaddeus Stevens, for example, launched a bitter attack in the House because freedmen were not specifically given grants of land. Complaints, however, were futile. The bills simply had too much support and were politically viable. When the Freedmen's Bureau Bill passed the House in its final form, only two Union Party members opposed. In the Senate no Republican had actually voted against it, and the Civil Rights Bill fared almost as well with only three Republican senators voting in the negative. Many of the president's most loyal supporters had joined in support and the pro-administration press was generally in favor.[32]

With such overwhelming party approval, coupled with what they thought were indications of Johnson's consent, few Republicans initially anticipated vetoes, and while the House considered the first of Trumbull's measures (the Freedmen's Bureau Bill), senators turned their attention to a constitutional amendment altering the basis of congressional representation. It was another issue over which radicals and conservatives had strong differences of opinion, but as they bickered with each other, Republicans gradually began to perceive a more serious disagreement between the majority of the Party and their "associate" in the White House. Apprehension grew general early in February, especially following the stormy visit paid to the chief executive by Frederick Douglass and other black leaders. There was sufficient reason to worry. On the same day the Freedmen's Bureau Bill was sent to the president and before he officially received it, Johnson intimated his serious reservations about the bill to Secretary Welles. Moreover, if Welles is to be believed, Johnson almost seems to have lost touch with reality. He spoke mysteriously of an "extraordinary intrigue" going on at the other end of Pennsylvania Avenue. Its intention was "subversion . . . of the government," getting rid of the president, and establishing a "sort of French Directory."[33]

Unaware of this conspiratorial turn in Johnson's thinking and his basic hostility, which was becoming more and more personal, most Republicans hoped that if a veto were in the offing, its rationale would be conciliatory. Meanwhile in the cabinet, Secretary of State Seward, deeply concerned with party unity, labored desperately to change the president's mind. When that proved fruitless the longtime Republican leader drafted a suggested veto message that would have assured Congress the president agreed with the general provisions of the bill but had objections to particulars. Johnson, in contrast, was in no mood for conciliation, and on February 19 he sent his own version of a veto message that ignored Seward's well-considered advice. Though he professed "to share with Congress the strongest desire to secure to the freedmen the full enjoyment of their freedom and property," his objections, in effect, made federal protection of such rights impossible. Not only did he believe an extension of federal power unconstitutional, but he also intimated that he would not approve Reconstruction measures while eleven states were still excluded from the Union by Congress.[34]

Republicans, especially moderate-conservatives like Trumbull, were naturally shocked and dismayed by the president's assertions. His position seemed to eliminate virtually any measure affecting the southern states based upon federal authority. The situation was made even worse on the following day, when the East Tennessean indulged in one of his frequent excesses of stump rhetoric. In an intemperate harangue responding to a serenade by supporters, he claimed, with typical hyperbole, that radical Republicans such as Sumner and Stevens were traitors as obnoxious as Jefferson Davis and his breed. Still, Trumbull and his moderate-conservative colleagues like John Sherman of Ohio and William Pitt Fessenden of Maine hoped that some kind of compromise was possible. Hopes proved vain. On March 27 Johnson returned the Civil Rights Bill, Trumbull's second measure, with a veto message couched in terms that were even less acceptable.[35]

This time not only were the president's objections phrased in nonnegotiable constitutional terms, but his appeal to racism was also blatant. Most important, he refused to consider any federal measures protecting freedmen. The bill, he argued, attempted to establish the "perfect equality of the white and colored races" by federal action. Its grant of federal citizenship to blacks, in fact, discriminated "against foreigners, and in favor of the negro. . . ." Perhaps illustrating the real heart of his objections, he brought up the totally extraneous subject of intermarriage — the most repulsive symbol of racial equality to virtually all racists. He admitted that the bill did not intend to repeal state laws governing marital unions between the races, but if Congress could "abrogate all State laws of discrimination," it could change the regulations on that touchy subject as well. The president continued to attack each portion of the measure separately. Near the end of his official tirade, he summed up his objections in a manner highlighting what he considered a clash between the interests of whites (in another context he might have called them "the people") and blacks:

> In all our history, in all our experience as a people living under Federal and State law, no such system as that contemplated by the details of this bill, has ever before been proposed or adopted. They establish for the colored race safeguards which go infinitely beyond any that the General Government has ever provided for the white race. In fact, the distinction of race and color is by the bill made to operate in favor of the colored and against the white race.[36]

Trumbull had made no secret of his feelings when Johnson vetoed the Freedmen's Bureau Bill. In a speech appealing to his colleagues to override, an effort that fell one vote short, he made plain his bitter disappointment. After all, he assumed he had been acting "in harmony" with the White House, yet the party's leader had apparently changed his mind:

The President believes it unconstitutional; I believe it constitutional. He believes that it will involve great expense; I believe it will save expenses. He believes that the freedmen will be protected without it; I believe he will be tyrannized over, abused and virtually re-enslaved without some legislation by the nation for his protection.

Still, with a remnant of understanding for the president's position, Trumbull noted that he had no objection to the administration's basic plan for restoration and regretted "exceedingly the antagonism which his message presents to the expressed view of Congress."[37]

Whatever sympathy left for Johnson in Trumbull's mind evaporated with the next veto — the Civil Rights Bill. If anything, his appeal to override, successful on this occasion, was couched in terms that were more harsh and revealed deep, personal anger. He described in some detail his discussions with the president and left no doubt that he felt he had been deceived — in short deliberately lied to — by his supposed ally. He wrote his wife several months later, "I have no faith in his good intentions. How could I have after he so deceived me about the Civil Rights Bill and the Freedmen's Bureau Bill." By the summer of 1866 Trumbull would tell his brother-in-law, "We have got to fight Johnson because he will fight us."[38]

The radicals, who had long since given up on Johnson, were ecstatic. The president, by his own action, had united the Republican Party against his administration as nothing else could. Sumner wrote in a speech, which was not delivered possibly out of an uncharacteristic desire to avoid offending his old party adversaries, for the moment allies: "I should take heart, when I see how Senators once lukewarm, indifferent, or perhaps hostile now generously unite in securing protection to the freedmen by act of Congress." Many of these reluctant converts, in contrast, were less than enthusiastic. Henry L. Dawes of Massachusetts, a leading moderate in the House, complained to his wife,

A few of our people are in their element now — perfectly happy. They can cry and howl and . . . alarm the country at the terrible crisis the President has involved us in, and he is fool enough, or wicked enough . . . to furnish them with material fuel for the flame, depriving every friend he has of the least ground upon which to stand and defend him.[39]

It is tempting to see the president's "foolishness" or "wickedness" as the product of a conscious attempt at deception. Certainly men like Trumbull felt they had simply been lied to by a leader they assumed thought as they did, and their sense of betrayal had a great deal to do with the unusually bitter, personal nature of the conflict that ensued. Eric L. McKitrick, in his analysis of Johnson's role in Reconstruction, maintains that Trumbull's speech attacking the Civil Rights veto "constitutes an important source document for one of the most unusual cases of alienation in our political history, a case almost without parallel in the effectiveness with which Executive and Legislative departments were to become, for a time sealed off from each other."[40] Certainly from this point, though there would be fruitless attempts at compromise, the real battle lines were drawn, and to a large extent the struggles on a national level revolved around the annoying personality of Andrew Johnson himself.

There was quite likely an element of truth in the charges of duplicity made by Johnson's former associates. It is not inconceivable that this veteran of numerous political wars deliberately allowed some of the more doctrinaire radicals to delude themselves concerning his real feelings. He never held a high opinion of abolitionists and, it is safe to assume, had few qualms about being less than candid with characters like Stearns, or perhaps even Sumner. But consciously lying to a man like Trumbull was another matter entirely. To have done so would have required an unusual degree of Machiavellian foresight.

Traditional defenders of Johnson find a different origin for these apparent misunderstandings. According to their view, the Republicans became the victims of an ancient prerogative of leadership, that of listening politely to all one's callers and then making one's own decisions. Even McKitrick, certainly no defender of Johnson, accepts a corollary of this argument. He sees the problem originating as a failure on the Tennessean's part to understand the nature of party politics. Johnson, "the outsider," never realized that his Republican visitors, especially men like Trumbull, presumed themselves "negotiating" with their party leader in order to arrive at some consensus that all could support. Profoundly ignorant of the niceties of party politics, the president simply ignored such meetings when he made his final decision.[41]

To accept completely McKitrick's view, however, requires that an observer agree with his one-dimensional portrait of the tailor-politician's personality and almost disregard Johnson's proven abilities as a prewar leader. To a degree, he was an "outsider"; yet, in view of his considerable national success, it is doubtful that his political talents were suited only to the stump wars of backwoods Tennessee. Equally relevant,

Johnson had certainly been in Washington long enough, as congress-man and senator, to absorb some understanding of the inner workings of party politics by osmosis if nothing else.

However, more important than quibbles with McKitrick's analysis of personality is the perspective that his view requires. McKitrick, as well as the president's contemporary enemies, seems to place primary blame for the misinterpretation of Johnson's intentions on personality, whether through ignorance or deception. Even traditional defenders emphasize a personal failure on the Republicans' part to understand the president. It is quite possible that all these views stress the wrong ele-ment in the obvious "misunderstanding." What the president did or did not say to individual congressmen or senators is of much less signifi-cance than what each participant assumed the words meant. Rather than being based on personality or deliberate deception, the confusion may well have originated in the nature of differing political ideologies and racial attitudes temporarily invisible to the participants. Racial at-titudes would be particularly important since thinking of this sort is rooted at a level of mind much closer to the unconscious or emotional than the rational. A person's assumptions concerning such matters are seldom thought out, and it is quite easy to assume that any *reasonable* man sees the world in the same way. Naturally then, disagreement on such matters would seem to be perversity or deliberate deception and, in this case, would result in both sides failing to grasp the meaning of their opponents' ideas. Eventually, when events themselves made the impact of their beliefs clear, acceptance was impossible, and the result-ing struggle was injected with unusual bitterness. In other words, the clash between Johnson and Trumbull, and even to some extent Stearns, began with what was, in effect, a failure to communicate. On matters involving race, these men spoke a different language.

The president, of course, believed that the final split with the moder-ates and the bitter dispute that followed was a simple question of right and wrong. In his own mind he was waging a constitutional battle, and he elected himself defender of the principles of that hallowed docu-ment. In the Freedmen's Bureau and Civil Rights vetoes, as well as in the flood of vetoes that followed, the majority of objections were pur-portedly based on constitutional grounds. Johnson never changed his basic argument. In fact, it appeared difficult for the former tailor, who significantly had no legal training, to say more than a few words with-out making some reference to the Constitution. His official address to the people upon leaving office, largely a self-serving defense of his policies, is a perfect example of this fetish-like incantation. The word "constitution" is repeated no fewer than forty-two times. Johnson also made clear that he recognized the political implications of his stubborn, strict-constructionist views:

> Doubtless, had I, at the commencement of my term in office, unhesitatingly lent its powers or perverted them to purposes and plans "outside of the Constitution," and become an instrument to schemes of confiscation and of general and oppressive disqualifications, I would have been hailed as all that was true, loyal, and discerning — as the reliable head of a party, whatever I might have been as the Executive of the Nation. Unwilling, however, to accede to propositions of extremists, and bound to adhere, at every personal hazard, to my oath to defend the Constitution, I need not, perhaps, be surprised at having met the fate of others whose only reward for upholding constitutional right and law have been the consciousness of having attempted to do their duty, and the calm and unprejudiced judgement of history.[42]

Judging from the content of othe president's panegyric appealing to "the calm and unprejudiced judgement of history," one might forget that a central part of his difficulties revolved around the freedmen. In the whole document — some eleven printed pages with over 5,000 words — terms referring to the black race — Negro, black, freedmen, or any equivalent — are never used. It was as if four million people had simply ceased to exist and the only real problem between the president and his enemies concerned the Constitution.[43] This perception was no accident; it was the way Johnson *consciously* defined the situation in his own mind as well as in public statements.

To comprehend this ability to simply ignore four million people, it is necessary to understand the relationship of racism and prewar Jacksonian ideology to the unsettled development of Reconstruction policy. Unlike his Republican associates, this southern disciple of Jackson had been obliged by his position to accept slavery and racism as a normal part of the social system. Before the war, northerners could conceivably view the American system without slavery; Johnson and other southern Democrats could not. In fact, the very nature of Johnson's strict version of Jacksonian ideology with its open, but white, hierarchy was in part a reflection of the compromise or, perhaps better, marriage between democracy and racism. Moreover, in the mechanic-politician's particular case his loyal defense of slavery, the economic institution, had never been as important as slavery, the social institution, which provided a sure means of racial separation and assured all whites a place in the "upper" class where democracy actually could exist. Since blacks had never truly been part of his democratic world of competing equals and were in his mind inherently inferior, it was impossible to envision their becoming real members of society and joining in the ascent up Jacob's ladder, without somehow damaging the real meaning of equality.

Johnson's own "climb" in politics had been an unusual amalgamation of the abstract principles of ideology and a practical, if very personalized, style of politics. Whatever the true nature of his numerous political conflicts, either pragmatic or ideological, he almost always defined his position in terms of high principles — usually attached to "democracy," the "Constitution," or ultimately "the people's will." In his inflexible mind it became impossible to separate this florid rhetoric from the realistic needs of his own political advancement. Opponents, whoever they were, became automatically "evil" because they stood in the way of such obvious "good." Once a battle was joined it was nearly impossible for good to compromise with evil.

This mode of thinking, simplifying and compartmentalizing politics, was exaggerated by his conspicuous tendency to personalize almost everything. When the tailor-turned-ideologue changed his liturgy to democracy, it had a deeply personal meaning. He was himself an example of the greatness of the *existing system*. His climb, he would have argued, came about because of "democracy" given form by the "Constitution" and expressed by "the people's will." He was able to rationalize deserting his fellow southerners essentially because he interpreted secession as an attack on democracy as embodied in the national government. But on another level, the rebels were not only traitors to the government but also traitors to Andrew Johnson *personally*.

In spite of what appeared to be a magnanimous policy toward the South during Reconstruction, he never forgave the men who betrayed him. In 1868, after the trauma of impeachment and the personal defeats suffered because of his pro-southern policies, he wrote his wartime friend Benjamin Truman a confidential and very candid letter in which he made statements that plainly contradicted his official benevolence:

> I shall go to my grave with the firm belief that Davis, Cobb, Toombs, and a few others of the archconspirators and traitors should have been tried, convicted, and hanged for treason. There was too much precious blood spilled on both sides not to have held the leading traitors responsible. If it was the last act of my life I'd hang Jeff Davis as an example. I'd show coming generations that, while the rebellion was too popular a revolt to punish many who

participated in it, treason should be made odious and arch-traitors should be punished. But I might lose my head, for Horace Greely, who made haste to bail out Jeff Davis, declares daily that I am a traitor. Just think of it.[44]

The importance of racism to Johnson's ideological conception of the world is amply illustrated by the degree to which the vindictive southern unionist was eventually willing to abandon his deep personal desire for revenge to preserve what he imagined was the basic social structure of a truly "democratic" society. He was not trying to deceive anyone with the harsh rhetoric and the calls for punitive measures against traitors. He was quite serious. However, Republicans, including the most radical, never understood that his hatred had a different origin from theirs. Republicans despised the leaders of secession, certainly, but that hatred had its origin in the position of the rebel leadership as representatives of the southern social system. In other words, the system, rather than men, was the real object of hatred. Johnson actually hated the individuals themselves. In the fanatical Jacksonian's mind, Jefferson Davis and his breed, not Andrew Johnson, betrayed the South and her system by abandoning democracy. They also betrayed Johnson personally and once again illustrated that they were unwilling to accept the tailor and his "kind" as social equals.

The same pattern of thought that had created the bitter and undying hatred of rebels was clearly at work during Reconstruction. It did not take Johnson long to develop a perception of circumstances identifying the "radicals," led by the "sinister" Thaddeus Stevens and the "fanatic" Charles Sumner, as a secret cabal intent on destroying the Constitution and by implication Andrew Johnson, who stood in their way. This unrealistic conspiratorial approach to problems was not crippling in all cases, as Johnson's considerable pre-Reconstruction success makes evident, nor did it mean that the practice of generally pragmatic politics was impossible. But when the place that racism occupied in his rigid ideology was injected into the situation, the president's mind became closed, and a realistic assessment of the problems of Reconstruction politics became for him impossible.

Slavery and the unique "place" it created for the black man had always been an important element in Johnson's perception of the existing "democratic" system — the system that had become his principal object of worship. He had abandoned the peculiar institution only when he had no other choice. Even then he had to rationalize slavery as a threat to democracy before accepting abolition. Certainly his original understanding of the Union war aims had been completely divorced from the question of the good or evil of slavery. In his thoughts immorality and slavery were never related. As he would later lecture to Frederick Douglass, abolition came only "as an incident to the suppression of a great rebellion." Freedom for blacks did not come about because it was a good thing in itself.[45]

Eventually, when his precarious wartime political position and his fanatical desire to crush the rebellion forced a public alteration in his attitude toward slavery, the familiar mental pattern took over and he became an advocate of abolition as a matter of "principle." During his interview with Douglass, the former slaveowner could inform the black leader without conscious duplicity that he opposed the institution first because it was a "great monopoly," and second because of "the abstract principle of slavery." Whatever the meaning of this last phrase, it still did not imply that slavery was morally wrong because it involved the oppression of blacks as a group of people, but because in some manner slavery, the *institution*, had proved itself a threat to democracy.[46]

Becoming president removed the element that had brought about even this halfway conversion to the antislavery cause. Now a power in his own right, the former slaveowner was no longer totally dependent on Lincoln and the Republicans for political support, and the rebellion, which had made everything else secondary, was visibly and convincingly crushed. As might be expected under the circumstances, Johnson moved slowly at first. He was obviously aware that his ideas were somewhat different from those of the more extreme antislavery radicals and, since he was unsure of his power or actual policy, it was simple political wisdom to humor such individuals, gathering as much support as possible. Gradually, as his confidence increased, the old Jacksonian could embark on a policy of his own. Moreover, with such a man it was natural that presidential decisions adhere closely to true beliefs. After all the presidency was, in a symbolic sense, the top rung of "Jacob's ladder"—the culmination of the most cherished dreams of an American politician, particularly Andrew Johnson. As president he would be much more apt to act with an eye toward history than toward political expediency.

In addition, the very nature of the office acted to increase Johnson's self-confidence and isolation from political reality. Following the death of Lincoln, men of many different persuasions rushed to offer aid and advice to the new chief executive. His correspondence is filled with letters of praise from all segments of the political spectrum, and the Republican press, during the early days of the administration, was avowedly pro-Johnson.[47] Such overwhelming expressions of support would unavoidably flatter the former tailor's never inconsiderable ego and help convince him of his personal popularity among "the masses." It was a dangerous assumption for a renegade Democrat who, like it or not, would have to work with a Republican majority in Congress.

Factionalism within the dominant party itself acted to increase these "delusions of grandeur." Political leaders representing various groups, often antagonistic, envisioned using the power of the presidency to enhance their own positions. Even when the direction of presidential Reconstruction became discernible and the product plainly unacceptable, it was not easy to break with the party leader. Both press and politician made excuse after excuse for the president's actions in trying to reconcile his policies with their own. Moreover, some Republicans, especially Secretary of State Seward and the Blair family, who were themselves bitter enemies, sought to use the president to strike at their old adversaries within the party. Their apparent willingness to support Johnson no matter what he did gave a false impression of his political strength. This illusion of widespread support became particularly important as the president's feud with the majority of the party became more harsh. His hopes were kept alive by joining with these mutually antagonistic allies in the quixotic attempt at forming a new center party based on administration policies. When the effort collapsed in the elections of 1866, it was too late for a man with Johnson's stubborn personality to abandon his course no matter what the cost.[48]

In a very real sense, then, Johnson's increasing isolation from political reality reinforced the tendency to act on his deep personal convictions, which in turn meant that the gulf separating the ideology of the president from the majority of the Republican Party would be exaggerated. The old Jacksonian, of course, was as blind as Trumbull and his moderate colleagues to the actual depth of that division. Just as in his early career, the president's rigid personality tended to ignore the subtle meanings of ideas contrary to his own. Opponents, in his estimation, were always self-serving; they were never men as deeply committed to their understanding of right as he was.

Stressing the importance of Johnson's ideology and its subtle marriage of racism and democracy does not mean that upon assuming office the new chief executive surveyed the situation and decided, in effect, that because Negroes were inferior he would follow a certain course. Racism seldom works in such a simplistic manner save in the warped mind of the most extreme fanatic. Equally relevant, the former slave-holder did not *consciously* harbor ill-feeling toward black people and, as with most racists, would never completely face the harsh implications of his own prejudice. After all, he had been a paternal slaveowner and liked to call attention to the fact. Like so many of his fellow southerners, he assumed that he was a special "friend of the colored man" who always had the best interest of the race at heart. He continually claimed when discussing his own slaves, "I have been their slave instead of their being mine."[49]

The image projected by Johnson's sincere paternalism played a critical role in clouding the perception of his initial policies. It was especially difficult for moderate and conservative Republicans, themselves paternalists of a different sort, to see through the facade of Johnson's fair-sounding words. In October 1865 the commander in chief made a speech to a regiment of black troops from the District of Columbia, which helped convince some people of his basic good will and desire to accept Negroes as a part of the American system. In the context of prewar ideology, however, his words, which sound so reasonable on the surface, reveal that his basic beliefs remained consistent.[50]

The skilled stump orator, as much at home before a black audience as a white, thanked the unit for its brave service to the country and, amid cheers, informed the Negro soldiers:

> This is your country as well as anybody else's country. . . . This country is founded upon the principles of equality, and at the same time the standard by which persons are to be estimated is according to their merit and their work; and you have observed no doubt, that for him who does his duty faithfully and honestly, there is always a just public judgement that will appreciate and measure out to him his proper reward.

Johnson seemed to be offering his black listeners a slice of the American dream. Yet as he continued he made clear, still using the language of high principle, that such an offer was provisional only. With the abolition of slavery a great part of the nation's problem had been solved, but an important dilemma still remained. Was it possible, "with all the prejudices of the whites," for the freedmen to become a part of the American system? Were "the digestive powers of the American Government sufficient" to ingest blacks and "make it work healthfully upon the system"? As far as he was concerned, he told his listeners, "Let us make the experiment and make it in good faith." If it could not be done and blacks and whites were forced to separate and become "distinct peoples," it would be the work of the "laws of Providence."[51]

Such statements might sound quite reasonable to most people unfamiliar with Johnson's prewar ideas about the ultimate verdict of providence. Certainly he had no intention of interfering with nature, and he wanted his listeners to understand that he did not "presume or pretend" he was "stronger than the laws . . . of nature" or "wiser than Providence itself." As always, he continued, "It is our duty to try and discover what these great laws are which are at the foundation of all things, and, having discovered what they are, conform our actions and our conduct to them."

In making his speech, the president inadvertently said a great deal about his true opinion of the potential "conduct" of the freedmen that illustrated his unconscious, but nevertheless real, conception of the "laws" of nature and providence. The new citizens, who would now have to govern themselves, were also given a lecture on the meaning of liberty:

> Liberty is not mere idea; a mere vagary. . . . It does not consist in idleness. Liberty does not consist in being worthless. Liberty does not consist in doing all things as we please, and there can be no liberty without law. In a government of freedom and of liberty there must be law and there must be obedience and submission to the law, without regard to color. (Cheers) Liberty (and may I not call you my countrymen) consists in the glorious privilege of work.[52]

Such warning to his fellow "countrymen" was a clear indication that the president unquestionably retained much of his prewar image of black men. Clearly he assumed that blacks lacked the ability to work without compulsion. This does not necessarily mean that Johnson was deliberately contradicting statements made late in the war in which he seemed to maintain that abolition would not undermine the value of black labor. He could not avoid being aware that blacks were capable of work, but he still plainly felt that their labor required a different motivation from white labor. In his mind a *natural* difference existed that somehow made Negroes less industrious — less capable of climbing Jacob's ladder than whites. He would never have envisioned the need to use quite the same tribute to work coupled with "submission" in speaking to a white audience. Whites worked to advance themselves because it was natural for them to do so.[53]

This was not the only belief held over from his slaveholding days. He also warned, "I have lived in a Southern State all my life and know what has too often been the case." Freedmen must now "Abstain from all licentiousness." Being free did not mean that people should frequent "low saloons and other places of disreputable character." Most important, they should esteem one thing higher than all others — "the solemn contract with all the penalties in the association of married life. Men and women should abstain from those qualities and habits that too frequently follow war." In short, blacks should stop being sexually immoral, which the president clearly implied they were, and form stable families. They would ultimately be judged by their conduct, not by the simple legal fact of being free. Nothing could be more absurd than "the idea of having a law passed in the morning that will make a white man a black man before night, and a black man a white man before day."[54]

These stereotyped perceptions of black people assumed considerable importance because of the nature of the president's Reconstruction plans. He began in early May 1865 by recognizing the provisional government of Virginia and then, late in the month, promulgating a plan for the reconstruction of North Carolina. In essence Johnson was following the practice established in wartime by Lincoln and designed to reconstruct state governments as quickly as possible with the help of "loyal" citizens on the scene. A provisional government would be established with a governor appointed by Washington, and, when conditions permitted, a constitutional convention would be held to restore a functioning state government. Significantly, just as in Tennessee, blacks would play no role in these new governments nor be allowed to vote in the initial elections. Governor Francis H. Pierpoint's unionist government in Virginia had never enfranchised blacks, and the North Carolina plan limited voters for the proposed constitutional convention to those "qualified and prescribed by the constitution and laws of the State of North Carolina in force immediately before the 20th day of May, A.D. 1861, the date of the so-called ordinance of secession."[55]

Given the complexity of Reconstruction, there was a remarkable ideological consistency in Johnson's public explanations for his policy. As always, difficult problems were best left to "the people" themselves whose decision, no matter what it might be, was endowed with the ultimate authority. During the war he had perceived himself as struggling to maintain this great principle, and he had continually promised that the Union war effort was simply intended to restore the system existing prior to secession. Moreover, his own practical experience in Tennessee gave a strong precedent for his approach. There, efforts at re-building the state government had been left largely to him and other Tennesseans.

This "illusion of voluntarism," as one historian has called it, remained a key element in the president's rationale, but it was plainly an illusion. Publicly the provisional governors were simply instructed to take what-ever action necessary to establish "a republican form of government." Private instructions were a different matter. Johnson made it clear to those concerned that he would insist that certain conditions be met. The new state conventions would have to declare the ordinances of se-cession null and void, repudiate the Confederate debt, and abolish slav-ery. The new legislature or the convention itself would also be required to ratify the Thirteenth Amendment before complete readmission.[56]

Johnson's "suggestions" illustrate that he was not completely blind to political reality. The restored states would have to convince a suffi-cient number in the North of southern loyalty to be accepted as part of a united nation and, most important immediately, convince enough senators and representatives to be admitted by Congress. Moreover, the president himself, as a southern unionist, wanted to insure that the last vestiges of moral and legal sanction for secession were re-moved, vindicating his own desertion of the South. Yet, insisting on any conditions at all — even if he succeeded in keeping the pressure at an unofficial level — underminded his argument for a strict construc-tionist, states-rights version of the Reconstruction process. Once the right of the federal government to determine conditions for readmis-sion was admitted, as Johnson himself did by requiring the ratification of the Thirteenth Amendment, the question actually became what con-ditions should be required rather than whether any conditions at all were "constitutional."

As far as most radical Republicans were concerned, the key pre-requisite for readmission was black suffrage, and the measure became more important as extremely visionary schemes such as land redistribu-tion became politically impossible. The demand was a logical exten-sion of freedom based on concepts of fairness shared by most Ameri-cans (assuming the added factor of race were excluded) and could even, from the Republican perspective, maintain the important illusion of "voluntarism." The southern people would still be in control of their own government; blacks would simply be part of these governments and theoretically able to protect themselves from unreasonable exploi-tation by the use of the franchise. Of course, political expediency was also at the heart of black suffrage. Most Republicans assumed, justifiably, that the majority of southern whites would vote Democratic. Joined with the "disloyal" Democrats in the North, the South might well become part of a new majority, which would endanger Republican control of the government and possibly the verdict of the war itself. From Johnson's point of view, obscured by the haze of his strict ideology reinforced by its admixture of racism, granting universal manhood suffrage without regard to race was not only unwise but could possibly be a danger to democracy almost as serious as secession. He was not oblivious to the powerful and influential support in favor of the measure and recognized, from the first, that some sort of compromise might well be necessary. There is little doubt that this recognition was behind the deliberately visible attempts, such as the interview with Stearns, to let it be known that he was willing, personally, to accept a limited suffrage proposal. Yet, perfectly satisfied with the contradiction, he also continued to insist that the federal government had no authority, under the Constitution, to prescribe suffrage. According to his logic it must be brought about by state governments.

Even if this strict constructionism was completely sincere, the president's reasoning and the procedure he followed were plainly questionable. He was well aware of the southern attitude toward black participation in politics, and it is hard to imagine that he actually expected southerners to accept the idea without resistance. He was, in effect, recommending to his provisional governors a measure that he had been unwilling to support in Tennessee when in a similar position.[57] Moreover, he gave a clear indication, especially to fellow southerners, that the adoption of "limited" black suffrage was simply a temporary concession to undercut the radical opposition to restoration. The implication was apparent. Once restored to the Union, state governments could do what they wished about suffrage — if desirable, revoke the privilege.

In the most often cited example of Johnson's support for limited black suffrage, a telegram to William L. Sharkey, provisional governor of Mississippi, the interplay between the issue and simple political expediency is clear. It was mid-August 1865, and Sharkey had just successfully organized a state convention. The president congratulated his appointee for his efforts and expressed the "hope" that as soon as possible Mississippi would ratify the Thirteenth Amendment. He then added:

> If you could extend the elective franchise to all persons of color who can read the constitution of the United States in English and write their names,

and to all persons of color who own real estate valued at not less than two hundred and fifty dollars and pay taxes thereon, you would completely disarm the adversary and set an example the other states will follow.

This you can do with perfect safety, and thus place the Southern States, in reference to free persons of color, upon the same basis with the Free States. I hope and trust your convention will do this, as a consequence the Radicals, who are wild upon negro franchise, will be completely foiled in their attempts to keep the Southern States from renewing their relations to the Union by not accepting their Senators and Representatives.[58]

By the time of this telegram, President Johnson unquestionably viewed anyone "wild upon negro franchise" as the "adversary." His public statements intimating a willingness to acquiesce in limited suffrage adopted by states was simply one means of "disarming" radical malcontents and thwarting their plot to keep southern states out of the Union. When the "restored" legislatures blithely disregarded his "suggestions" concerning suffrage, he did nothing; in fact, following the ignored hint to Sharkey, he never mentioned the subject to any other provisional governor. When the new governments attempted to evade his other "conditions," however, he carefully and firmly applied the necessary pressure. In September 1865, for example, the Alabama convention seemed to be balking over some of the measures he felt were necessary. The president had prominent men from Alabama send telegrams from Washington over the U.S. military telegraph to influentual men involved. It is hard to avoid the conclusion that Johnson shared the reluctance of most southerners to tolerate *any* admission of the freedmen to the electorate. Certainly, he felt strongly enough about the subject to accept what he must have known was a considerable political risk that could jeopardize his whole policy.[59]

Significantly, identifying the infatuation with black suffrage as the heart of opposition to his policies made it quite easy for Johnson to simply extend his reasoning to what was a dangerous perversion of the actual case. Anyone who opposed his policies upon any ground would automatically become "wild upon negro franchise." Seen through the inflexible logic of his version of Jacksonianism, support for black suffrage with its implication of racial equality was, by definition, opposition to democracy and the American system of government and, therefore, as much treason as the southern rebellion itself.

Moderate and conservative Republicans, scarcely fanatical advocates of universal manhood suffrage, were not immediately classed as the enemy. Indeed, had Johnson done so early in his administration, he would have undoubtedly proceeded more carefully and perhaps even made more initial concessions. He assumed that he had their support just as the moderates felt they had his support. However, a clear majority of the party expected a Reconstruction process that somehow guaranteed basic human rights for the freedman. Trumbull and his moderate colleagues always assumed a black man had certain "natural" rights as a human being. Imprisoned in his Jacksonian straitjacket and having no illusions about the "humanness" of Negroes, Johnson never understood this distinction between "natural" and "political" rights. Equality and political participation were in his mind the same thing. A strong stand for any kind of legally protected citizenship for freedmen would be dangerously close in his conception to the heresy of black suffrage. Moreover, Republicans, who were also northerners, had political reasons for anxiety about the precipitate return of seceding states. Ironically, the abolition of slavery destroyed the 3/5 ratio, which meant that the South would actually have increased representation in Washington. Obviously the North would demand some kind of adjustment. As a southerner, Johnson was naturally less concerned and viewed the northern fears as hypocritical.

Whether or not these potential points of conflict would ultimately result in a separation of the executive from the party depended to a great extent upon how presidential Reconstruction was perceived. If loyalty could truly be restored and the freedmen treated fairly by the new southern governments, less radical Republicans would be in no position to complain and would presumably support the president. Unfortunately, objective judgment was unlikely, especially from Andrew Johnson. Aside from the normal human tendency to discount criticism of one's own policies, the former southern mechanic retained an image of the Negro that made it likely he would believe only those who saw blacks through a similar set of blinders.

When men like Salmon P. Chase and Carl Schurz, ostensibly political allies of the president touring the South at his behest, wrote voluminous and essentially negative reports concerning southerners, most importantly their undesirable treatment of the freedmen, the words fell on deaf ears. These men, sympathetic to the plight of blacks and backers of the alarming heresy, simply did not know black people. Johnson assumed he did. It did not take long for Chase, Schurz, and others who told similar tales to join the president's growing list of enemies.[60]

On the other hand, Harvey M. Watterson, a fellow southerner also traveling at White House request, had a view of blacks similar to Johnson's. The newspaper man sent back highly positive accounts in his carefully numbered dispatches. If he was to be believed, the former rebels were rapidly and sincerely returning to loyalty while blacks, as was to be expected, were not behaving at all well in the new conditions, especially when under the influence of outside agitators like those in the Freedmen's Bureau.[61] This same clash between positive and negative opinion was evident in the hundreds of other reports, both written and oral, that reached the White House, but there is little doubt as to which were heard. Watterson and his ilk told the president what he wanted to hear, in fact, what he already knew to be the case. His own perception was inescapably determined by his deep personal prejudice.

The manner in which Johnson's racial attitudes operated on his mind to distort the information he received and produce an irrational response is amply illustrated by his exaggeration of minor rumors emanating from his home state. In August 1865 the president sent a message to General George Thomas in Nashville, complaining about abuses perpetrated by the Freedmen's Bureau in Pulaski. Officers were reportedly exceeding their jurisdiction and seizing property, which would result in "great prejudice" against the government. The exact source of information that caused the president to single out Pulaski is not completely clear. Undoubtedly he received numerous protests about Bureau activities from all over the South. However, at least one rumor reported to the president which he failed to share with Thomas had little to do with the operation of the Bureau: A white officer in Pulaski was supposed to have married a black woman. The rumor turned out to be erroneous. But Thomas, unaware of the supplementary reason behind the president's sudden interest in one small Tennessee town, investigated and reported back with only praise for the local federal officials and their efforts.[62]

The president, of course, was far from satisfied. His concern was as much with the irrational images any conception of racial equality triggered in his mind as with the actual operation of the Bureau. The real origin of his anger at institutions like the Bureau is made conspicuous in another series of telegrams exchanged with Thomas. In late August and early September, Johnson began bombarding the general with inquiries about one of his chief sources of apprehension—the conduct of black troops. Apparently some Tennesseans, including Governor Brownlow, were complaining about the presence of Negro soldiers.[63]

One of the resulting presidential telegrams, sent on September 4, reveals the depth of the president's racial hostility and the distorted pictures such feelings produced in his mind:

> I have information of the most reliable character that the negro troops stationed at Greenville [sic], Tenn, are under little or no restraint and are commiting depredations throughout the country, domineering over and in fact running the white people out of the neighborhood. Much of this is said to be attributable to the officers who countenance and rather encourage the negroes in their insolence, and in their disorderly conduct. The negro soldiery take possession of, and occupy property in the town at discretion, and have even gone so far as to have taken my own house and converted it into a rendezvous for male and female negroes who have been congregated there, in fact making it a common negro brothel. It was bad enough to be taken by traitors and converted into a rebel hospital, but a negro whore house is infinitely worse. As to the value of the property I care nothing for that, but the reflection that it has been converted into a sink of pollution, and that by our own forces, is, I confess, humiliating in the extreme. The people of East Tennessee above all others are the last who should be afflicted with the outrages of the negro soldiery. . . . It would be far better to remove every negro soldier from East Tennessee and leave the people to protect themselves as best they may.[64]

Thomas, undoubtedly shocked by the strange wire, replied three days later, suggesting several alternatives but reminding his chief that if he withdrew the Negro troops he had no white troops with which to replace them. Perhaps Thomas had hoped by delaying his reply that the president would have forgotten the whole, obviously silly, business. Johnson did not forget. After receiving the general's report he immediately sent another long, angry telegram complaining about the number of Negro troops, the danger of "insurrection," and certain "mischievous persons" inciting the Negroes. Thomas apparently had had enough nonsense and, taking advantage of his close wartime friendship with the president, sent his own long and candid wire the following day. There was, in his opinion, not "the least foundation for fearing an insurrection" by his black troops. "As a general rule," he assured the president, "the Negro Soldiers are under good discipline. . . . I believe in the majority of cases of collision between whites and negro Soldiers that the man has attempted to bully the negro, for it is exceedingly repugnant to the Southerners to have negro Soldiers in their midst and Some are So foolish as to vent their anger upon the Negro because he is a soldier." Thomas reiterated his difficulty in acquiring sufficient white troops and offered as a word of caution that certain "evil-minded persons" were always willing to "misrepresent and exaggerate every event however trifling."[65]

Converting the house of the president of the United States into a brothel was no mere "trifling," and the general could not completely ignore Johnson's outrage. He investigated the report concerning the "violated" house and sent the information to the president on September 18. The house was actually occupied by a white family placed there by Johnson's son-in-law, Judge Patterson. The family had been continuous occupants and could hardly be proprietors of a Negro bawdy house. Thomas also informed his chief that he had investigated the anxiety about Negro insurrection in Georgia, Alabama, Tennessee, and Kentucky and was able to confirm his last report that there was "not the least probability of such an occurrence unless precipitated by the discontented whites." Some whites had "maltreated their neighbors" and "naturally fear that the negroes will attempt revenge." Others were simply "jealous that the poor negro is at last a free man." Thomas was sure that the efforts of the local head of the Freedmen's Bureau would "very soon restore peace and quiet as the status of the negro is the only subject about which the dissatisfied spirits in rebeldom can grumble."[66]

Unfortunately there was a "dissatisfied spirit" in Washington who could never completely accept the new status of the Negro as a free *man*. In spite of sober judgments like those of General Thomas, President Johnson was incapable of seeing beyond the image of black people he had held throughout his adult life. When Trumbull and his conservative colleagues could not avoid perceiving the glaring failures of presidential Reconstruction, especially the lack of protection for freedmen, they assumed that Johnson was aware of the same problems. He simply was not, or did not consider southern treatment of freedmen a problem. Republicans proceeded, rationally from their perspective, to remedy the difficulties with the Freedmen's Bureau Bill and the Civil Rights Bill. Justice and fairness to any "people," even if they were inferior, was a principle of American life that Trumbull and his fellow moderate and conservative Republicans were not prepared to abandon even for political expediency. Andrew Johnson vetoed these bills for reasons that also appeared rational from his point of view. Not only did these bills seem unnecessary, but they also had to be vetoed to protect whites. No matter how much he may have hated individual rebels, he could not bring himself to force all the southern people to suffer the supreme indignity of being made equal to blacks, albeit symbolically.

This deep basic difference in "principle" had been for all practical purposes unrecognized by either Johnson or the moderate Republicans. Initially both assumed that they were working toward the same general goals, but when the uncomfortable truth became obvious Johnson, just as the moderate Republicans, felt betrayed. Trumbull and his ilk had deceived him, or so it seemed. It was natural for the president, with his tendency to personalize every difference, to leap to the erroneous conclusion that such men were actually radicals in disguise. They were now revealing themselves by their malignant opposition to his "constitutional" policies and their insistence on unnecessary measures protecting the freedmen. Their initial cooperation seemed a simple smoke screen hiding personal animosity and fell designs to subvert democracy with dangerous experiments like black suffrage.

The personal nature of the split between Johnson and his former "associates" helped obscure their many points of agreement and made continual efforts at compromise unlikely to succeed. As always, a battle against "personal" enemies steeled Johnson's resolve, and in this particular case, ideology gave an added reason for resistance. His own policies had forced the moderates into the waiting arms of the radicals. The Republican Party now stood for a policy, especially the extended franchise, that was by Johnson's definition a threat to the American system for which he had already sacrificed so much. Unable to separate the radicals from the conservatives, he had to fight the majority of the Republican Party. Johnson's perception of democracy, inseparable from the reconciliation of racism with equality, meant that his struggle, waged with undeniable personal courage and considerable political skill, was against simple human justice and, ironically, against democracy as Americans of a century later would understand it. This steadfast advocate of white equality did everything within the limited power of the presidency to prevent the establishment of real "human" equality.

Chapter 6

Vindication?

I want my reputation to go down clear. There was not a colored man in Tennessee freed by Mr. Lincoln's emancipation proclamation. Who did it? I did, on the steps of the Capitol in Nashville, in the midst of the excitement and perils of that hour, while the missiles of death were flying. I, myself, proclaimed that slavery no longer existed in Tennessee; that every man was free by the inherent principles in him.

Andrew Johnson
April 1869[1]

There is little doubt that Andrew Johnson's "reputation" as a liberator is somewhat questionable. In the last half of the twentieth century few professional historians would accept his claim to even a scrap of Lincoln's mantle, and most would probably rate his overall performance as chief executive as something less than satisfactory. There is also little doubt that this present assessment of the embattled president has been influenced, if not determined, by the change in the general attitude toward race that took place following the Second World War. In earlier decades when Claude Bowers' jeremiad, *The Tragic Era*, dominated the public perception of Reconstruction and the followers of William A. Dunning reigned supreme among the academically inclined, Johnson was seen quite differently, and racism was a respectable idea held by many if not a majority of white Americans. This simple ratio between racial attitude and interpretation is something that we modern "revisionists" should remind ourselves of when passing judgment on our predecessors as well as the historical characters we seek to analyze.

Racism is a type of belief that burrows deeply into the psyche of an individual and his society, exerting its powerful influence indirectly rather than directly on decisions. It seldom stands alone as the *conscious* motive for any action taken; instead it entwines itself within the individual's image of the world and distorts reality. Moreover, since it is part of one's world view it becomes omnipresent and seems to infect almost every aspect of thought, even those remote from the subject of race. The racist becomes a person who sees the world through a carnival mirror. While such people may be able to function quite well and seem rational to those who share their mirror world, the twisted reflection, so apparent to outsiders, guarantees a twisted response. Naturally, such people are incapable of coming to grips with the real source of their feelings and often explain motivation with an elaborate rationale that seems designed as much to convince themselves as others.

Unfortunately, historians have proven no more immune than their subjects, as the formerly respected Dunning school amply illustrates. Hardly exhibiting the customary traits of the extreme racist, these men and women were rational, reasonably objective, professional historians, whose work was conducted within the most respected canons of scholarship. Certainly they would have been personally offended by the contemporary meaning of the word "racist" with all its negative connotations and yet, almost without exception, they held a stereotypical conception of blacks that simply assumed such people were in some manner inferior to whites. One might quibble over whether or not their view included a concept of inherent inferiority, but the fact remains that whatever its particular components, the perspective led to, or perhaps even required, a distorted interpretation of Reconstruction.

Imagine for a moment that the basic premise of the extreme racist is accurate. Black people represent a different order of creature (perhaps human) forever inferior by the verdict of nature. The federal government's apparent commitment to racial equality during Reconstruction then becomes a crass form of hypocrisy—indeed a kind of "tragedy." In particular, the attitude of the more radical Republicans would seem absurd. Such men, who one assumes were rational human beings, must have been acting from less than admirable motives unconnected with race, for example economic or political. Andrew Johnson, on the other hand, while inept politically would appear to be struggling, as he so often claimed, to protect the American constitutional system from those who either for personal gain or malignant hatred sought to change the system contrary to the dictates of nature.

Johnson's conscious interpretation of the situation, the reasons that he honestly believed lay behind his actions, was based on a perspective similar to that of the historians who, more than a half century later, temporarily provided the "vindication" he so craved. He was even less likely to understand the influence of his racial attitudes than they were.

Racism had become too much a part of his conception of reality; it was a key part of the foundation for his idealized vision of American democracy, the vision that provided the driving force behind his whole political career. For this self-proclaimed champion of the South's "common people," assaulting white supremacy threatened the validity of the American experiment.

Given Johnson's basic beliefs, the pivotal break with the moderate Republicans over the Freedmen's Bureau and the Civil Rights Bill, correctly identified by Eric L. McKitrick as the turning point in Reconstruction, was obviously rooted in more than political ineptness.[2] Moderates like Trumbull, clearly racists of a different sort, were not seeking true equality for freedmen. Instead, acting from essentially humanitarian motives — or perhaps what might be better described as a sense of fair play — they envisioned some sort of second-class citizenship for blacks, a position analogous to that occupied by women in nineteenth-century society, protected but certainly not equal. To a man who thought as Johnson, imprisoned in his extreme egalitarian version of American society, second-class citizenship was not citizenship at all. The moderate position appeared to the president simply untenable, a smoke screen for radicalism.

The radical minority of the Republican Party, who saw the world from a totally different perspective, agreed with the president's rejection of second-class citizenship. Some of these men undoubtedly held views of race much closer to the modern conception and genuinely hoped to provide at least symbolic equality for black people. Others might well have been influenced by the prospect of political and economic advantage or war-inspired hatred as the president imagined. But whatever the basic motivation, radical opinion represented a majority of neither the party nor the nation. Visionary schemes like those of Thaddeus Stevens for redistributing land in the South never had a chance politically.[3] The only approach upon which a majority of Republicans could eventually agree involved black participation in politics, particularly in the South. Obviously political survival was an impelling consideration, but the commitment could be made acceptable only because of their understanding of the American political system rooted in antebellum political ideology, an ideology directly opposed to that of the president.

In the mind of most nineteenth-century Americans, the ballot played an important role in citizenship, but it was an ingredient whose meaning varied greatly depending on one's conception of the total system.

Most Republicans, like Lincoln, came from a Whig tradition and never accepted the shibboleths of extreme Jacksonianism. They did not insist that political participation automatically and almost magically conferred on a citizen a *status* that made him equal to all others. Even if they had accepted such ideas, Republicans lived in regions with only a small number of blacks. Never having rationalized the exclusion of such people within a rigid egalitarian system, they could perceive little danger in admitting a few inferiors.

Johnson, it should always be remembered, defined himself and his society in terms of politics, politics buttressed by his self-conscious egalitarianism. All that he accomplished, all that he had become, he owed to the political system and its *gift* of equality. Most important, as a southerner he had constructed an elaborate rationalization in which the system required racial exclusion as a matter of necessity. He could easily envision the government he worshipped being overwhelmed and destroyed by the sudden influx of inferiors. Just as the pseudo-aristocrats of the South had sought to destroy democracy and its grant of equality with secession, it appeared to Johnson that the Republicans threatened real equality by including blacks within democracy.

The depth of Johnson's personal feeling about the Negro's admission to the democratic masses, "the people," is illustrated by a strange incident that occurred far off center stage in 1864, while he was military governor. A rumor began to circulate in Nashville to the effect that two blacks, one of which was a slave, had been elected to office in Wilson County. Though erroneous and possibly the product of Confederate sympathizers, the rumor infuriated Johnson. He ordered Judge Mason M. Brien to inquire into the matter and if possible seize the poll books. Brien was also to arrest "all the parties in any manner connected with this expression of contempt for the Government and its efforts to restore civil law in Tennessee, and have said parties sent under guard to this City for such disposition as may be here after determined upon."[4]

The core of the struggle between the president and Congress, which has been so ably chronicled by modern revisionist scholarship, rested on this issue fueled by the extreme nature of Johnson's racism. The program created by Congress, based on the Reconstruction Act of 1867 and supported by the Fourteenth and Fifteenth Amendments to the Constitution, represented "an expression of contempt" for Andrew Johnson and all that he stood for. His emotional commitment to ideology only reinforced his naturally volatile style of politics and guaranteed that the rhetorical defense of his position would grant little quarter, but rhetoric was not the only weapon in Johnson's political arsenal.

Given the real nature of the struggle, the usual interpretation of Johnson's course during the early months of Reconstruction, which stresses some measure of political incompetence, might need serious qualification. If scholars like Michael Les Benedict are right and by the war's end black suffrage had actually become a goal for a majority of Republicans, the president's actions contain a healthy admixture of pragmatism and surprising self-control. Johnson himself certainly believed that black suffrage was the goal of many Republicans, and his program was admirably designed to forestall such a disaster without appearing to do so in principle. It nearly succeeded. But the blind resistance of his fellow southerners doomed his efforts, and the president, suffering from a related blindness, could never accept the program's failure or understand Republican objections as anything other than an attack on the American system itself. Moreover, any feasible compromise would ultimately be a defeat because compromise with Congress meant some form of black suffrage.[5]

Following his political isolation and the failure of his quixotic attempt at forming a third party around himself in 1866, Johnson was still not willing to concede. Though the deck was stacked against him and he obviously made political blunders, such as his ill-fated "swing around the circle tour," the political warfare he waged from within the limited powers of the nineteenth-century presidency exhibited considerable skill. It was his success as an irritant to the ascendant Congress rather than his failure that led to impeachment.[6] Even here, the Republicans were forced to act more from frustration than political calculation. As a result their efforts were based on weak foundation that ended in the failure to remove him from office.

More significant, however, was the ultimate failure of the program upon which the Republicans based their hopes and the future of black Americans. Perhaps Andrew Johnson understood "the people," especially those in the South, better than his adversaries ever could. Though it would take longer, the congressional effort at Reconstruction, even with black suffrage, placed the future of the freedmen in the hands of southern whites as surely as the president's more direct version. Never grasping the complexity and depth of southern racism, most Republicans were unable to imagine what would be required to alter the basic attitudes of the southern people. To establish justice in a society where the majority is committed to injustice is a formidable task, particularly where the forms of democracy are preserved. Only extreme radicals, who had little chance of convincing a majority of Americans, had the moral courage and political foresight to come close to understanding the commitment required. Most white Americans in the nineteenth century, North or South, were unwilling to abandon, even temporarily, the revered principle of majority rule or their own feelings of racial superiority for the sake of black people.

Johnson's failure on the national level came, in part, because he underestimated the extent of northern anger triggered by the South's refusal to make minimal gestures of simple fairness to the freedmen and, in part, because of his own overemphasis of the symbolic nature of suffrage. His political instincts were nevertheless still sound, and he left office determined to seek personal "vindication." Appropriately, the old warrior accomplished this goal through a remarkable political resurrection in his home state by joining in the first successful overthrow of a Republican government in the South.

Unlike the rest of the Confederacy, Tennessee had not been included in the Reconstruction Act of 1867. The provisional government established there by Johnson in the last days of his tenure as military governor reduced the necessity for federal intervention. The temporary ascendancy of this "radical" regime, led by Johnson's ancient enemy William G. Brownlow, was possible only because the military governor himself had established voting restrictions that eliminated conservative unionists as well as ex-Confederates. Still, the course of Tennessee's Republican government during the early months of its existence was hardly radical, and a hesitant move toward black suffrage had been subtly quashed with Johnson's help before he ever left the state.[7]

It soon became evident to Brownlow and his supporters that the president's program of restoration would be fatal to their interests. Not only were their senators and representatives denied seats in Congress along with those from Johnson's other creations but also the conservative unionists, who had been denouncing the president since his apparent conversion to emancipation, gleefully joined his third-party movement. Loyal Tennessee Republicans had no choice but to repudiate their former leader and seek allies among the radicals in Washington. Their efforts seemed politically sound and had an immediate payoff. Tennessee was readmitted to the Union after ratifying, with some difficulty, the Fourteenth Amendment. For Governor Brownlow there was even personal satisfaction in dissolving the unnatural alliance with his old

foe. In his famous wire notifying the Clerk of the Senate of the Fourteenth Amendment's ratification, the parson could not conceal his pleasure and concluded with relish, "Give my regards to the dead dog in the
White House."[8]

Unfortunately for the future of Tennessee Republicanism, the occupant of the White House was far from dead politically, and, more important, support from the northern radicals would prove costly. The
native unionist element contained many adherents who were extremely
hostile to the idea of political participation by the freedmen. In fact,
Johnson's timely intervention against limited black enfranchisement
during the ad hoc convention establishing a provisional goverment had
been as politically necessary as it was ideologically gratifying. Any
move by the government intended to benefit black people weakened
the fragile unity among the state's loyalists, yet just such measures were
the price for support from congressional Republicans.

Each time Brownlow was forced by circumstances to extend privileges to former slaves, he suffered defections from the ranks of white
Republicans. These losses sapped the strength of the party, and for the
governor, whose personal antipathy toward Negroes was at least as
deep as Johnson's, having his administration depend on black votes
must have been galling in the extreme.[9] It was possible only because
of his undying hatred toward the secessionists and because it provided
the only feasible alternative that guaranteed immediate political survival. His desperate measures were much like Johnson's own conversion to emancipation under similar circumstances.

Even with black votes and extensive disenfranchisement of the white
opposition, Brownlow's hold on power was at best temporary. He faced
the same problems that would later plague his counterparts in other
"reconstructed" states, not the least of which was overt political violence. The infamous Ku Klux Klan was actually founded in Tennessee
and led a campaign of terror against the state government. Brownlow
characteristically resisted with vigor and even used a "black and tan"
state militia to combat lawlessness, but his efforts, while determined,
were doomed in a state where a majority actively supported or at least
acquiesced to political coercion.[10] Most important, however, since even
the radical Republicans never intended permanent restrictions on white
voters, political power would eventually shift to the will of the majority, which clearly opposed that part of the Reconstruction program
designed to benefit black people.

By the time Andrew Johnson returned home to his apparent retire-

ment, the foundation of Republican control had already cracked. Brownlow had himself elected to the United States Senate and his successor,
the Speaker of the State Senate, DeWitt C. Senter, was determined to
capture the leadership of the party for himself. The parson described
the new chief executive as a "loyal man, capable, tried, and trusty," but
the opinion was not shared by a majority of the faithful. The Republican state convention meeting in May 1869 selected the new governor's
bitter personal rival, William B. Stokes, as its nominee for the post in
the impending election. Angered by the rejection, Senter refused to accept the convention's verdict and declared himself the official candidate
of Tennessee Republicanism.

Naturally, the conservative opposition was pleased and, rather than
nominating one of their own, waited for the candidates to bid for their
support. The highest bidder was Governor Senter. On June 5, he an-
nounced his conversion to universal manhood suffrage and proceeded to
replace all county registrars unfriendly to his new departure. Massive
registration of formerly disenfranchised Confederates followed in clear
violation of the law and guaranteed a white conservative majority.[11]

It was a situation tailor-made for the former president, and he immediately took to the stump to campaign for Senter. Johnson not only
saw the race as an opportunity to strike at his enemies in Washington
and their whole program of Reconstruction, but also as a chance to enhance his own position in hopes of being elected to the United States
Senate, a post he had fixed on as the symbol of his political exonera-
tion.[12] During some of his speeches he made it clear that the flexibility
that had always lain beneath the veneer of principle had never left him.
The man who had fought so hard against the elements in the Republican program designed to help the freemen suddenly remembered that
he had *personally* freed the slaves in Tennessee and took the opportunity to remind the new black voters.[13] Like other southern conservatives
struggling against Republican rule, the ex-president had to face the simple fact that black suffrage was a reality in spite of his best efforts. It
was only political wisdom to use it against the enemy if possible.[14]
Moreover, while there was a touch of cynicism in Johnson's appeal, he
and other southern conservative leaders could follow such a course because even in their own minds racism had never been consciously identified as the motive for action. As formerly paternal masters, such men
actually believed themselves the real "friends" of the freedmen even if
black voters with a firmer grip on practical reason thought otherwise.

Surprisingly, Senator Brownlow, the very symbol of Tennessee radicalism, followed a course similar to his archenemy. From his safe haven in Washington, the parson threw his support to Senter even after it became apparent that the governor's ambition would destroy Republican control of the state. When his attitude was denounced with considerable justification by the radical faction, Brownlow denied the charge of apostasy with familiar passion and bristled at the accusation that he had once more joined an "alliance" with Andrew Johnson. In fact, the senator did remain a loyal, if inconsequential, supporter of the Grant administration and continued his eternal feud with his East Tennessee rival.[15] But personal hatred notwithstanding, there was an undeniable similarity between the two unionist leaders that says a great deal about Reconstruction in Tennessee and elsewhere. In spite of their love of rhetorical excess, neither Andrew Johnson nor William G. Brownlow was capable of being a social revolutionary. To actually "reconstruct" Tennessee or any other southern state, nothing less than a *social* revolution was required, a revolution that had at least a chance of leading to a fundamental change in white minds.

Ironically it was the secessionists, in 1860, who attempted a revolution, a political revolution; southern unionists had sought to preserve — a goal that by its very nature limited alternatives. Granted, many northern radicals, by ideological conviction, and a portion of southern unionists, by necessity, became temporary advocates of a kind of revolution, but emancipation and suffrage proved poor weapons within a democracy. To effect real change in the American system, the battle had to be waged within the minds of white Americans, and it was a battle for which the nineteenth century was ill-equipped. The existing understanding of the human personality and human social systems provided few tools with which to combat racism, and it was racism, after all, that lay at the heart of the nation's problems.

The fall of Republicanism in Tennessee, while certainly pleasing to the ex-president, did not bring the immediate personal "vindication" he craved. His enemies, with some deft political maneuvers, were able to prevent his election to the Senate in 1869. However, his defeat, like his defeat in the battles over Reconstruction, was temporary. In 1874 the Tennessee Legislature, dominated by conservatives, sent him to Washington to replace his perennial adversary, Senator Brownlow. His return to the institution that had nearly convicted him of "high crimes and misdemeanors" came appropriately at the time when the last governments erected in the South by his congressional enemies were crumbling. His final political speech was a typical Johnsonian assault on the last futile measures of the Grant administration to shore up the Republican government of Louisiana.[16]

This unintentional farewell address illustrated more than remarkable perseverance; it was an example of surprising ideological consistency. There was more polish here than in the harangues the young tailor had launched at his East Tennessee neighbors years earlier, but even with different issues the message remained the same. American democracy, the American system that made all white men aristocrats, must be preserved. As for blacks, whose place within that supposedly democratic society became for a brief time its most crucial challenge, they were simply ignored.[17] In the ex-president's mind, their place could never really change whether they were free or enslaved.

The attitude was not simply political inertia; it had become an immutable part of his personality. In the last letter he ever wrote, addressed to his daughter Mary, the old patriarch made it clear that he still saw himself as the paternal head of a multi-colored extended family just like the mythical families of the pseudo-aristocrats he so often professed to hate. He planned to visit his daughter and would probably bring William, one of his ex-slaves. William was eager to see Liz and the children, and Johnson wished to give him the opportunity. Through the trials of Civil War and Reconstruction, the Johnson "family," black and white, was still together.[18]

The collapse of Reconstruction provided Johnson with the kind of "vindication" he would have understood, but in view of his justifiably rough treatment at the hands of modern historians that "vindication" is laced with tragedy. Like the black Americans who were its obvious victims, Andrew Johnson was also a victim of the racism that infected his society, an infection created by his own and other white minds. Racism, while obviously not the conscious motive for the individual decisions he made before, during, or after Reconstruction, was a necessary ingredient in every decision he made — a necessary part of his vision of the world. In Johnson's case, the demands of his driven personality and the political ideology that he came to worship made the impact of racism more damaging to the nation and to his historical reputation.

In this sense, racism is the "key" to understanding Johnson's actions and, by simple extension, Reconstruction itself. Of course it would be inaccurate to imagine what happened as an example of a pure cause-and-effect relationship. Racism is far too complex. If its involvement in Andrew Johnson's life illustrates anything, it is that as a pattern of thought racism means little until transformed into action through the medium of an individual personality. It is quite conceivable that a person could share many of the same basic assumptions about the nature of black people and act in a manner very different from Andrew Johnson. On the other hand, without his racist beliefs it is unlikely that Johnson would have acted as he did.

Notes

PROLOGUE

1. Philip S. Foner, *The Life and Writings of Frederick Douglass* (4 vols., New York, 1955), 4:20–21.

2. Arna W. Bontemps, *Free at Last: The Life of Frederick Douglass* (New York, 1971), 244–45; Foner, *Frederick Douglass*, 4:18–20.

3. The following account including direct quotations, unless otherwise cited, is taken from a transcript of the meeting in Foner, ibid., 182–91. Foner's account is basically the same as that found in Edward McPherson, *The Political History of the United States of America During the Period of Reconstruction* (Washington, 1887), 52–55. Both accounts are based on a report in the *New York Tribune*, Feb. 8, 1866. See also, William Wells Brown, *The Negro in the American Rebellion* (Boston, 1867), 388; Benjamin Quarles, *Frederick Douglass* (Washington, 1948), 226.

4. *New York Tribune*, Feb. 12, 1866. For an explanation of the ideological positions of the various wings of the Republican Party during Reconstruction, see Michael Les Benedict, *A Compromise of Principle: Congressional Republicans and Reconstruction, 1863-1869* (New York, 1974), 21–58.

5. P. Ripley to Manton Marble, Feb. 8, 1866, quoted in John H. and La-Wanda Cox, *Politics, Principle, and Prejudice, 1865-1866: Dilemma of Reconstruction America* (New York, 1969), 163.

6. Booker T. Washington, *Frederick Douglass* (Philadelphia, 1906), 246–47.

CHAPTER 1

1. Herbert Marcuse, *One Dimensional Man: Studies in the Ideology of Advanced Industrial Society* (Boston, 1964), provides a poignant critique of the empirical approach in modern thought.

2. See Thomas F. Gossett, *Race: The History of an Idea in America* (Dallas, 1963), for an example of the concentration on ideology in explaining racism.

3. Gordon W. Allport, *The Nature of Prejudice* (New York, 1954), 17–26.

4. Harmannus Hoetink, *Slavery and Race Relations in the Americas: Comparative Notes on their Nature and Nexus* (New York, 1973), 192.

5. Frantz Fanon, *Black Skins, White Masks* (New York, 1967), 188.

6. Fawn M. Brodie, *Thomas Jefferson: An Intimate History* (New York, 1974), 466; Winthrop Jordan, *White over Black: American Attitudes Toward the Negro, 1550–1812* (Chapel Hill, N.C., 1968), 429–81.

7. Thomas Jefferson, *Notes on the State of Virginia*, William Peden, ed. (Chapel Hill, N.C., 1955), 140–43, 162–63. The most often cited example of Jefferson's attitude toward talented blacks is his exchange of correspondence with Benjamin Banneker. Jordan, *White over Black*, 449–57; Henry E. Baker, "Benjamin Banneker, the Negro Mathematician and Astronomer," *Journal of Negro History*, 3 (1918), 99–118.

8. William Stanton, *The Leopard's Spots: Scientific Attitudes toward Race in America, 1851–59* (Chicago, 1960), 4, 41–53, 65–66, 161–83; George M. Fredrickson, *The Black Image in the White Mind: The Debate on Afro-American Character and Destiny, 1817–1914* (New York, 1971), 28–29; Gossett, *Race*, 60.

9. Ibid.; Stanton, *Leopard's Spots*, 100–103.

10. A good discussion of the early use of the legend of Ham as support for the concept of black inferiority is found in Jordan, *White over Black*, 16–20. A summary of the biblical argument in the antebellum defense of slavery is found in a pamphlet by the Baptist writer, Thornton Stringfellow. For an excerpt, see Eric L. McKitrick, ed., *Slavery Defended: The Views of the Old South* (Englewood Cliffs, N.J., 1963), 86–98.

11. See Leon F. Litwack, *North of Slavery: The Negro in the Free States, 1790–1860* (Chicago, 1961); Eugene H. Berwanger, *The Frontier Against Slavery: Western Anti-Negro Prejudice and the Slavery Extension Controversy* (Urbana, Ill., 1967); and Fredrickson, *Black Image*, for discussions of racial attitudes outside the South.

12. Chase C. Mooney, *Slavery in Tennessee* (Bloomington, Ind., 1957), 102; Kenneth M. Stampp, *The Peculiar Institution: Slavery in the Ante-Bellum South* (New York, 1956), 32. Over one-half of the slaves in the United States lived in the seven states of the deep South and among the slave states the percentage of the slave population varied greatly. In Tennessee the peak figure was 24.8 percent reached in 1860. At the same time South Carolina had a slave population of 57 percent.

13. Mooney, *Slavery in Tennessee*, 4–6, 102. See also, Mary Emily Robertson Campbell, *The Attitude of Tennesseans Toward the Union, 1847–1861* (New York, 1961), 14–19, for an interesting statistical discussion of Tennessee's slave population.

14. Eric Russell Lacy, *Vanquished Volunteers: East Tennessee Sectionalism from Statehood to Secession* (Johnson City, Tenn., 1965), 16–107; Mooney, *Slavery in Tennessee*, 65–69, 77–81.

15. Ibid., 69–73.

16. Frederick Law Olmsted, *The Cotton Kingdom: a Traveller's Observations on Cotton and Slavery in the American Slave States* (2 vols., New York,

1861) 2:126–42; Olmstead, *The Slave States,* Harvey Wish, ed. (New York, 1959), 211.

17. John Eaton, *Grant, Lincoln and the Freedmen: Reminiscences of the Civil War with Special Reference to the Work for the Contrabands and Freedmen of the Mississippi Valley* (New York, 1897), 119; Harvey Wish, ed., *Ante-Bellum: Writings of George Fitzhugh and Hinton Rowan Helper on Slavery* (New York, 1960), 22–39.

18. Olmstead, *Cotton Kingdom,* 110–11, 134–37. Wilbur J. Cash also felt that slavery created a "savage and ignoble hate for the Negro" in the common white and, though recognizing the importance of economic factors, stressed status as the key to support of slavery by the lower classes. W. J. Cash, *The Mind of the South* (New York, 1941), 38–41, 86.

19. John Dollard, *Caste and Class in a Southern Town* (New York, 1937), 75–79.

20. Alexis de Tocqueville, *Democracy in America,* Phillipps Bradley, ed. (2 vols., New York, 1945), 1:359–60; Berwanger, *Frontier Against Slavery,* 3–6.

21. J. S. Buckingham, *The Slave States of America* (2 vols., London, 1842), 2:237–44. "Major Malony" was probably John Maloney, proprietor of a local inn and one-time mayor of Greeneville. Richard H. Doughty, *Greeneville: One Hundred Year Portrait (1715–1875)* (Kingsport, Tenn., 1975), 70.

22. Oliver P. Temple, *Notable Men of Tennessee from 1833 to 1875: Their Times and Their Contemporaries* (New York, 1912), 362–63.

23. Doughty, *Greeneville,* 37–43. For a perceptive analysis of the leadership class in the antebellum frontier regions, see Thomas P. Abernethy, *From Frontier to Plantation in Tennessee: A Study of Frontier Democracy* (Chapel Hill, N.C., 1932) 359–64.

24. Doughty, *Greeneville,* 61–62; Temple, *Notable Men,* 369–74, 400; Abernethy, *Frontier to Plantation,* 337–44, 261–62.

25. Doughty, *Greeneville,* 47; Mooney, *Slavery in Tennessee,* 66–69, 192.

26. Doughty, *Greeneville,* 47; Mooney, *Slavery in Tennessee,* 66–69; *American Economist and East Tennessee Statesman* (Greeneville, Tenn.), May 1, 1824. Most issues carried advertisements for local businesses and, though *The Genius of Universal Emancipation* was itself advertised, seldom if ever made any direct mention of slavery.

27. Ibid., July 15, 1824.

28. Ibid.

CHAPTER 2

1. Harriot S. Turner, "Recollections of Andrew Johnson," *Harper's Monthly Magazine,* 120 (1910), 170. See also, Robert W. Winston, *Andrew Johnson: Plebeian and Patriot* (New York, 1928), 104–105, for a slightly different version

of the quotation. Though most observers attribute the substance of the state-ment to Harris, John Bell Brownlow claims the remark was made originally by William T. Haskell, a Murfreesboro politician. Brownlow to O. P. Temple, Apr. 21, 1894, Oliver P. Temple Papers, Univ. of Tenn. Lib., Knoxville.

2. Winston, *Andrew Johnson*, 516. See Lloyd Paul Stryker, *Andrew John-son, A Study in Courage* (New York, 1929) and Milton Lomask, *Andrew John-son, President on Trial* (New York, 1960) for examples.

3. U.S. Government Pub., *Memorial Addresses on the Life and Character of Andrew Johnson Delivered in the Senate and House of Representatives, January 12, 1876* (Washington, 1876), 11–15 and *passim*.

4. First Inaugural Address, Oct. 17, 1853, in Leroy P. Graf and Ralph W. Haskins, eds., *The Papers of Andrew Johnson* (hereinafter cited as *Papers* with appropriate volume number) (7 vols. to date, Knoxville, 1967–87), 2:177.

5. Ibid., 1:xix; Temple, *Notable Men*, 357–68, 455–67.

6. Ibid., 372–74; Winston, *Andrew Johnson*, 58–75; Margarita Spaulding Gerry, "Andrew Johnson in the White House: Being the Reminiscences of Wil-liam H. Crook," *Century Magazine*, 126 (1908), 877. For examples of Johnson's pointed humor, see Johnson to Blackston McDannel, Jan., 1845; Speech on the Admission of Texas and Other Matters, Jan. 21, 1845; Johnson to David T. Patterson, July 10, 1845, in *Papers*, 1:185, 191, 217–18.

7. Harold D. Lasswell, *Power and Personality* (New York, 1948), 21–48.

8. Winston, *Andrew Johnson*, 3–8. Winston goes to considerable lengths to prove that Jacob Johnson was far from "a person of no consequence." His description, however, only succeeds in creating the image of a man apparently satisfied, even happy, in the role of servant to "his betters."

9. Ibid., 9; Notice of Runaway Apprentices, June 24, 1824, in Papers, 1:3; Temple, *Notable Men*, 452.

10. Winston, *Andrew Johnson*, 11–14.

11. Ibid., 15–23.

12. Ibid., 10.

13. *Papers*, 1:xix.

14. Temple, *Notable Men*, 357, 456; Winston, *Andrew Johnson*, 11, 14; Gerry, "Reminiscences of W. H. Crook," 665; Turner, "Recollections of Andrew Johnson," 169; Frank Cowan, *Andrew Johnson, President of the United States: Reminiscences of His Private Life and Character by One of His Secretaries* (Greenesburgh, Pa., 1894), 2–6; Notice of Runaway Apprentices, June 24, 1824, in *Papers*, 1:3.

15. J. B. Brownlow to Temple, enclosure, n.d., Temple Papers. Though his assertion may be the product of hindsight, Brownlow claims that the slave-owners in particular looked down on Johnson.

16. Abernethy, *Frontier to Plantation*, 286. It may be possible that John-son's trade was a special handicap. One observer states that tailoring has "from

time out of mind been regarded as an effeminate, unmanly occupation." If such were actually the case, it would add another element to Johnson's feelings of inferiority and clearly be related to his aggressive behavior. Gaillard Hunt, "The President's Defense: His Side of the Case, as Told by his Correspondence," *Century Magazine*, 85 (1913), 427.

17. Winston, *Andrew Johnson*, 23; *Papers*, 1:xxiii; Johnson to Valentine Sevier, June 7, 1832, in ibid., 14. Another letter was addressed to Alexander Williams himself, informing the Greeneville leader of legislative business and signed, "Your friend." Johnson to Alexander Williams, Jan. 27, 1836, in ibid., 16–17.

18. Ibid., xxiii–xxv; Temple, *Notable Men*, 367–68; Abernethy, *Frontier to Plantation*, 351, 362.

19. Temple, *Notable Men*, 366–67.

20. Ibid; Winston, *Andrew Johnson*, 32–33; *Papers*, 1:xxv.

21. Temple, *Notable Men*, 366–67. Johnson's attachment to Calhoun did not disappear. In 1843 he wrote Robert B. Reynolds, a Knoxville lawyer, that he had "no hesitancy in speaking out for John C. Calhoun against the world." Johnson to Robert B. Reynolds, Sept. 9, 1843, in *Papers*, 1:121–22. See Abernethy, *Frontier to Plantation*, 300, 309–11, for a different assessment of Johnson's conversion.

22. Winston, *Andrew Johnson*, 69–75; Temple, *Notable Men*, 383–90. This tale, taken largely from Winston's account, may be more legend than truth. The story was apparently current in Washington during Johnson's presidency. William H. Crook, tells a similar version with a different time frame. Gerry, "Reminiscences of W. H. Crook," 665. See also Speech at Murfreesboro, May 1, 1855, and Speech at Pulaski, May 11, 1855, in *Papers*, 2:271–307, for two of the most important speeches in the canvass.

23. J. B. Brownlow to Temple, enclosure, n.d.; J. B. Brownlow to Temple, Sept. 8, 1892, Temple Papers.

24. Temple, *Notable Men*, 373.

25. *Nashville Union*, May 21, 1849; *Papers*, 1: appendix 4:678.

26. Remarks Concerning Senate Homestead Bill, Mar. 22, 1860; Johnson to A. O. P. Nicholson, Nov. 22, 1858, in ibid., 3:484, 196. A good example of Johnson's technique of using factual information is found in a speech at Evan's Crossroads, Greene County, 1849. The subject was slavery and the Democrat, using a blinding array of statistics and quotes impossible for his audience to follow, proved that Whigs were encouraging abolition. Speech at Evan's Crossroads, Greene County, May 26, 1849, in ibid., 498–507.

27. Eric L. McKitrick, *Andrew Johnson and Reconstruction* (Chicago, 1960), 89–91.

28. Speech at Bristol (Democratic Version), May 21, 1859, in *Papers*, 3:278. See ibid., 1:xx–xxvii, for a brief evaluation of Johnson's two terms as Governor.

For a more detailed analysis, see Hubert Blair Bently, "Andrew Johnson, Governor of Tennessee, 1853–57" (Ph.D. dissertation, University of Tennessee, 1972).

29. Speech at Nashville, July 15, 1856, in *Papers*, 2:413.

30. Ibid., xxiv; Winston, *Andrew Johnson*, 128–41; Ralph W. Haskins, "Andrew Johnson and the Preservation of the Union," East Tennessee Historical Society's *Publications*, 31 (1961), 43–60.

31. J. B. Brownlow to Temple, enclosure, n.d., Temple Papers.

32. Johnson to Mary Johnson, Dec. 7, 1850, in *Papers*, 1:592–93.

33. Johnson to Robert Johnson, Jan. 15, 1860, ibid., 3:383. Johnson's continual use of the first-person pronoun was obsessive and at times the subject of ridicule. In his inaugural speech as vice-president, given while clearly under the influence of alcohol, he used the personal pronoun "I" twenty-seven times. On the same day in his address, Lincoln used the term only once. Cox and Cox, *Politics, Principle, and Prejudice*, 96.

34. Temple, *Notable Men*, 371; *Papers*, 3:xxiii–xxvi.

35. Ibid., 1:xxviii; Temple, *Notable Men*, 457; Winston, *Andrew Johnson*, 17–20. J. B. Brownlow has a particularly colorful description of Johnson treating a group of potential voters at a public house. According to the description, "Johnson was always perfectly indifferent to the *quality* of the whiskey he drank, he smacked his lips and enjoyed the meanest whiskey hot and fresh from the still, with the fusil oil on it, and stuff which would vomit a gentleman. . . ." It may not have been Johnson's taste, but his desire to "be one of the boys" that lay behind such activities. J. B. Brownlow to Temple, Sept. 8, 1892, Temple Papers.

36. Temple, *Notable Men*, 462. Numerous observers commented on Johnson's neatness. For one of the better descriptions, see Benjamin C. Truman, "Anecdotes of Andrew Johnson," *Century Magazine*, 85 (1913), 435–36.

37. Johnson to Robert Johnson, Oct. 20, 1859, in *Papers*, 3:301–302.

38. First Inaugural Address, Oct. 17, 1853, in ibid., 2:176.

39. Remarks on the War with Mexico and Other Matters, May 29–30, 1846, in ibid., 1:311.

40. Remarks at Opening of State Agricultural Fair, Oct. 12, 1857, in ibid., 2:506.

41. For a discussion of Johnson's pardoning policy, see McKitrick, *Johnson and Reconstruction*, 142–52. Some historians have speculated, with considerable justification, that Johnson's desire for acceptance by the southern aristocracy played a role in his policy. Kenneth M. Stampp, *The Era of Reconstruction, 1865–1877* (New York, 1967), 70–71; Michael Pierce, "Andrew Johnson and the South, 1865–1867" (Ph.D. dissertation, North Texas State University, 1970), 25. Johnson's "chivalrous" attitude toward the ladies was noted by several contemporary observers. Gerry, "Reminiscences of W. H. Crook," 657; Truman, "Anecdotes of Andrew Johnson," 436–37. For a different but equally revealing view, see Turner, "Recollections of Andrew Johnson," 168–76.

42. Johnson to Railroad Agent, Gurleysville, Alabama, June 22, 1869, in Clement C. Clay Papers, Duke University Library, Durham; K. T. Daniel to Johnson, June 23, 1869; Mrs. V. C. Clay to Johnson, July 22, 1869 in Johnson Mss., Lib. of Cong.; Temple, *Notable Men,* 439–50; Mary Ozelle Bible, "The Post Presidential Career of Andrew Johnson" (Master's Thesis, University of Tennessee, 1936).

43. Abernethy, *Frontier to Plantation,* 357.

CHAPTER 3

1. Speech on Homestead Bill, May 20, 1858, in *Papers,* 3:165.

2. Winston, *Andrew Johnson,* 104–105, gives an account of Johnson's trip and subsequent weeks of struggle in East Tennessee.

3. Thomas Shackelford to Johnson, June 4, 1865, Johnson Mss., L.C. In the process of writing the president requesting an appointment, Shackelford recalls in detail their private conversation four years earlier.

4. Ibid.

5. William L. Barney, *The Road to Secession: A New Perspective on the Old South* (New York, 1972), 43.

6. Speech on the Gag Resolution, Jan. 31, 1844, in *Papers,* 1:140.

7. Speech on the Admission of Oregon, Jan. 31, 1846, in ibid., 285.

8. Exchange with Daniel Clark, Mar. 27, 1860, in ibid., 3:495.

9. John E. Patterson to Johnson, July 2, 1861, in ibid., 4:537–38.

10. Shackleford to Johnson, June 4, 1865, Johnson Mss., L.C.

11. Fay W. Brabson, *Andrew Johnson: A Life in Pursuit of the Right Course, 1808–1875* (Durham, N.C., 1972), 17. Colonel Brabson, a Greeneville native, had the bills of sale for the two slaves in his possession; he had also interveiwed William Johnson, born to Dolly while she was Johnson's slave. For an account of Johnson's economic status, see *Papers,* 1:xxii–xxiii.

12. Winston, *Andrew Johnson,* 102; *Cincinnati Daily Commercial,* Mar. 28, 1862, quoting *Nashville Banner,* Mar. 15, 1862; *New York Times,* Mar. 15, 1863; *Life, Speeches and Services of Andrew Johnson* (Philadelphia, 1865), 95–98; and Charles Johnson to Johnson, Jan. 29, 1860, in *Papers,* 3:404–405.

13. Winston, *Andrew Johnson,* 103.

14. Charles Johnson to Johnson, Jan. 29, 1860, in *Papers,* 3:404–405.

15. For discussions of Charles Johnson and his problems, see Winston, *Andrew Johnson,* 96; Brabson, *Andrew Johnson,* 46; and *Papers,* 2:xxx.

16. Winston, *Andrew Johnson,* 103. Johnson was very sensitive to any insinuation that he was weak in his support for slavery because he did not own many slaves. For a typical Johnsonian reply to such a charge, see Speech on Popular Sovereignty and the Right of Instruction, Feb. 23, 1858, in *Papers,* 3:60–61.

17. Ibid.; *Knoxville Daily Press and Herald,* Apr. 1, 1869; and Bill of Sale for Negro Slave, May 6, 1857, in *Papers,* 2:471, 471n.

18. Johnson to Robert Johnson, Apr. 16, 1854, in ibid., 231, 232n; Brabson, *Andrew Johnson,* 48–49.

19. Stampp, *The Peculiar Institution,* 327.

20. See Stanley Elkins, *Slavery: A Problem in American Institutional and Intellectual Life* (Chicago, 1959), 81–133, for another perspective on the process of "infantilization" as the product of slavery.

21. For discussions of the importance of sex in racist mythology, see Allport, *The Nature of Prejudice,* 348–55; Jordan, *White Over Black,* 136–78; and Claude H. Nolan, *The Negro's Image in the South* (Lexington, Ky., 1968), 29–39.

22. Exchange with Palfrey of Massachusetts on the Negro, Apr. 15, 1848, in *Papers,* 1:418–20, 420n–21n.

23. "The Moses of the Colored Men" Speech, Oct. 24, 1864, in ibid., 7:251–53. See also, Frank Moore, ed., *Speeches of Andrew Johnson, President of the United States with a Biographical Introduction* (Boston, 1866), xxxv–xxxvii; *Nashville Times,* Oct. 24, 1864; *Nashville Dispatch,* Oct. 26, 1864.

24. "The Moses of the Colored Men" Speech, Oct. 24, 1864, in *Papers,* 7:251–53.

25. Johnson to Robert Reynolds, Sept. 9, 1843, in *Papers,* 1:121, 122n.

26. Excerpt from Mayor's Book, Jan. 18, 1834, in ibid., 15–16; Mooney, *Slavery in Tennessee,* 20; Lacy, *Vanquished Volunteers,* 100–101.

27. Resolutions for the Establishment of the State of Frankland, Dec. 7, 1841, in *Papers,* 1:61; Lacy, *Vanquished Volunteers,* 114; Ezekiel Birdseye to Garrit Smith, Nov. 27, 1841, in W. Freeman Galpin, ed., "Letters from an East Tennessee Abolitionist," East Tennessee Historical Society's *Publications,* 3 (1931), 145–49. See also Samuel Cole Williams, *The Lost State of Franklin* (Johnson City, Tenn., 1929), 277–79; and Stanley J. Folmsbee, *Sectionalism and Internal Improvements in Tennessee, 1796–1845* (Knoxville, 1939), 219, 229.

28. Robert H. White, *Messages of the Governors of Tennessee* (8 vols., Nashville, 1952–72), 3:615–16; Resolutions on Congressional Districting, Oct. 5, 1842, in *Papers,* 1:85–86.

29. Johnson to the Freemen of the First District of Tennessee, Oct. 15, 1845, in ibid., 254–56. Johnson himself pointed out this fact during an exchange with John Bell in the Senate. Exchange with John Bell, Feb. 24, 1858, in ibid., 3:87. For an interesting discussion of one of these intrastate battles, see Roger W. Shugg, *Origin of Class Struggle in Louisiana: A Social History of White Farmers and Laborers During Slavery and After, 1840–1875* (Baton Rouge, 1939), 130–44.

30. Johnson to the Freeman of the First District of Tennessee, Oct. 15, 1845, in *Papers,* 1:254–57.

31. Speech on the Gag Resolution, Jan. 31, 1844; Speech at Evans' Crossroads, Greene County, May 26, 1849, in ibid., 133–41, 144, 500.

32. Speech on the Gag Resolution, Jan. 31, 1844, in ibid., 144.

33. Ibid., 143.

34. See Speech on the Admission of Texas and Other Matters, Jan. 21, 1845; Speech on the Whigs and Expansion, June 5, 1850, in ibid., 187–207, 539–43; Speech on the Homestead Bill, Apr. 29, 1852, in ibid., 2:43.

35. See Speech at Nashville, July 15, 1856, in ibid., 395–436; Speech on Popular Sovereignty and the Right of Instruction, Feb. 23, 1858; Speech on Harper's Ferry Incident, Dec. 12, 1859, in ibid., 3:43–89, 318–52.

36. Johnson to Sam Milligan, Dec. 28, 1852, in ibid., 2:101–102; Speech on the Whigs and Expansion, June 5, 1850, in ibid., 1:544–45; Johnson to A. O. P. Nicholson, June 27, 1856; Speech at Nashville, July 15, 1856; Johnson to Thomas B. Childress, Aug. 7, 1856, in ibid., 2:388, 431, 438.

37. Johnson's attitude toward Douglas is particularly revealing. In the early 1850s the Tennessee Congressman did not think highly of the budding politician from Illinois, who in his opinion was "the candidate of the *cormorants* of our party . . . a mere hot bed production, a precocious politician wormed into, and kept in existence by a Set of interested plunders. . . ." Douglas' break with the Buchanan administration over the admission of Kansas only reinforced such feelings. But as the election of 1860 approached, Johnson found a community of interest with Douglas. There was quiet cooperation between Johnson men and supporters of Douglas in Tennessee and at the Charleston convention, where Johnson instructed his followers to avoid a break with the Douglas forces. Publicly, however, Johnson maintained his opposition to the Illinois Democrat. Johnson to David Patterson, Apr. 4, 1852, in ibid., 30–31; Johnson to Robert Johnson, Jan. 23, 1855, Jan. 12, 1860, Apr. 8, 1860, and Apr. 22, 1860; William Henry Maxwell to Johnson, Feb. 2, 1860; Frank C. Dunnington to Johnson, Feb. 13, 1860, in ibid., 3:7–8, 380, 410–12, 426, 517–18, 573.

38. Winston, *Andrew Johnson*, 118; Johnson to George W. Jones, Mar. 15, 1860; Johnson to Harry T. Phillips, Aug. 15, 1859, in *Papers*, 3:466–67, 290.

39. Ibid., 2:xviii, xxv; ibid., 3:xxvii; Temple, *Notable Men*, 392.

40. Speech on Popular Sovereignty and the Right of Instruction, Feb. 23, 1858, in ibid., 3:60–61.

41. Johnson to Horace Greely, Dec. 14, 1851, in ibid., 1:631–33; Speech to New York Land Reformers, May 27, 1852, in ibid., 2:57–61. For a discussion of Johnson and the Homestead Bill, see Winston, *Andrew Johnson*, 128–41. See also Speech on Homestead Bill, May 20, 1858, and Speech on Amendment to Homestead Bill, Apr. 11, 1860 in *Papers*, 3:132–69, 524–47.

42. Winston, *Andrew Johnson*, 138. For Johnson's bitter reaction to Buchanan's veto, see Speech on Homestead Bill Veto, June 23, 1860, in *Papers*, 3:627–42.

43. Speech on the Admission of Texas and Other Matters, Jan. 21, 1845, in ibid., 1:205.

44. *Acts of the State of Tennessee*, 30th General Assembly, 1 Sess., 1853–54,

121; Johnson to William McLain, Apr. 11, 1856, and Nov. 11, 1856, in *Papers*, 2:381, 448.

45. Johnson to William McLain, Apr. 11, 1856, in ibid., 381.

46. Ibid., 3:373n, 381n; John Hope Franklin, *From Slavery to Freedom* (New York, 1967), 221; *Tennessee House Journal, 1859–1860*, 237–38, 456–58, 486, 1033; Robert Johnson to Johnson, Jan. 10, 1860; Johnson to Robert Johnson, Jan. 12, 1860, in *Papers*, 3:377, 379.

47. Bently, "Andrew Johnson," 545–49; *Memphis Bulletin*, Oct. 23, 1856, quoted in *Nashville Republican Banner*, Nov. 1, 1856. See also Harvey Wish, "The Slave Insurrection Panic of 1856," *Journal of Southern History*, 5 (May 1939), 206–22.

48. Springfield Citizens to Johnson, Dec. 6, 1856, in *Papers*, 2:456–57; Thomas Shackelford to Johnson, June 4, 1865, Johnson Mss., L. C.; Turner, "Recollections of Andrew Johnson," 160. Mrs. Turner, who was a child at the time, remembers the incident in question as having occurred following the John Brown raid. However, her memory was probably inaccurate. At the time of Brown's incursion, Johnson was Senator, not Governor. Moreover, the month involved would suggest that her recollection actually involved events during the troubles of 1856.

49. Johnson to Elbridge G. Eastman, May 27, 1849, in *Papers*, 1:509.

50. Speech on Amendment to Homestead Bill, Apr. 11, 1860, in ibid., 3:525–26.

51. Johnson to John L. Dawson, Feb. 23, 1859; Johnson to George W. Jones, March 13, 1860, in ibid., 258, 466. The question of exactly what constituted an abolitionist is a source of considerable controversy. For reasonable discussions of the meaning of the term, see Aileen S. Kraditor, *Means and Ends in American Abolitionism: Garrison and his Critics on Strategy and Tactics, 1834–1850* (New York, 1969), 8, and Dwight Lowell Dumond, *Antislavery Origins of the Civil War in the United States* (Ann Arbor, 1939), 37.

52. David Donald, "Toward a Reconsideration of Abolitionists," in *Lincoln Reconsidered: Essays on the Civil War Era* (New York, 1956), 19–36.

53. Johnson to the Freemen of the First Congressional District of Tennessee, Oct. 15, 1845, *Papers*, 1:220–48; Winston, *Andrew Johnson*, 101–102. For a discussion of religion as an influence on abolitionism, see Gilbert Hobbs Barnes, *The Anti-Slavery Impulse, 1830–1844* (New York, 1933), 3–16.

54. First Inaugural Address, Oct. 17, 1853, in *Papers*, 2:173–78.

55. Ibid., 176. For two contrasting views on the influence of Transcendentalism on abolitionism, see Elkins, *Slavery*, 140–93; Kraditor, *Means and Ends in American Abolitionism*, 11–38.

56. See George Fitzhugh, *Sociology for the South or the Failure of Free Society* (Richmond, 1854); Fitzhugh, *Cannibals All! or Slaves Without Masters* (Richmond, 1857). For contrasting interpretations of Fitzhugh's ideas, see Harvey Wish, *George Fitzhugh: Propagandist of the Old South* (Baton Rouge, 1943), and Eugene D. Genovese, *The World the Slaveholders Made* (New York, 1971), 118–244.

57. First Inaugural Address, Oct. 17, 1853, in *Papers*, 2:176.

58. See Barney, *The Road to Secession*, 49–50, for an interesting comment on the relationship between democracy and racism.

59. Speech at Evans' Crossroads, Greene County, May 26, 1849, in *Papers*, 1:499–500.

60. *Charleston Courier*, Dec. 12, 1840; Hinton Rowan Helper, *The Impending Crisis of the South: How to Meet It* (New York, 1857).

61. See Speech on Harper's Ferry Incident, Dec. 12, 1859, in *Papers*, 3:334–38, for an example of Johnson's use of statistical evidence in support of slavery. For a brief discussion of Helper's career, see Wish, *Ante-Bellum* 22–26.

62. Speech on the Gag Resolution, Jan. 31, 1844, in *Papers*, 1:136.

63. Address to the State Democratic Convention, Nashville, Jan. 8, 1856, in ibid., 2:353–54.

64. Speech on Harper's Ferry Incident, Dec. 12, 1859, in ibid., 3:319–21.

CHAPTER 4

1. "The Moses of the Colored Men" Speech, Oct. 24, 1864, in *Papers*, 7:251.

2. Clifton R. Hall, *Andrew Johnson, Military Governor of Tennessee* (Princeton, 1916), 154–55.

3. "The Moses of the Colored Men" Speech, Oct. 24, 1864, in *Papers*, 7:252–53.

4. Cox and Cox, *Politics, Principles, and Prejudice*, 232. The Coxes' work is an excellent example of modern scholarship in which the race theme assumes a central role in Reconstruction.

5. For a discussion of Johnson's influence in the state Democratic Party, see *Papers*, 3:xxiv–xxv. For a discussion of the Homestead Bill, see Speech on Homestead Bill, May 20, 1858, in ibid., 132–66; Winston, *Andrew Johnson*, 119, 135–39. For an indication of Robert Johnson's optimism concerning his father's presidential hopes, see Robert Johnson to Johnson, Apr. 10, 1860, in *Papers*, 3:523.

6. Winston, *Andrew Johnson*, 121–27; *Papers*, 3:xxvii; Robert Johnson to Johnson, May 8, 1860, in ibid., 588–89. Johnson's reaction to Buchanan's veto was bitter. Speech on Homestead Bill Veto, June 23, 1860, in ibid., 627.

7. For discussions of Johnson's stand against secession, see Haskins, "Andrew Johnson and the Preservation of the Union," 43–60; Leroy P. Graf, "Andrew Johnson and the Coming of the War," *Tennessee Historical Quarterly*, 19 (1960), 208–21; George C. Rable, "Anatomy of a Unionist: Andrew Johnson in the Secession Crisis," ibid., 22 (1973), 332–54.

8. Speech on Transcontinental Railroads, Jan. 25, 1859, in *Papers*, 3:232.

9. Johnson to Abraham L. Gammon, July 31, 1860, in ibid., 653.

10. Speech on Secession, Dec. 18–19, 1860, in ibid., 4:4.

11. Speech on the Seceding States, Feb. 5–6, 1861, in ibid., 242–44.

12. Johnson to Sam Milligan, Jan. 13, 1861, in ibid., 160–61.

13. Joint Resolution for Amendments on Presidential, Senatorial, and Judicial Selection, Dec. 13, 1860; Resolution Proposing "Unamendable" Amendments Affecting Slavery, Dec. 13, 1860, in ibid., 3:692–95, 696; Speech on Secession, Dec. 18–19, 1860, in ibid., 4:3–5.

14. Remarks on War Aims Resolution, July 25, 1861, in ibid., 597–99.

15. Johnson to Robert Johnson, Dec. 6, 1860; Sam Milligan to Johnson, Dec. 13, 1860, in ibid., 3:688, 690–91. For discussions of Lincoln's approach, see Richard N. Current, *The Lincoln Nobody Knows* (New York, 1958); Benjamin Quarles, *Lincoln and the Negro* (New York, 1962); Abraham Lincoln to O. H. Browning, Sept. 22, 1861, in T. Harry Williams, ed., *Abraham Lincoln: Selected Speeches, Messages, and Letters* (New York, 1957), 166–68.

16. Fourth Debate with Stephen A. Douglas at Charleston, Illinois, Sept. 18, 1858, in Roy P. Basler, ed., *The Collected Works of Abraham Lincoln* (8 vols., New Brunswick, N.J., 1953), 3:145–46. For an extensive comparison of Lincoln and Johnson, see William T. M. Riches, "The Commoners: Andrew Johnson and Abraham Lincoln to 1861" (Ph.D. dissertation, University of Tennessee, 1976).

17. Current, *Lincoln Nobody Knows*, 216. Lincoln's colonization policy is discussed in Quarles, *Lincoln and the Negro*, 108–23.

18. Current, *Lincoln Nobody Knows*, 216.

19. McKitrick, *Johnson and Reconstruction*, 43–48. O. P. Temple makes some interesting comments about the impact of Johnson's unionism on the Greene County Whigs. He feels that many of Johnson's old enemies in his home county switched sides rather than support the same position as their ancient nemesis. Temple, *Notable Men*, 374–75.

20. Salmon P. Chase to Johnson, Jan. 11, 1861, in *Papers*, 4:152; Haskins, "Andrew Johnson and the Preservation of the Union," 53–55, 58; J. Milton Henry, "The Revolution in Tennessee, February, 1861 to June, 1861," *THQ* 17 (1959), 105–14; James L. Baumgardner, "Andrew Johnson and the Patronage" (Ph.D. dissertation, University of Tennessee, 1968), 22–23; T. Harry Williams, *Lincoln and the Radicals* (Madison, Wi., 1941), 68–69.

21. Schuyler Colfax to Johnson, July 5, 1862, in *Papers*, 5:541. For an example of Johnson's aggressive support of the Lincoln administration, see Speech in Support of Presidential War Program, July 27, 1861, in ibid., 4:606–49.

22. Hall, *Andrew Johnson, Military Governor*, 19–31; Peter Maslowski, *Treason Must Be Made Odious: Military Occupation and Wartime Reconstruction in Nashville, Tennessee, 1862–1865* (Millwood, N.Y., 1978), 20–26.

23. Lincoln to Johnson, July 11, 1862, *Papers*, 5:551–53. For a discussion of Johnson's feuds with Generals Buell and Rosecrans, see Maslowski, *Treason Must Be Made Odious*, 37–49.

24. Colfax to Johnson, July 5, 1862, in *Papers*, 5:541. For a discussion of Lincoln's intentions concerning Reconstruction, see LaWanda Cox, *Lincoln and Black Freedom: A Study in Presidential Leadership* (Columbia, S.C., 1981).

25. Don Carlos Buell to Johnson, Mar. 11, 1862, in *The War of Rebellion: A Compilation of Official Records of the Union and Confederate Armies* (hereinafter cited as *OR*) (170 vols., in 128, Washington, 1880–1901), Ser. 1, 10:612; *Cincinnati Daily Commercial*, Mar. 19, 1862; Speech in Nashville, Mar. 13, 1862, in *Papers*, 5:202–204.

26. Ibid., 203; Appeal to the People of Tennessee, Mar. 18, 1862; Speech to Davidson County's Citizens, Mar. 22, 1862; Speech at Nashville, May 12, 1862, in ibid., 210–12, 222–41, 379–87. See also, *Life, Speeches, and Services of Andrew Johnson*, 95–98; *Cincinnati Daily Commercial*, Mar. 28, 1862.

27. Speech at Nashville, July 4, 1862, in *Papers*, 5:534–40; *Nashville Daily Union*, July 6, 1862.

28. James M. McPherson, *The Struggle for Equality: Abolitionists and the Negro in the Civil War and Reconstruction* (Princeton, 1964), 97, 109, 111–12; Montgomery Blair to Johnson, April 29, 1862, in *Papers*, 5:347–48.

29. Quarles, *Lincoln and the Negro*, 101–23.

30. McPherson, *Struggle for Equality*, 107–108; Proclamation Revoking General Hunter's Order of Military Emancipation of May 9, 1862, May 19, 1862, in Basler, *Collected Works of Lincoln*, 5:222–23.

31. Johnson to Lincoln, May 22, 1862; Horace Maynard to Johnson, June 7, 1862, in *Papers*, 5:411, 451–52.

32. Appeal to the Border State Representatives to Favor Compensated Emancipation, July 12, 1862, in Basler, *Collected Works of Lincoln*, 5:317–19. Lincoln began writing his first draft of the proclamation in the early days of July and apparently did not inform anyone until he told Seward and Welles on July 13. Quarles, *Lincoln and the Negro*, 107.

33. Ibid.

34. Ibid., 127.

35. Maslowski, *Treason Must Be Made Odious*, 34–37. See Johnson to Lincoln, Apr. 9, 12, May 18, 1862, in *Papers*, 5:289, 301, 403.

36. Maslowski, *Treason Must Be Made Odious*, 34–37, 161; Hall, *Andrew Johnson, Military Governor*, 48.

37. Johnson to George H. Thomas, August 16, 1862, in *Papers*, 5:617.

38. Maslowski, *Treason Must Be Made Odious*, 37–49.

39. John V. Cimprich, Jr., *Slavery's End in Tennessee, 1861–1865* (University of Ala., 1985), 100; *Knoxville Register*, Oct. 5, 1862.

40. Herman Belz, *Reconstructing the Union: Theory and Policy during the Civil War* (Ithaca, N.Y., 1969), 105–6; Lincoln to Johnson, Oct. 21, 1862, in *Papers*, 6:33–34.

41. Hall, *Andrew Johnson, Military Governor*, 48–49, 87–89; *Nashville Daily Union*, Dec. 8, 1862; *Memphis Bulletin*, Nov. 28, Dec. 27, 1862; Cim-

prich, *Slavery's End*, 100–101; Writ of Election for Congressional Districts, Dec. 8, 1862, in *Papers*, 6:92.

42. *Memphis Bulletin*, Nov. 9, 1862; William B. Campbell to Johnson, Nov. 2, 1862; Petition to the President, Dec. 4, 1862, in *Papers*, 6:46–47, 85–86.

43. Ibid., 86n; James G. Blaine, *Twenty Years of Congress from Lincoln to Garfield* (2 vols., Norwich Conn., 1884), 1:446.

44. Johnson to Lincoln, Jan. 11, 1863, in *Papers*, 6:114; *OR* Ser. 1, 20:317.

45. *Papers*, 6:xlviii.

46. Maslowski, *Treason Must Be Made Odious*, 166–73.

47. Johnson to Lincoln, Jan. 11, 1863, in *Papers*, 6:114.

48. *Nashville Daily Union*, Dec. 3, 1862. The *Nashville Daily Union* began publication in April 1862 under the editorship of S. C. Mercer, a radical unionist from Kentucky. Until 1864 when it was taken over by conservatives, the paper consistently advocated a slightly more radical position than the Governor on questions concerning blacks. For example, on March 13, 1862 it contained an editorial praising Lincoln's Emancipation Proclamation and in April began to advocate the use of black troops. Both positions anticipated Johnson's public statements. Maslowski, *Treason Must Be Made Odious*, 55; *Nashville Daily Union*, Mar. 13 and Apr. 1, 1863.

49. Hall, *Andrew Johnson, Military Governor*, 92–93; W. D. Foulke, *The Life and Public Service of Oliver P. Morton* (2 vols., Indianapolis, 1899), 1:213.

50. *Nashville Daily Union*, Mar. 3, 1863; *New York Times*, March 8, 1863. The accounts of Johnson's speeches were published in different newspapers with slight variations in wording. The above quotes were taken directly from these newspaper versions. For other versions, see Speech at Indianapolis, Feb. 26, 1863; Speech at Cincinnati, Feb. 27, 1863; Speech to the Ohio Legislature, Mar. 3, 1863; Speech at Harrisburg, Pa., Mar. 6, 1863; Speech at Philadelphia, Mar. 11, 1863; Speech to the Loyal League, New York City, Mar. 14, 1863; Speech at Baltimore, Mar. 20, 1863; and Speech to Washington Union Meeting, Mar. 31, 1863, in *Papers*, 6:148–61, 165–69, 168–93, 200–204.

51. *New York Times*, Mar. 2, 1863.

52. Ibid.

53. Lincoln to Johnson, Mar. 26, 1863, *Papers*, 6:194–95.

54. Clipping enclosed in Johnson, Horace Maynard, and Allen A. Hall to Lincoln, Mar. 27, 1863, ibid., 198; *Nashville Daily Union*, Mar. 26, 1863.

55. Johnson to Eliza Johnson, Mar. 27, 1863; Johnson, Maynard, and Hall to Lincoln, Mar. 27, 1863, in *Papers*, 6:195–96, 198.

56. Maslowski, *Treason Must Be Made Odious*, 81–82; *Nashville Daily Union*, Apr. 23, 1863; Hall, *Andrew Johnson, Military Governor*, 93–94.

57. Ibid., 95–98.

58. Ibid., 99–101; Maslowski, *Treason Must Be Made Odious*, 83–84. For

a discussion of Etheridge's activities, see Herman Belz, "The Etheridge Conspiracy of 1863: A Projected Conservative Coup," *JSH*, 36 (1970), 549–67.

59. Hall, *Andrew Johnson, Military Governor*, 98–99.

60. Speech at Franklin, Aug. 23, 1863, in *Papers*, 6:331–39; *Memphis Bulletin*, Sept. 8, 1863; *Nashville Daily Union*, Aug. 25, 1863.

61. Speech at Nashville, in *Papers*, 6:344–45; *Nashville Daily Union*, Sept. 1, 1863.

62. Ibid.

63. Charles A. Dana, *Recollections of the Civil War: With the Leaders at Washington and in the Field in the Sixties* (New York, 1898), 106; J. S. Goodrich to Johnson, Sept. 7, 1863, Johnson Mss., L.C.

64. Lincoln to Johnson, Sept. 11, 1863, in *Papers*, 6:362–63.

65. Johnson to Lincoln, Sept. 17, 1863, in ibid., 377–78.

66. The Johnson papers are filled with letters concerning problems over the changing status of freedmen. For interesting examples, see Fanny Drane to Johnson, Jan. 15, (1863); Thomas B. Johnson to Johnson, Aug. 8, 1863; William J. Kelly to Johnson, Sept. 9, 1863; Edmund Cooper to Johnson, Nov. 1, 1863, in ibid., 120, 318–19, 360–61, 446–47.

67. Appendix, ibid., 762–64; *Nashville Times and True Union*, Jan. 7, 1865.

68. Eaton, *Grant, Lincoln, and the Freedmen*, 44–45.

69. Appendix, *Papers*, 6:762–64, 764n.

70. Maslowski, *Treason Must Be Made Odious*, 97–102; Joseph G. McKee and M. M. Brown to Johnson, Nov. 3, [1863], *Papers*, 6:450–51; George L. Sterns to Edwin M. Stanton, Sept. 25, 1863 in *OR*, Ser. 3, 3:840. The most complete discussion of the treatment of the freedmen in Tennessee is found in Cimprich, *Slavery's End*, 19–80.

71. Ibid.

72. Ibid., 44.

73. Lincoln to Johnson, Sept. 11, 1863, in *Papers*, 6:362–63; Maslowski, *Treason Must Be Made Odious*, 102–103; Frank Preston Stearns, *The Life and Public Services of George Luther Stearns* (Philadelphia, 1907), 308. For a discussion of Lincoln's decision to use black troops, see Quarles, *Lincoln and the Negro*, 153–67.

74. Johnson to Stanton, Sept. 17, 1863; Johnson to Rosecrans, Sept. 17, 1863, in *Papers*, 6:376–77.

75. Stanton to Johnson, Sept. 18, 1863, in ibid., 378, 379.

76. Lincoln to Johnson, Sept. 18, 1863, in ibid., 378.

77. Maslowski, *Treason Must Be Made Odious*, 102–117; Johnson to Lincoln, Sept. 23, 1863, in *Papers*, 6:384. What might have happened had Johnson resisted Lincoln at this point is illustrated by the example of Kentucky. State authorities vigorously opposed black recruitment, but it eventually went on over their objections and beyond their control. It should be remembered that

the Kentucky governor was an elected official, not a presidential appointee. Quarles, *Lincoln and the Negro*, 63–67.

78. Johnson's Testimony re: Condition of Negroes, Nov. 23, 1863, in *Papers*, 6:488–92.

79. Ibid.

80. Ibid.

81. For a view of Johnson's ideas on "Restoration," see Speech on Restoration of State Government, Jan. 21, 1864, in ibid., 574–90.

82. Ibid.

83. Ibid.; Johnson to Brownlow, Apr. 6, 1864; Johnson to James R. Hood, Apr. 6, 1864, ibid., 663–64.

84. Acceptance of Vice-presidential Nomination, July 2, 1864, in ibid., 7:7–11; Johnson to William Dennison, Chairman, and others, Committee of the National Union Convention, July 2, 1864, in John Savage, *The Life and Public Services of Andrew Johnson, Seventeenth President of the United States* (New York, 1866), 299–300.

85. Johnson to M. Blair, Nov. 24, 1863, in *Papers*, 6:492; *Baltimore Gazette*, Jan. 10, 1867. For a discussion of the radical theories current in the summer and fall of 1863, see Belz, *Reconstructing the Union*, 131–35.

86. Johnson to J. A. Hurlbut, Oct. 3, 1863, in *Papers*, 6:402–403.

87. Speech on Restoration of State Government, Jan. 21, 1864, in ibid., 582.

88. B. B. French to Johnson, Feb. 8, 1866, in Johnson Mss., L.C.

89. Foner, *Life and Writings of Frederick Douglass*, 4, 184; Speech on Restoration of State Government, Jan. 21, 1864, in *Papers*, 6:574–90.

90. Hall, *Andrew Johnson, Military Governor*, 163–70.

91. Milligan to Johnson, Oct. 21, 1863, in *Papers*, 6:428–29.

92. Benedict, *Compromise of Principle*, 41–43.

93. *Nashville Daily Union*, June 1, 1864; *Nashville Times and True Union*, May 31, 1864. The convention's resolution is an almost exact copy of a resolution passed by a mass meeting of unionists in Knoxville in April. According to O. P. Temple, Johnson was the author. *Knoxville Whig and Rebel Ventilator*, Apr. 23, 1864; Temple, *Notable Men*, 408; Cimprich, *Slavery's End*, 113.

CHAPTER 5

1. *New York Citizen*, Feb. 23, 1867. Quotation taken from an interview by pro-Johnson editor Charles G. Halpine.

2. For a detailed discussion of the various theories of Reconstruction, see Belz, *Reconstructing the Union*.

3. For contemporary accounts of the initial Republican response to Johnson, see George W. Julian, "George W. Julian's Journal—Assassination of Lin-

coln," *Indiana Magazine of History*, 11 (1915), 335–36; Blaine, *Twenty Years of Congress*, 2:14.

4. For discussions of Reconstruction historiography, see Howard K. Beale, "On Rewriting Reconstruction History," *AHR*, 45 (1940), 807–27; Bernard Weisberger, "The Dark and Bloody Ground of Reconstruction Historiography," *JSH*, 25 (1959), 427–47.

5. Hans L. Trefousse, *Impeachment of a President: Andrew Johnson, the Blacks, and Reconstruction* (Knoxville, 1975), 5–6.

6. McKitrick, *Andrew Johnson and Reconstruction*, 85–92; Benedict, *A Compromise of Principle*, 107.

7. See James G. Randall and Richard N. Current, *Lincoln the President* (4 vols., New York, 1945–55), 4:130–36, for a discussion of Lincoln's role in selecting the vice-presidential candidate.

8. The Blair family represented the old "Democratic" wing of the Republican Party and would naturally have more in common with a staunch Jacksonian than former Whigs. Also, having their power base in border states they shared many attitudes, especially those concerning race, with the Tennessean. The role played in Reconstruction by this strange family, who like moths were always attracted to any glimmer of power, needs further examination. The best discussion is probably found in Cox and Cox, *Politics, Principle, and Prejudice*, 52–62. See also, McKitrick, *Andrew Johnson and Reconstruction*, 71–72, 136; William E. Smith, *The Francis Preston Blair Family in Politics* (2 vols., New York, 1959), vol. 2.

9. Alexander K. McClure, *Old Time Notes of Pennsylvania* (2 vols., Philadelphia, 1905), 1:14; Fawn M. Brodie, *Thaddeus Stevens: Scourge of the South* (New York, 1959), 220.

10. Charles E. Hamlin, *Life and Times of Hannibal Hamlin, by His Grandson* (Cambridge, 1899), 472; Brodie, *Thaddeus Stevens*, 217. For a discussion of Stearns career, see Stearns, *George Luther Stearns*.

11. Ibid., 309.

12. Johnson to Stanton, Sept. 17, 1863, in *Papers*, 6:376.

13. Stearns to Johnson, Sept. 26, 1864, Johnson Mss., L.C. See also, Stearns to Johnson, Sept. 26, 1864 in *Papers*, 7:192–93, for a brief discussion of Stearns' letter.

14. Stearns to Johnson, June 9, 1864, in *Papers*, 6:721.

15. Sumner to Stearns, May 4, 1865, in Stearns, *George Luther Stearns*, 344.

16. Ibid., 258–60; McPherson, *The Political History of the United States*, 48–49. The Stearns interview was published in the *Boston Daily Advertiser*, Oct. 23, 1865.

17. The idea of a great "amphitheater" of democracy was one of Johnson's favorite rhetorical flourishes. See Speech on the Seceding States, Feb. 5–6,

1861, in *Papers*, 4:237; Speech of President Andrew Johnson in Front of the White House at Washington, Feb. 22, 1866, Johnson Mss., L.C.

18. McPherson, *Struggle for Equality*, 336–37; Stearns, *George Luther Stearns*, 360–62, 376–77.

19. Benedict, *A Compromise of Principle*, 21–58, 104.

20. Ibid., 41; Eric Foner, *Free Soil, Free Labor, Free Men: The Ideology of the Republican Party before the Civil War* (New York, 1970), 261–300.

21. See Benedict, *A Compromise of Principle*, 135–40, for a discussion of the moderate-conservative position during presidential Reconstruction.

22. Acceptance of Vice-presidential Nomination, July 2, 1864, in *Papers*, 7:7; Johnson to William Dennison, Chairman, and others, Committee of the National Union Convention, July 2, 1864, in Savage, *Life and Public Services of Andrew Johnson*, 297–300; Message of the President of the United States to the Two Houses of Congress at the Commencement of the First Session of the Thirty-ninth Congress, Dec. 4, 1865, Johnson Mss., L.C. For a discussion of the actual author of Johnson's first message, see Benedict, *A Compromise of Principle*, 132.

23. Ibid., 39, 102; Mark M. Krug, *Lyman Trumbull: Conservative Radical* (New York, 1965), 228–70; *Cong. Globe*, 38 Cong., 1 Sess., 1706.

24. Krug, *Lyman Trumbull*, 87–106; *Papers*, 3:350n; *Cong. Globe*, 36 Cong., 1 Sess., 1, 5–15.

25. Ibid.

26. Speech on Harper's Ferry Incident, Dec. 12, 1859, *Papers*, 3:318–28.

27. Ibid.

28. *Cong. Globe*, 36 Cong., 1 Sess., 100–107.

29. Speech on Harper's Ferry Incident, Dec. 12, 1859, in *Papers*, 3:328–29.

30. Benedict, *A Compromise of Principle*, 111, 121; Howard K. Beale, ed., *Diary of Gideon Welles: Secretary of the Navy Under Lincoln and Johnson* (3 vols., New York, 1960), 2:322; R. King Cutler to Trumbull, Dec. 6, 1865, Lyman Trumbull Mss., L.C.

31. Benedict, *A Compromise of Principle*, 147.

32. Ibid., 149–50; *Cong. Globe*, 39 Cong., 1 Sess., 298–99, 655, 658, 688.

33. Benedict, *A Compromise of Principle*, 155; Beale, *Diary of Gideon Welles*, 432.

34. Benedict, *A Compromise of Principle*, 155; LaWanda and John H. Cox, "Andrew Johnson and his Ghost Writers," *Mississippi Valley Historical Review*, 48 (1961), 465–73; Cong. Globe, 39 Cong., 1 Sess., 915–17; Freedmen's Bureau Veto Message, Feb. 19, 1866, Johnson Mss., L.C.

35. Speech of President Andrew Johnson in Front of the White House at Washington, Feb. 22, 1866, in ibid.; McKitrick, *Andrew Johnson and Reconstruction*, 298–314; Benedict, *A Compromise of Principle*, 156–63.

36. *New York Times*, Mar. 28, 1866; James D. Richardson, ed., *Messages*

and Papers of the Presidents of the United States, 1789–1897 (10 vols., Washington, 1896–99), 6:405–16.

37. *Cong. Globe*, 39, Cong., 1 Sess., 936–43.

38. Ibid., 1755–61; Lyman Trumbull to Julia Jayne Trumbull, May 29, 1866, quoted in Krug, *Lyman Trumbull*, 243–44; Trumbull to Dr. William Jayne, July 2, 1866, quoted in ibid., 244.

39. Charles Sumner, *The Works of Charles Sumner* (15 vols., Boston, 1870–83), 10:274–75; Henry L. Dawes to Mrs. Electa Dawes, Mar. 31, 1866, quoted in Benedict, *A Compromise of Principle*, 166–68.

40. McKitrick, *Andrew Johnson and Reconstruction*, 316.

41. Howard K. Beale, *The Critical Year: A Study of Andrew Johnson and Reconstruction* (New York, 1930), 25; McKitrick, *Andrew Johnson and Reconstruction*, 217–18, 317.

42. *Address of Andrew Johnson to the People of the United States, March 4, 1869* (Washington, 1869), Johnson Mss., L.C.

43. Ibid.

44. Johnson to Benjamin Truman, Aug. 3, 1868, quoted in Truman, "Anecdotes of Andrew Johnson," 438–40.

45. Foner, *Frederick Douglass*, 187.

46. Ibid., 186.

47. McKitrick, *Andrew Johnson and Reconstruction*, 19–21. For examples of typically supportive letters to Johnson, see James M. Ashley to Johnson, Apr. 15, 1865; Benjamin F. Butler to Johnson, Apr. 25, 1865; George Bancroft to Johnson, Apr. 26, 1865; Hannibal Hamlin to Johnson, May 3, 1865, Johnson Mss., L.C.

48. A good example of the Republican attempt at conciliation was the effort by Senator John Sherman of Ohio to work out a compromise following Johnson's veto of the Freedmen's Bureau Bill. See Benedict, *A Compromise of Principle*, 112, 158–60. The efforts and motives of Secretary Seward and the Blair family have been described in detail in Cox and Cox, *Politics, Principle, and Prejudice*, 50–87. See also, McKitrick, *Andrew Johnson and Reconstruction*, 175–86, 394–420.

49. Foner, *Frederick Douglass*, 184–85.

50. *Harper's Weekly*, 9 (Oct. 28, 1865), 674; McKitrick, *Andrew Johnson and Reconstruction*, 184.

51. *New York Times*, Oct. 11, 1865.

52. Ibid.

53. Speech on Restoration of State Government, Jan. 21, 1864, *Papers*, 6:574–90.

54. *New York Times*, Oct. 11, 1865.

55. Benedict, *A Compromise of Principle*, 196–207; OR, Ser. 3, 5:13–15; Richardson, *Messages and Papers of the Presidents*, 6:13–14.

56. Benedict, *A Compromise of Principle*, 104–105, 127. There is little doubt that Johnson was serious about his own conditions for readmission. The president made his wishes clear to his provisional governors. For examples of White House pressure, see Johnson to James Johnson, Oct. 28, 1865; Johnson to W. L. Sharkey, Nov. 1, 1865, Tel. Sent by Pres., Off. Rec. Sec. of War, RG 107, 2, 1865.

57. Hall, *Andrew Johnson Military Governor*, 167–70. See Ch. 4.

58. Johnson to Sharkey, Aug. 15, 1865, Johnson Mss., L.C. For varying interpretations of the motivation behind the Johnson telegram, see Cox and Cox, *Politics, Principle, and Prejudice*, 157; Winston, *Andrew Johnson*, 334; Benedict, *A Compromise of Principle*, 107; James W. Garner, *Reconstruction in Mississippi* (New York, 1901), 112; Pierce, "Andrew Johnson and the South," 29–30.

59. Cox and Cox, *Politics, Principle, and Prejudice*, 157; F. W. Sykes and others to Governor Parsons and Governor Fitzpatrick, Sept. 19, 1865; F. W. Sykes to Clark and Speak, Sept. 21, 1865; F. W. Sykes and Levi W. Lawler to Lewis E. Parsons, Sept. 21, 1865, Tel. Sent by Pres., Off. Rec. Sec. of War, RG 107, 2:1865.

60. McKitrick, *Andrew Johnson and Reconstruction*, 162–64.

61. Ibid., 164.

62. Johnson to Thomas, Aug. 14, 1865, in *OR*, Ser. 1, 49:1100; Mrs. John A. Jackson to Johnson, Sept. 2, 1865, Johnson Mss., L.C.; Thomas to Johnson, Aug. 16, 1865, Tel. Rec. by Pres., RG 107, 4:1865–66.

63. Brownlow to Johnson, Aug. 16, 1865, Johnson Mss., L.C.

64. Johnson to Thomas, Sept. 4, 1865, Tel. Sent by Pres., Off. Rec. Sec. of War, RG 107, 2:1865–66.

65. Thomas to Johnson, Sept. 7, 1865, Tel. Rec. by Pres., RG 107, 4:1865–66; Johnson to Thomas, Sept. 8, 1865, Tel. Sent by Pres., Off. Rec. Sec. of War, RG 107, 2:1865; Thomas to Johnson, Sept. 9, 1865, Tel. Rec. by Pres., RG 107, 4:1865–66.

66. Thomas Johnson, Sept. 19, 1865, Johnson Mss., L.C.

CHAPTER 6

1. *Knoxville Daily Whig*, 4, 1869.

2. McKitrick, *Andrew Johnson and Reconstruction*, 274–324.

3. Brodie, *Thaddeus Stevens*, 232–35.

4. Johnson to Mason M. Brien, May 15, 1864, in *Papers*, 6:697–98.

5. Benedict, *A Compromise of Principle*, 41–42.

6. The best discussions of the motivation behind impeachment are found in Trefousse, *Impeachment of a President* and Michael Les Benedict, *The Impeachment and Trial of Andrew Johnson* (New York, 1973).

7. Thomas B. Alexander, *Political Reconstruction in Tennessee* (Nashville, 1950) is probably the best extant account of Reconstruction in Tennessee. See also Patton, *Unionism and Reconstruction in Tennessee, 1860–1869*.

8. *Nashville Daily Press and Times*, July 2, 1866; Alexander, *Political Reconstruction in Tennessee*, 111.

9. See E. Merton Coulter, *William G. Brownlow: Fighting Parson of the Southern Highlands* (Chapel Hill, 1936), 291–93, for a discussion of Brownlow's attitude toward blacks. See also Patton, *Unionism and Reconstruction*, 124–43.

10. Alexander, *Political Reconstruction in Tennessee*, 178. See also, Allen W. Trelease, *White Terror: The Ku Klux Klan Conspiracy and Southern Reconstruction* (New York, 1971), for the best modern account of Klan activities.

11. Ibid., 199–225.

12. Bible, "The Post Presidential Career of Andrew Johnson," 11–26; Winston, *Andrew Johnson*, 495–97.

13. *Knoxville Daily Whig*, Apr. 4, Aug. 3, 1869; *Knoxville Daily Press and Herald*, Apr. 4, 7, 8, 10, 11, 14, 21, 1869.

14. See Michael Perman, *The Road to Redemption: Southern Politics, 1869–1879* (Chapel Hill, N.C., 1984), 3–21, for an account of the strategy of southern conservatives in 1869.

15. Alexander, *Political Reconstruction in Tennessee*, 222–23; Coulter, *William G. Brownlow*, 386–95.

16. Winston, *Andrew Johnson*, 496–506.

17. *Cong. Record*, 44 Cong., 1 Sess. and special sess., 121–27.

18. Johnson to Mary Johnson, July 26, 1875, Johnson Correspondence, 1865–75, Tennessee State Library and Archives, Nashville.

Selected Bibliography

A. UNPUBLISHED MANUSCRIPTS

Clement C. Clay Papers. Duke University Library. Durham, N.C.
Andrew Johnson Correspondence, 1865–1879. Tennessee State Library and Archives. Nashville.
Andrew Johnson Papers. Manuscript Division, Library of Congress. Washington, D.C.
Official Records of the Office of the Secretary of War. Record Group 107, National Archives. Washington, D.C.
Oliver P. Temple Papers. University of Tennessee Library. Knoxville.
Lyman Trumball Papers. Manuscript Division, Library of Congress. Washington, D.C.

B. PUBLISHED MANUSCRIPTS

Basler, Roy P., ed. *The Collected Works of Abraham Lincoln.* 8 vols. New Brunswick, N.J., 1953.
Foner, Philip S. *The Life and Writings of Frederick Douglass.* 4 vols. New York, 1955.
Galpin, W. Freeman, ed. "Letters from an East Tennessee Abolitionist," East Tennessee Historical Society's *Publications,* 3 (1931), 145–49.
Graf, LeRoy P., and Ralph W. Haskins, eds. *The Papers of Andrew Johnson,* 7 vols. Knoxville, 1967–1987.
Life, Speeches and Services of Andrew Johnson. Philadelphia, 1865.
McKitrick, Eric L., ed. *Slavery Defended: The Views of the Old South.* Englewood Cliffs, N.J., 1963.
McPherson, Edward, comp. *The Political History of the United States of America During the Period of Reconstruction.* Washington, D.C., 1887.
Moore, Frank, ed. *Speeches of Andrew Johnson, President of the United States with a Biographical Introduction.* Boston, 1866.
Richardson, James D., ed. *Messages and Papers of the Presidents of the United States, 1789–1897.* 10 vols. Washington, D.C., 1896–1899.

White, Robert H., ed. *Messages of the Governors of Tennessee.* 8 vols. Nashville, Tenn., 1952–1972.

Williams, T. Harry, ed. *Abraham Lincoln: Selected Speeches, Messages, and Letters.* New York, 1957.

C. PUBLIC DOCUMENTS

Acts of the State of Tennessee.

Memorial Addresses on the Life and Character of Andrew Johnson Delivered in the Senate and House of Representatives, January 12, 1876. Washington, D.C., 1876.

Tennessee House Journal.

U.S. Congressional Globe.

U.S. Congressional Record.

The War of Rebellion: A Compilation of the Official Records of the Union and Confederate Armies. 170 vols. Washington, D.C., 1880–1901.

D. MEMOIRS, DIARIES, AND COMMENTARIES

Beale, Howard K., ed. *Diary of Gideon Welles: Secretary of the Navy Under Lincoln and Johnson.* 3 vols. New York, 1960.

Blaine, James G. *Twenty Years of Congress from Lincoln to Garfield.* 2 vols. Norwich, Conn., 1884.

Buckingham, J. S. *The Slave States of America.* 2 vols. London, 1842.

Cowan, Frank. *Andrew Johnson, President of the United States: Reminiscences of His Private Life and Character by One of His Secretaries.* Greenesburgh, Pa., 1894.

Dana, Charles A. *Recollections of the Civil War: With the Leaders at Washington and in the Field in the Sixties.* New York, 1898.

Eaton, John. *Grant, Lincoln and the Freedmen: Reminiscences of the Civil War with Special Reference to the Work for the Contrabands and the Freedmen of the Mississippi Valley.* New York, 1897.

Fitzhugh, George. *Cannibals All! or Slaves Without Masters.* Richmond, 1857.

———. *Sociology for the South or the Failure of Free Society.* Richmond, 1854.

Gerry, Margarita Spalding. "Andrew Johnson in the White House: Being the Reminiscences of William H. Crook," *Century Magazine,* 126 (1908), 863–72.

Helper, Hinton Rowan. *The Impending Crisis of the South: How to Meet It.* New York, 1857.

Jefferson, Thomas. *Notes on the State of Virginia,* ed. William Peden. Chapel Hill, N.C., 1955.

Julian, George W. "George W. Julian's Journal—Assassination of Lincoln," *Indiana Magazine of History*, 11 (1915), 324-37.

McClure, Alexander K. *Old Time Notes of Pennsylvania*. 2 vols. Philadelphia, 1905.

Olmstead, Frederick Law. *The Cotton Kingdom: A Traveller's Observations on Cotton and Slavery in the American Slave States*. 2 vols. New York, 1861.

————. *The Slave States*, ed. Harvey Wish. New York, 1959.

Sumner, Charles. *The Works of Charles Sumner*. 15 vols. Boston, 1870-1883.

Tocqueville, Alexis de. *Democracy in America*, ed. Phillips Bradley. 2 vols. New York, 1945.

Truman, Benjamin C. "Anecdotes of Andrew Johnson," *Century Magazine*, 85 (1913), 435-40.

Turner, Harriot S. "Recollections of Andrew Johnson," *Harper's Monthly Magazine*, 120 (1910), 168-76.

Wish, Harvey, ed. *Ante-Bellum: Writings of George Fitzhugh and Hinton Rowan Helper on Slavery*. New York, 1960.

E. NEWSPAPERS AND MAGAZINES

American Economist and East Tennessee Statesman. Greeneville, Tenn.
Baltimore Gazette.
Boston Daily Advertiser.
Charleston Courier.
Cincinnati Daily Commercial.
Harper's Weekly.
Knoxville Daily Press and Herald.
Knoxville Daily Whig.
Knoxville Register.
Knoxville Whig and Rebel Ventilator.
Memphis Bulletin.
Nashville Banner.
Nashville Daily Press and Times.
Nashville Daily Union.
Nashville Dispatch.
Nashville Republican Banner.
Nashville Times.
Nashville Times and True Union.
Nashville Union.
New York Citizen.
New York Times.
New York Tribune.

F. SECONDARY SOURCES

Abernethy, Thomas P. *From Frontier to Plantation in Tennessee: A Study of Frontier Democracy*. Chapel Hill, N.C., 1932.

Alexander, Thomas B. *Political Reconstruction in Tennessee*. Nashville, 1950.

Allport, Gordon W. *The Nature of Prejudice*. New York, 1954.

Baker, Henry E. "Benjamin Banneker, the Negro Mathematician and Astronomer," *Journal of Negro History*, 3 (1918), 99–118.

Banton, Michael. *Race Relations*. London, 1967.

Barnes, Gilbert Hobbs. *The Anti-Slavery Impulse, 1830–1844*. New York, 1933.

Barney, William L. *The Road to Secession: A New Perspective on the Old South*. New York, 1972.

Baumgardner, James L. "Andrew Johnson and the Patronage." Ph.D. dissertation, University of Tennessee, 1968.

Beale, Howard K. *The Critical Year: A Study of Andrew Johnson and Reconstruction*. New York, 1969.

——. "On Rewriting Reconstruction History," *American Historical Review*, 45 (1940), 807–27.

Belz, Herman. "The Etheridge Conspiracy of 1863: A Projected Conservative Coup," *Journal of Southern History*, 36 (1970), 465–73.

——. *Reconstructing the Union: Theory and Policy During the Civil War*. Ithaca, N.Y., 1969.

Benedict, Michael Les. *A Compromise of Principle: Congressional Republicans and Reconstruction, 1863–1869*. New York, 1974.

——. *The Impeachment and Trial of Andrew Johnson*. New York, 1973.

Bentley, Hubert Blair. "Andrew Johnson, Governor of Tennessee, 1853–1857." Ph.D. dissertation, University of Tennessee, 1972.

Berwanger, Eugene H. *The Frontier Against Slavery: Western Anti-Negro Prejudice and the Slavery Extension Controversy*. Urbana, Ill., 1967.

Bible, Mary Ozelle. "The Post Presidential Career of Andrew Johnson." Master's thesis, University of Tennessee, 1936.

Bontemps, Arna W. *Free at Last: The Life of Frederick Douglass*. New York, 1971.

Brabson, Fay W. *Andrew Johnson: A Life in Pursuit of the Right Course, 1808–1875*. Durham, N.C., 1972.

Brodie, Fawn M. *Thaddeus Stevens: Scourge of the South*. New York, 1959.

——. *Thomas Jefferson: An Intimate History*. New York, 1974.

Brown, William Wells. *The Negro in the American Rebellion*. Boston, 1867.

Campbell, Mary Emily Robertson. *The Attitude of Tennesseans Toward the Union, 1847–1861*. New York, 1961.

Cash, Wilbur J. *The Mind of the South*. New York, 1941.

Cimprich, John Vincent, Jr. *Slavery's End in Tennessee, 1861–1865*. University of Alabama, 1985.

Commanger, Henry Steele. *The Study of History.* Columbus, Ohio, 1965.

Coulter, E. Merton. *William G. Brownlow: Fighting Parson of the Southern Highlands.* Chapel Hill, N.C., 1936.

Cox, LaWanda. *Lincoln and Black Freedom: A Study in Presidential Leadership.* Columbia, S.C., 1981.

Cox, LaWanda and John H. "Andrew Johnson and his Ghost Writers," *Mississippi Valley Historical Review,* 48 (1961), 465–73.

————. *Politics, Principle, and Prejudice, 1865–1866: Dilemma of Reconstruction America.* New York, 1969.

Current, Richard N. *The Lincoln Nobody Knows.* New York, 1958.

Donald, David, ed. *Lincoln Reconsidered: Essays on the Civil War Era.* New York, 1956.

Dollard, John. *Caste and Class in a Southern Town.* New York, 1937.

Doughty, Richard H. *Greeneville: One Hundred Year Portrait (1715–1875).* Kingsport, Tenn., 1975.

Dumond, Dwight Lowell. *Antislavery Origins of the Civil War in the United States.* Ann Arbor, 1939.

Elkins, Stanley. *Slavery: A Problem in American Institutional and Intellectual Life.* Chicago, 1959.

Fanon, Frantz. *Black Skins, White Masks.* New York, 1967.

Folmsbee, Stanley J. *Sectionalism and Internal Improvements in Tennessee, 1796–1845.* Knoxville, 1939.

Foner, Eric. *Free Soil, Free Labor, Free Men: The Ideology of the Republican Party before the Civil War.* New York, 1970.

Foulke, W. D. *The Life and Public Service of Oliver P. Morton.* 2 vols. Indianapolis, 1899.

Franklin, John Hope. *From Slavery to Freedom.* New York, 1967.

Fredrickson, George M. *The Black Image in the White Mind: The Debate on Afro-American Character and Destiny, 1817–1914.* New York, 1971.

Gardiner, Patrick. *The Nature of Historical Explanation.* Oxford, 1961.

Garner, James W. *Reconstruction in Mississippi.* New York, 1901.

Genovese, Eugene D. *The World the Slaveholders Made.* New York, 1971.

Gossett, Thomas F. *Race: The History of an Idea in America.* Dallas, 1963.

Graf, LeRoy P. "Andrew Johnson and the Coming of the War," *Tennessee Historical Quarterly,* 19 (1960), 208–21.

Hall, Clifton R. *Andrew Johnson, Military Governor of Tennessee.* Princeton, 1916.

Halperin, Bernard. "Andrew Johnson, the Radicals and the Negro, 1865–1866." Ph.D. dissertation, University of California, Berkeley, 1966.

Hamlin, Charles E. *Life and Times of Hannibal Hamlin, by his Grandson.* Cambridge, 1899.

Haskins, Ralph W. "Andrew Johnson and the Preservation of the Union," *East Tennessee Historical Society's Publications,* 31 (1961), 43–60.

Henry, J. Milton. "The Revolution in Tennessee, February, 1861 to June, 1861," *Tennessee Historical Quarterly*, 17 (1959), 99–117.

Hoetink, Harmannus. *Slavery and Race Relations in the Americas: Comparative Notes on their Nature and Nexus*. New York, 1973.

Hunt, Gaillard. "The President's Defense: His Side of the Case, as Told by his Correspondence," *Century Magazine*, 85 (1913), 422–34.

Jordan, Winthrop. "Modern Tensions and the Origins of American Slavery," *Journal of Southern History*, 28 (1962), 18–30.

———. *White over Black: American Attitudes Toward the Negro, 1550–1812*. Chapel Hill, N.C., 1968.

Kovel, Joel. *White Racism: A Psychohistory*. New York, 1970.

Kraditor, Aileen S. *Means and Ends in American Abolitionism: Garrison and his Critics on Strategy and Tactics, 1834–1850*. New York, 1969.

Krug, Mark M. *Lyman Trumbull: Conservative Radical*. New York, 1965.

Lacy, Eric Russell. *Vanquished Volunteers: East Tennessee Sectionalism from Statehood to Secession*. Johnson City, Tenn., 1965.

Lasswell, Harold D. *Power and Personality*. New York, 1948.

Litwack, Leon F. *North of Slavery: The Negro in the Free States, 1790–1860*. Chicago, 1961.

Lomask, Milton. *Andrew Johnson, President on Trial*. New York, 1960.

McKitrick, Eric L. *Andrew Johnson and Reconstruction*. Chicago, 1960.

McPherson, Edward. *The Struggle for Equality: Abolitionists and the Negro in the Civil War and Reconstruction*. Princeton, 1964.

Marcuse, Herbert. *One Dimensional Man: Studies in the Ideology of Advanced Industrial Society*. Boston, 1964.

Maslowski, Peter. *Treason Must Be Made Odious: Military Occupation and Wartime Reconstruction in Nashville, Tennessee, 1862–1865*. Millwood, N.Y., 1978.

Mooney, Chase. *Slavery in Tennessee*. Bloomington, Ind., 1957.

Myrdal, Gunnar, et al., eds. *An American Dilemma: The Negro and American Democracy*. New York, 1944.

Noel, Donald L., ed. *The Origins of American Slavery and Racism*. Columbus, Ohio, 1972.

Nolan, Claude H. *The Negro's Image in the South*. Lexington, Ky., 1968.

Patton, J. W. *Unionism and Reconstruction in Tennessee, 1860–1869*. Chapel Hill, N.C., 1934.

Perman, Michael. *The Road to Redemption: Southern Politics, 1869–1879*. Chapel Hill, N.C., 1984.

Pierce, Michael. "Andrew Johnson and the South, 1865–1867." Ph.D. dissertation, North Texas State University, 1970.

Quarles, Benjamin. *Frederick Douglass*. Washington, D.C., 1948.

———. *Lincoln and the Negro*. New York, 1962.

Rable, George C. "Anatomy of a Unionist: Andrew Johnson in the Secession Crisis," *Tennessee Historical Quarterly*, 32 (1973), 332–54.

Randall, James G. and Richard N. Current. *Lincoln the President.* 4 vols. New York, 1945–1955.

Riches, William T. M. "The Commoners: Andrew Johnson and Abraham Lincoln to 1861." Ph.D. dissertation, University of Tennessee, 1976.

Savage, John. *The Life and Public Services of Andrew Johnson, Seventeenth President of the United States.* New York, 1866.

Shugg, Roger W. *Origin of Class Struggle in Louisiana: A Social History of White Farmers and Laborers During Slavery and After, 1840–1875.* Baton Rouge, 1939.

Smith, William E. *The Francis Preston Blair Family in Politics.* 2 vols. New York, 1959.

Stampp, Kenneth M. *The Era of Reconstruction, 1865–1877.* New York, 1967.

———. *The Peculiar Institution: Slavery in the Ante-bellum South.* New York, 1956.

Stanton, William. *The Leopard's Spots: Scientific Attitudes toward Race in America, 1851–59.* Chicago, 1960.

Stearns, Frank Preston. *The Life and Public Services of George Luther Stearns.* Philadelphia, 1907.

Stryker, Lloyd Paul. *Andrew Johnson, A Study in Courage.* New York, 1929.

Temple, Oliver P. *Notable Men of Tennessee from 1833 to 1875: Their Times and Their Contemporaries.* New York, 1912.

Trefousse, Hans L. *Impeachment of a President: Andrew Johnson, the Blacks, and Reconstruction.* Knoxville, 1975.

Trelease, Allen W. *White Terror: The Ku Klux Klan Conspiracy and Southern Reconstruction.* New York, 1971.

Van den Berghe, Pierre L. *Race and Racism: A Comparative Perspective.* New York, 1967.

Weisberger, Bernard. "The Dark and Bloody Ground of Reconstruction Historiography," *Journal of Southern History*, 25 (1959), 427–47.

Williams, Samuel Cole. *The Lost State of Franklin.* Johnson City, Tenn., 1929.

Williams, T. Harry. *Lincoln and the Radicals.* Madison, Wisconsin, 1941.

Winston, Robert W. *Andrew Johnson: Plebeian and Patriot.* New York, 1928.

Wish, Harvey. *George Fitzhugh: Propagandist of the Old South.* Baton Rouge, 1943.

———. "The Slave Insurrection Panic of 1856," *Journal of Southern History*, 5 (May 1939), 206–22.

Index

206 Andrew Johnson and the Negro

Tennessee (*continued*)
  constitutional convention of
    1834, 15, 58; Democratic Party
    in, 34, 35, 39, 60, 64, 82, 89;
    emancipation in, 98–108, 116–
    18, 157; free blacks in, 66–68,
    111, 119; Freedmen's Bureau in,
    153, 155; General Assembly, 15,
    30, 40, 58, 66, 165; intrastate
    sectionalism, 15, 58, 59, 60, 84;
    Manumission Society, 15, 20;
    Reconstruction in, 106, 107,
    117–19, 127, 148–54, 160, 162–
    65; Republican Party, 162–65;
    secession crisis, 46, 85, 89; slave
    rebellion hysteria (1856), 69;
    slavery in, 14–16, 19, 20, 58, 59,
    85, 101, 108, 111, 113, 116, 119,
    157, 170n; treatment of freedmen
    in, 108–11; unionists, 85, 99–
    105, 116, 118–20, 162, 184n;
    University of, xv, xvi; Whig
    Party in, 32, 34, 59, 60, 89, 90,
    100
Texas: annexation of, 66
Thirteenth Amendment, 149
Thomas, George H., 98, 153–55
Thoreau, Henry David, 72
"three-fifths principle," 59, 60, 152
Tocqueville, Alexis de, 17
Toombs, Robert, 142
The Tragic Era, 157
Trancendentalism, 72, 73
Trefousse, Hans, xviii, 124
Trelease, Allen W., xv
Truman, Benjamin, 142
Trumbull, Julia Jayne, 138
Trumbull, Lyman, 131–34, 136–40,
    145, 151, 155, 156, 159

Turner, Harriot S., 178n
Turner, Nat: rebellion of, 16
Types of Mankind, 13

Union Party, 80, 81, 116, 120, 122,
    125
Unionism, 53, 82–84, 89–91, 95–
    109, 113, 116–27, 143, 149

Van Buren, Martin, 33
Virginia: Provisional Government
    of, 148

War Democrats, 90, 125
Washington, Booker, T., 6
Washington, D.C., 101, 103–5
Watterson, Harvey M., 152, 153
Webster, Daniel, 27
Weld, Theodore Dwight, 70
Welles, Gideon, 134, 136, 181n
West Tennessee, 15, 84, 104, 105;
    slavery in, 15
Wheatly, Phyllis, 12
Whig Party, 19, 32, 55, 125, 160,
    173n, 180n, 185n; Lincoln and,
    88, 90, 160; in Tennessee, 32, 34,
    59, 60, 89, 90, 100
White, Hugh Lawson, 33, 34
White Over Black, 170n
William: Johnson family slave, 166,
    175n
Williams, Alexander, 19, 32, 42,
    173n
Wilson County, Tenn., 160
Winston, Robert, 25, 51, 172n,
    173n
Winthrop, Robert C., 63
Wisconsin, 1
Word, Sarah, 29